MW00629355

Spaces of Capital / Spaces of Resistance

GEOGRAPHIES OF JUSTICE AND SOCIAL TRANSFORMATION

SERIES EDITORS

Nik Heynen, University of Georgia
Mathew Coleman, Ohio State University
Sapana Doshi, University of Arizona

ADVISORY BOARD

Deborah Cowen, University of Toronto
Zeynep Gambetti, Boğaziçi University
Geoff Mann, Simon Fraser University
James McCarthy, Clark University
Beverly Mullings, Queen's University
Harvey Neo, National University of Singapore
Geraldine Pratt, University of British Columbia
Ananya Roy, University of California, Los Angeles
Michael Watts, University of California, Berkeley
Ruth Wilson Gilmore, CUNY Graduate Center
Jamie Winders, Syracuse University
Melissa W. Wright, Pennsylvania State University
Brenda S. A. Yeoh, National University of Singapore

Spaces of Capital /
Spaces of Resistance

MEXICO AND THE GLOBAL POLITICAL ECONOMY

CHRIS HESKETH

THE UNIVERSITY OF GEORGIA PRESS
Athens

© 2017 by the University of Georgia Press
Athens, Georgia 30602
www.ugapress.org
All rights reserved
Set in 10/12.5 Minion Pro by Graphic Composition, Inc., Bogart, Georgia

Most University of Georgia Press titles are
available from popular e-book vendors.

Printed digitally

Library of Congress Cataloging-in-Publication Data

Names: Hesketh, Chris, 1981– author.
Title: Spaces of capital/spaces of resistance : Mexico and the global political economy /
    Chris Hesketh.
Description: Athens : University of Georgia Press, [2017] | Series: Geographies of justice
    and social transformation ; 37 | Includes bibliographical references and index.
Identifiers: LCCN 2017014292 | ISBN 9780820351742 (hardback : alk. paper) |
    ISBN 9780820352848 (pbk. : alk. paper) | ISBN 9780820351759 (ebook)
Subjects: LCSH: Economic development—Political aspects—Mexico. | Economic
    development—Political aspects—Latin America. | Geopolitics. | Space in economics. |
    Economics—Sociological aspects.
Classification: LCC HC135 .H4534 2017 | DDC 330.972/7—dc23
    LC record available at https://lccn.loc.gov/2017014292

For my grandma and grandpa

CONTENTS

ACKNOWLEDGMENTS

This book would not have been possible without the support, advice, and company of a number of people.

I would like to gratefully recognize the support of the Economic and Social Research Council (ESRC) studentship that funded the initial research (ref: ES/F005377/1). Publishers' permission to draw from the following material was gratefully received: "From passive revolution to silent revolution: Class forces and the production of state, space and scale in modern Mexico," *Capital & Class*, 34 (3) (2010): 383–407; "The clash of spatializations: Geopolitics and class struggle in Mexico," *Latin American Perspectives*, 40 (4) (2013): 70–87; "Producing state space in Chiapas: Passive revolution and everyday life," *Critical Sociology*, 42 (2) (2016): 211–28.

At the University of Georgia Press I would like to thank Nik Heynan and Melissa Wright for their advice and helpful comments on the project in its earlier stages. Mick Gusinde-Duffy has also been instrumental is seeing the project through to fruition.

In Mexico I would like to thank John Holloway and Gustavo Esteva for their early help in getting my research off the ground. I owe a particular debt of gratitude to Oliver Fröhling and Tom Hansen for their invaluable support in helping to provide points of contact and arranging transportation. I would also like to thank all the interviewees, who were very giving of their time. My thanks to the communities of Oaxaca and Chiapas for providing such hospitable and inspiring places from which to conduct research. In (re)presenting your struggles I hope I have done justice to them.

This project was started at the University of Nottingham, where the Centre for the Study of Social and Global Justice (CSSGJ) provided a fantastic setting in which to interact with great colleagues and to broaden my intellectual horizons through discussion and debate. Participants in the Marxist reading group helped me clarify my ideas, and I am grateful to all comrades who participated in this fantastic collective enterprise, but I owe particular thanks to Andreas Bieler, Sara Motta, Phillip Roberts, and Cemal Burak Tansel.

A special mention must also be made of Adam Morton. Despite moving to the other side of the world, he has remained fantastically supportive of my work, offering comment, critique, and good humor as and when needed.

At my new home at Oxford Brookes I would like to thank all my colleagues, who often provide much-needed social respite from the rigors of mental labor. In particular, thanks go to Steve Hurt, Mikko Kuisma, Tina Managhan, Victoria Browne, Doerthe Rosenow, and Maia Pal.

I owe a final debt of gratitude to my family. Since this research began, this family has been extended both with nieces and nephews and with my own children. For Molly and Nikhil, now that the book is finished I will look forward to some much-needed time to play. I would like to reserve special thanks for my wife, Sirisha, for her never-ending support and patience. Finally, I would like to dedicate this book to the memory of my grandma and grandpa. Sadly, we lost them before this work was completed, but I know they would have been proud to see it published.

Spaces of Capital / Spaces of Resistance

INTRODUCTION

On January 1, 1994, in the southern Mexican state of Chiapas, an indigenous rebel group calling itself the Ejército Zapatista de Liberación Nacional (EZLN, Zapatista Army of National Liberation) rose up in response to the government's new economic orientation, which had culminated most visibly with the signing of the North American Free Trade Agreement (NAFTA), due to come into effect on that very day. Since then, the Zapatistas have taken over (or "recuperated," as they put it) thousands of hectares of privately held lands and constructed an autonomous form of governance. The Zapatistas do not recognize state laws, and they do not accept government programs and money. When one enters Zapatista territory one is greeted with a sign that reads, "Aquí, manda el pueblo" (Here, the people command).

In the summer of 2006, in another southern Mexican state, Oaxaca, the violent dislodgement of the annual teachers' *plantón* (encampment) led to the creation of a broad collection of social movements, trade unions, and civil society organizations under the banner of Asamblea Popular de los Pueblos de Oaxaca (APPO, Popular Assembly of the Peoples of Oaxaca). Barricades were erected and public buildings and symbols of power were taken over after a state of "ungovernability" was declared. Since this time, social movement activism, centered on opposition to neoliberal development projects and localized authoritarianism, has proliferated in Oaxaca. There have also been attempts to reinvent community and reorient development by drawing on the state's indigenous cultural practices.

Both of these ongoing cases represent efforts to craft new geographical relations of power. They call into question the legitimacy of the state as the arbiter of social life, as well as the efficacy and desirability of a purely representative form of democracy. Moreover, these cases question the viability of capitalist social relations. In light of such questions, as well as numerous developments within Latin America, Jean Grugel's (2002: 170) assertion that the rise of neoliberalism in the region has rendered "utopian debates" about politics irrelevant seems premature, to say the least. Rather, what we are witnessing is the reinvention of utopia (Motta 2006).

This book seeks to explore these spaces of resistance, understand why they have arisen, and synthesize what they mean for comprehending (geo)politics today. I argue that to fully understand these movements in Chiapas and Oaxaca we have to be attentive to their specific local histories. However, these specific histories must be contextualized with reference to state formation and socio-economic development within Mexico. The development trajectory of Mexico, meanwhile, is informed by the particular regional dynamics of Latin America as a whole, including the shared legacy of colonization, state-led industrialization, and neoliberal transition. As should be obvious, this suggests that Latin America must likewise be placed within the broader context of the global political economy, based as it is on surplus value extraction in the form of capital accumulation, which has constantly sought to extend its logic into the region. It is at this point that we have to begin to push our inquiry into the spatial and its role within the global political economy by establishing the nexus between capitalist social relations and the production of space, as well as the counterspaces produced in opposition to this.

Drawing from the methodology of Neil Brenner (2004: 18–21), this book constructs its analysis on three separate levels: the abstract level, the meso level, and the concrete level. As Brenner (2004: 21) notes, these are not to be thought of as ontologically separate; instead, they represent "analytically distinct, if dialectically intertwined, epistemological vantage points." As its name suggests, the abstract level involves drawing together key systemic features of a system and outlining a theoretical framework within which we can operate in order to conduct our empirical investigation. The meso level, by contrast, is concerned with broad periodizations of institutional configurations that coalesce within time and space, underpinning dominant ideas about and practices of development. Lastly, the concrete level looks at the precise ways in which these wider forces unfold within specific contexts either at a national or a subnational level. Saskia Sassen (2007: 7) has rightly pointed out that studying the global "entails not only a focus on what is explicitly global in scale. It also calls for a focus on locally scaled practices and conditions articulated within global dynamics." It is at these scales that we can observe disjunctures and contradictions within material social practices and also think about processes of resistance and alternatives that are constructed within these interstices. Following Henri Lefebvre (1976: 18), this work is thus attentive to the differences and tensions involved in the production of scalar hierarchies. Indeed, this attentiveness is vital to performing an original analysis of the emergent spaces of resistance inspired by indigenous subjectivities. Noel Castree (2004: 137n6) has stated that "few, if any critical geographers have focused in-depth on the broader, international context for specific indigenous struggles." This book is a response to this lacuna.

In addressing questions of place, space, and scale, the book develops the perspective of historical-geographical sociology (see also Hesketh and Morton 2014). All three components can be justified as follows. With regard to geography, David Harvey (2006a: xix) famously argued that historical materialism cannot exist without a solid appreciation of the dialectics of spatiotemporality, hence the agenda-setting advancement of what he called "historical-geographical materialism." Nevertheless, historical sociology, despite major spatiotemporal claims, often fails to deliver spatial analysis of one of its major terms, "uneven and combined development" (e.g., Lacher 2006; Rosenberg 2006, 2010; Teschke 2003). Space is "there," but it is redundant and unexplored, a mere happenstance of developmental unevenness and combination.[1] This book seeks to correct this oversight with a clear spatial focus. The detailed historical emphasis, meanwhile, is justified primarily for two interrelated reasons. First, as Karl Marx (1852/2000: 329) attested, "The tradition of all the dead generations weighs like a nightmare on the living." Historical investigation helps, therefore, not only to denaturalize the present by showing how it has grown out of past conditions but also to examine how past and present conditions could inform future trajectories (Ollman 2003: 2–3, 124). In the words of Joel Wainwright (2008), this allows us to "decolonise development" by showing how the very term "development" has become a synonym for the furtherance of capitalist rule (see also Ruccio and Gibson-Graham 2010). Second, it allows us to focus on the production of the agents of resistance and transformation, contextualizing these subjectivities and explaining why they arise in specific places and times. In relation to the sociological component, Beverley Silver (2003: 20, 6) has argued that a key intellectual task is to identify subaltern responses to capitalist development, emphasizing that the recomposition of capital on a global scale also leads to the recomposition of labor. This book, while reasserting the importance of class struggle within the global political economy, argues, through its focus on indigenous resistance, that class struggle must be widened from its focus solely in regard to resistance at the point of production. Instead, the method of historical-geographical sociology can highlight how alternative histories and practices of constructing social relationships can provide a useful well of experiences to draw upon that can be reconfigured as important tools for social movements and communities in the contemporary age (see also Hesketh 2016).

Contributions of the Book

The book offers a number of contributions. First, it demonstrates the continued importance of the spatial and spatial planning within the global political economy, drawing attention to the role that uneven and combined development plays within this process and extending the concept to multiple scales of analysis. As previously mentioned, this work gives the particular empirical cases of uneven development a more specific geographical rendering than has been present hitherto (following the revival of the term "uneven and combined development" in debates within the international relations discipline). The book highlights how the continual production of space through the transformation of the biophysical environment is a prerequisite for the current economic system to function. It also provides a detailed account of the social agency of such a process, as well as linking this process to crises in economic, political, and environmental spheres.

Second, the book deploys the theoretical insights of Antonio Gramsci and Henri Lefebvre in a novel way to aid in understanding processes of modern state formation in Latin America and, in even more detail, Mexico and two specific federal states within Mexico (Oaxaca and Chiapas). In particular, I draw upon Gramsci's notions of passive revolution and hegemony to show how spatial and scalar configurations have been historically produced within Mexico and for what social purpose. Stephen Gill (2008: 58) has argued that the concepts "passive revolution" and "hegemony" should be thought of as "end-points in a continuum of actual historical (and indeed possible) transformations." Hegemony, as theorized by Gramsci (1971: 57, Q 19, §24), is about the intellectual and moral leadership that a class is able to exercise within (and across) a society.[2] Crucially, the concept is used to transform our notion of the "political," or where we see "politics" being practiced. This is because the state and civil society are theorized as being inextricably connected (Sassoon 1980: 111). Hegemony is used both to explain the dominant position of the bourgeoisie and to theorize the task of subaltern classes in constructing an alternative. Passive revolution, meanwhile, refers to processes in which aspects of the social relations of capitalist development are either instituted or expanded, resulting in both "revolutionary" rupture and a "restoration" of social relations across different scales and spatial aspects of the state (Gramsci 1971: 106–14, Q 15, §§11, 17, 15, 25, 59, 62; Hesketh and Morton 2014: 150). It therefore involves a state-led process of "modernization" that, while often offering certain gains, ultimately serves to exclude the subaltern classes from meaningful participation (Gramsci 1971: 114–18, Q 10ii, §61; Sassoon 2001: 8; Thomas 2013: 23). In contrast to hegemony, passive revolution refers less to the strength of a dominant class and more to the weakness of its adversaries in forming such alternatives (Sassoon 1980: 204).

Stefan Kipfer (2013: 85) has noted that Gramsci's key concepts were developed through their historical and geographical specificity, and I continue this methodology throughout the book. Therefore, I offer a spatially nuanced explanation of hegemony and hegemonic processes that draws from the work of the new cultural historical studies in Mexico, which emphasize "everyday forms of state formation" (Joseph and Nugent 1994; Lomnitz-Adler 1992; Mallon 1995). In contrast to approaches that stress a purely "national" level to the operation of hegemonic projects (Jessop 1990: 196–219), this book demonstrates the interplay between global, regional, national, and localized articulations of power in the production of space and scale. This is done by developing the novel notion of "uneven and combined hegemony." The purpose of this concept is also to offset a contemporary trend within current Mexican studies literature that focuses on power dynamics solely at the local level without linking this scale to wider processes of class formation (see, among others, Bobrow-Strain 2007; Cornelius, Eisenstadt, and Hindley 1999; Smith 2009).

The book also makes claim to originality by offering a subnational examination of passive revolution as a means of constructing such state space. While the concept of hegemony has been successfully "decentered" by a number of scholars (Mallon 1995; Winnant 1994), the same has not been done for passive revolution. Instead, analysts of passive revolution have largely remained fixed on its broader regional significance or national manifestations (e.g., see Modonesi 2013; Morton 2013; Munck 2013). Chapters 5 and 6 seek to demonstrate, therefore, that attention to forms of "intimate class culture" (Lomnitz-Adler 1992: 28) in a subnational setting has important implications for the articulations of passive revolutionary transformation, as well as the "anti–passive revolutionary" strategies of movements of resistance (Sassoon 1980: 216).

Lastly, the book underscores the contestations involved in the production of space and looks toward the potential for alternative geographical projects based upon the epistemologies of the excluded (Merrifield 2013; Santos 2006). These issues have often been elided in more structuralist accounts of capital, where a detailed engagement with specific resistance movements has not been undertaken (e.g., see Harvey 2006a, 2010; Smith 2008). However, I have maintained a focus on resistance that stresses its dialectical nature rather than a separate dualistic history. Concretely, this means not postulating a fully autonomous sphere of action for social movement activism but rather examining the relational character to the dominant exercise of power, as well as its contestation and subversion (Modonesi 2010: 42, 45). This emphasis on the dialectic is missing from some of the landmark analyses within geographical studies that focus more on a radical politics of language in constructing the social world to achieve transformation (e.g., Gibson-Graham 2006a, 2006b).

The book lays particular stress on the agency of indigenous communities and movements in the struggles over place and space. Indigenous subjectivities have largely been excluded from dominant debates about development in Latin America, frequently being regarded as an anachronism that would be absorbed through the twin processes of mestization and proletarianization.[3] However, in recent decades (and in particular since the quincentennial remembrance of Spanish conquest), indigenous resistance has risen to prominence throughout the region (Postero 2004; Yashar 1999, 2005). Indigenous movements are now the leading social force of popular mobilization in Latin America, providing a cosmovision often in direct antagonism to capitalist social relations of production (Robinson 2008: 303; Zibechi 2012: 13). Subsequently, many of the long-held axioms of traditional leftist thought, such as the centrality of the state and the working class (defined in terms of a fixed sociological category) as the agent of political transformation, have been challenged. Among a number of new trends that are observable in Latin America is the manner in which social movements have become more territorially rooted while frequently, but not exclusively, seeking autonomy from the state and political parties (Zibechi 2012: 14–15). I explore the reasons behind this strategic evolution, and I discuss its potentialities and problems in a globalized context.

As mentioned earlier, the book draws its empirical focus from resistance movements that have emerged in the southern states of Oaxaca and Chiapas, most notably since the neoliberal reforms of Carlos Salinas de Gortari (1988–94). One of the chosen case studies, the Zapatistas, has already been extensively written about, yet relatively scant consideration has been devoted to analyzing the spatial and scalar dimensions of their political praxis, which I have remedied through my research. The other case study examines the state of Oaxaca. While in recent years this state has seen more scholarly reflections on state formation (see, e.g., Chassen-López 2004; Overmyer-Valázquez 2006; Smith 2009), these studies have focused on the period leading up to the Mexican Revolution or the era immediately following it. The analysis brought to bear in this book offers a detailed engagement that deals with contemporary state formation and resistance in Oaxaca but also considers these aspects from the perspective of the longue durée. Such an approach offers an important contribution to debates surrounding the historical sociology of international relations, which have hitherto taken a largely Eurocentric bent (e.g., Lacher 2006; Rosenberg 2006, 2013; Teschke 2003). As noted above, within Mexican studies there is an emergent literature on subnational political processes, and calls have been made for further comparative research across Mexico (Otero 2004: 342). This is important to avoid what Stein Rokkan (1970) has called "whole nation bias" or what John Agnew (1994) terms "the territorial trap." Richard Snyder (2001: 94) has further argued that "subnational comparisons better equip researchers to handle the spatially uneven nature of major processes of political and economic transformation." However, as will be explained in the section below on methodology, this approach does not entail having to adopt the positivist comparative method championed by Snyder that conceives the social world as made up of separable and controllable units of analysis.

Intellectual Production and the Social Purpose of Academic Inquiry

Before beginning any investigation, it is necessary to critically reflect on the motivations and intended social purpose of such an undertaking. Robert Cox (1981: 128) famously opined, "Theory is always for someone or some purpose. . . .

[T]here is no such thing as theory in itself, divorced from a standpoint in time and space." All academic interventions are thus conceived of as serving a social function of a particular kind, whether the authors recognize that function or not. This conforms to the definition of an intellectual offered by Antonio Gramsci (1971: 10–17, Q 12, §1) as anyone who seeks to organize, direct, educate, and inform. In agreement with Marx's famous eleventh thesis on Ludwig Feuerbach (1845/2000: 173), scholarly activity is not a passive description of the world; instead, it seeks to aid efforts to change the world.[4] As Lefebvre (1961/2008: 19) pointed out, "Critique implies possibilities, and possibilities as yet unfulfilled. It is the task of critique to demonstrate what these possibilities and this lack of fulfilment are." This work thus makes no claim for neutrality and rejects the separation between subject and object. Rather, it is consciously anticapitalist in its orientation for reasons that will become clear as the argument progresses. Nevertheless, we must recognize that there exists a major debate as to how an anticapitalist politics is best articulated (for a discussion, see Hesketh 2016). For some, it is essential to focus on and display more clearly the logic of capital, as this is the dominant mode of production within the global economy (Bernstein 2010: 1–2; Harvey 2010: 4; Ollman 2003: 4; Wood 1995: 238). However, an opposing position argues that in constructing alternatives, it is vital to loosen the grip of unilinear trajectories of development, as such perspectives can result in a highly capitalocentric viewpoint (Gibson-Graham 2006a). Such a view claims that theory should "proliferate possibility, not foreclose it," if it is to play a part in emancipatory activity (Gibson-Graham 2006b: 126). This book adopts a position between these two debates. In concurrence with Kipfer (2002: 147), I postulate that searching for alternatives while exploring capitalist survival are internally related, not mutually exclusive, spheres of concern.

Globalization and Its Discontents: Lost in Space

Over the last two decades much scholarly debate has turned to analyzing processes of neoliberal restructuring, commonly referred to as "globalization." One theorist has defined this process as an "epochal shift" that is reconfiguring the world's previous spatial order (Robinson 2004b: 4). In William Robinson's view, economic restructuring has led to a situation whereby "transnational space" now exerts a hegemonic influence over national space. The import of this development is that it implies (in Robinson's thinking) that resistance must now operate at this level as well (Robinson 2003, 2004b, 2008). Indeed, this call for a transnational form of resistance has also been asserted in the influential works of Michael Hardt and Antonio Negri (2000, 2005) and explored in concrete detail with regard to its practicalities (Bieler 2012, 2013). In contrast to this, other theorists have called for a politics of "localization," or a dispersal of power as a means to deal with emergent global problems (Hines 2000; Zibechi 2010). Others have questioned the very narrative of globalization, claiming that it is a disempowering discourse that hides the fact that the state retains key powers in order to regulate these "global" forces should it choose to do so (Hirst and Thompson 1999; Weiss 1998). Another school—the so-called global transformationalists—claims that reforms to global capitalism below the nation-state level and at the supranational level will serve to curb its current excesses and serve to humanize it while still being able to utilize the power of the market to create a form of global social democracy (Held 2004; Held and McGrew 2002). An adequate understanding of the spatial dynamics of capital accumulation thus becomes an urgent task if we are to address questions of how an alternative political economy can begin to articulate itself. This process-based perspective is imperative if we are not to engage in a form of "spatial fetishism" (Harvey 1996: 353; Massey 2005: 101). As David Harvey (1990: 218) counsels, "Any project to transform society must grasp the complex nettle of transformation of spatial and temporal conceptions and practices." It is precisely this challenge that my research seeks to undertake.

Certainly, the global restructuring of space that has occurred since the 1970s is not without contradiction and friction. The unresolved tensions encapsulated within this process are summed up perfectly by Henri Lefebvre (1991: 351), who asks, "How and why is it that the advent of a world market, implying a degree of unity at the level of the planet, gives rise to a fractioning of space—to a proliferation of nation-states, to regional differentiation and self-determination, as well as to multinational states and transnational corporations, which, although they stem this strange tendency towards fission, also exploit it in order to reinforce their own autonomy? Towards what space and time will such interwoven contradictions lead us?"

Building upon this question, I draw upon the concept of uneven and combined development as a vital explanatory tool with which to understand the production of space and as a "prime law of the modern world" (Lefebvre 1961/ 2008: 3). Propelling this is capital's need to embed itself into the physical environment in order to produce surplus value. However, due to the nature of the class conditions that exist within capitalist social relations, capital must also remain in motion, seeking out new profitable areas for accumulation (Harvey 2006a: 380; Brenner 1998). Neil Smith (2008: 155–59, 187) has outlined how uneven development involves a contradictory dynamic, leading to the equalization of the conditions of production across space, on the one hand, while accentuating the differentiation of space, on the other. The spatial, in other words, should be seen as the *geographical expression of class struggle*, or, as Lefebvre (1991: 55) decisively put it, "Today, more than ever, the class struggle is inscribed in space." This astute observation will be a leitmotif of the book, demonstrated and further validated through empirical investigation.

It is precisely this issue of spatial transformation and contestation in the present that is in fact missing from the recent literature on uneven and combined development within the historical sociology of international relations. Justin Rosenberg (2006: 316; 2013), for example, has sought to extend the term so that the world (and therefore world history) can be understood as an ontological whole. Uneven and combined development in this usage therefore collapses the false distinction between domestic and international but nevertheless allows us to focus on its very real sociological constitution (Rosenberg 2006: 327). Extending this analysis, Rosenberg has sought to provide a social theory of the international by stressing that uneven and combined development is in fact a general abstraction that is foundational to what development actually is (for a debate around this issue, see Callinicos and Rosenberg 2008). Uneven and combined development is thus posited as a universal law of human history (Rosenberg 2010: 179–84; 2013).[5] This argument is made by extending the philosophical arguments back to hunter-gatherer societies and the original establishment of political societies. Elsewhere, the term has gained currency in examining the geopolitics of the interstate system through an analysis of social property relations (Lacher 2006; Teschke 2002, 2003, 2005). As Ian Bruff (2010) summarizes, this has meant that the current literature is most comfortable when intellectual efforts are devoted to the study of precontemporary history, which marks the research focus's substantive field of inquiry.[6] However, Neil Smith (2006: 181–84) has trenchantly argued that this has the danger of removing the social purpose of the concept of uneven and combined development, which was originally deployed by Leon Trotsky "to analyse and evaluate the possibilities and trajectories of revolution." Smith thus contends that approaches to the concept that are despatialized are also thus depoliticized (see also Rioux 2015). Mindful of this point, I seek to be cognizant of both spatial concerns and movements of resistance throughout the book.

Methodological Issues

As has already been mentioned, in exploring the spaces of capital and the spaces of resistance, this book develops an approach based on historical-geographical sociology. More specifically, it draws influence from both Michael Burawoy's (1998) "extended case method" and Philip McMichael's (1990, 2000) notion of "incorporated comparison."[7] The extended case method is sharply distinguished from positivist science, which seeks to separate subject and object, as well as fact and value. Instead, this method does not deny that we bring our own assumptions to the study of key academic questions. Rather, this method stresses these assumptions are "more like prisms than templates and they are emergent rather than fixed" (Burawoy 1998: 11). The extended case method is an explicitly critical method of inquiry, forming situated knowledge that is consciously interventionist in the social world. The purpose of the extended case method is thus to draw links between the unique and the general and to move from the micro to the macro, thereby extending outward from one spatial scale to another (Burawoy 1998: 5). Closely related to this standpoint of seeking causal connections between cases is the method of incorporated comparison. This method takes some inspiration from the "encompassing" comparative methodology associated with scholars such as Immanuel Wallerstein (1974) and Charles Tilly (1984) in that it seeks to show the interconnections between social phenomena across time and space. However, the incorporated comparative method takes neither the whole (the world system) nor its constituent parts (regions, countries, etc.) as fixed units of analysis. Instead, this method is attentive to the dialectical relation between the whole and the parts and does not claim either as the prime locus of explanation. In McMichael's (1990: 386) words, the incorporated comparison method "progressively constructs the whole as a methodological procedure by giving context to historical phenomena." The stress is on the cumulative process of history. Comparison, therefore, "is 'internal' to historical inquiry, whereby process instances are comparable because they are historically connected and mutually conditioning" (McMichael 2000: 671). This approach has the advantage of allowing us to appreciate the totality of capitalist relations while being attentive to capitalism's different articulations at different spatial scales. Borrowing a turn of phrase from Gramsci (1971: 117, Q 10ii, §61), capitalism can thus be thought of as a "universal concept with geographical seats."

Following the critical orientation of my research, I have focused on Latin America because that region has and continues to offer the most compelling sites of resistance and alternatives to neoliberal capitalism. It has provided some of the most dynamic and innovative experiments in radical democracy, from the participatory budget and inception of the World Social Forum (WSF) process in Porto Alegre, Brazil, to the many significant social movements, including, among others, the Zapatistas (Mexico), the Movimento dos Trabalhadores Sem Terra (MST, Landless Workers' Movement, Brazil), and the Movimiento de Trabajadores Desocupados (MTD, Unemployed Workers' Movement, Argentina). The "pink tide" phenomenon saw Left or left-of-center governments returned to Venezuela, Bolivia, Brazil, Argentina, Ecuador, Uruguay, and Nicaragua. Such governments may now be under challenge (Modonesi 2015). Furthermore, these leftist governments have not always lived up to their radical rhetoric and aspirations (Hesketh and Morton 2014; Webber 2011). However, they have managed to place the idea of socialism into the public consciousness and help to "interrupt" neoliberalism (Goodale and Postero 2013). Moreover, it must not be forgotten that this shift to the left was frequently a process driven from below by social movements (Ciccariello-Maher 2013). These movements remain key agents in the making of history (Cox and Nilsen 2014).

I focused more narrowly on Mexico for a number of reasons. It was the only country in Latin America before 1950 to undergo a profound, protracted, and bloody revolution, yet in spite of this it has also been the Latin American country that has most vigorously pursued the path of capitalist development (Weinert 1981: 115; Hansen 1971: 95). This development was further enhanced by the signing of NAFTA in 1994, a strong indication of the country's commitment to a neoliberal accumulation strategy. Moreover, and of necessity related to this commitment, Mexico has produced some of the most visible and vibrant resistance movements, all of which have sought to contest and remake political space and inspire global ideas about how neoliberalism can be challenged and concepts such as "globalization" and "revolution" can be reimagined (Holloway and Peláez 1998). Mexico thus provides fertile ground for considering the twin pillars of this research: the spaces of capital and the spaces of resistance. I have chosen Oaxaca and Chiapas as case studies because they have been key sites of resistance in recent years, and their social struggles have resonated both throughout Mexico and in the wider world. Their struggles also remain ongoing and open-ended.

Book Summary

The book proceeds as follows.

Chapter 1 begins by underscoring why a concern with the spatial is important. It also makes the case for focusing on two concepts related to the tradition of historical-materialist thought, namely, class struggle and mode of production. Once the reasons for this focus have been established, the chapter outlines a theory of the production of space. A discussion of the characteristics of feudal/absolutist space is then offered before the chapter goes on to consider what is distinctive about the production of space under capitalist social relations of production. The contradictions involved in actual or attempted capitalist transformations of spaces are highlighted, and the role of space for a politics of resistance is briefly discussed.

Chapter 2 turns to an analysis of the production of space in Latin America. It highlights the manner in which Latin America has both been integrated into and itself been a site through which the global economy has been produced. It explores the region's development trajectory in terms of a contradictory spatial project and draws attention to the manner in which particular spatial divisions of labor have been constructed within the region. In particular, it highlights the rise of neoliberalism in Latin America as an attempt to offset contradictions inherent in the capitalist mode of production by means of a spatial fix, drawing attention to the class basis involved in such a process.

Chapter 3 deepens this analysis of state, space, and class formation through an investigation of modern Mexico. Here Gramsci's key concepts of passive revolution and hegemony are utilized to explain the nation's development trajectory while situating those concepts and that trajectory within the conditions of worldwide capitalist development.

Chapters 4 and 5 offer detailed case studies of the states of Oaxaca and Chiapas, respectively. These chapters analyze how spatial reconfigurations have come about, reflecting both the changing way in which these states became integrated within the global political economy and the changing accumulation strategies of the national state. I examine subnational forms of passive revolution in each case in order to explore localized processes of state formation. Furthermore, both chapters include a detailed discussion of movements of resistance and their attempts to defend place and produce alternative geographical spaces that are not based on the logic of capital. These chapters thus provide an excavation of spatial history in order to reveal its sedimented layers, which continue to influence current topographies and contribute to recent ruptures.

CHAPTER ONE

Geographical Politics and the Politics of Geography

The spatial is not just a matter of lines on a map; it is a cartography of power.
—Doreen Massey, *For Space*

This chapter seeks to critically engage with debates surrounding the production of space under capitalist social relations of production. The aim is to construct a theoretical framework whereby changes in the geography of the global economy and, moreover, resistance to those changes can be understood. Furthermore, the framework developed here should allow us to examine these changes through a multiscalar analysis. Rather than simply focusing on global, national, or local changes, this chapter seeks to develop an approach that can integrate analyses on a variety of spatial scales. In short, the chapter aims to serve as a tool of analysis, helping to explain why struggles over space, and what particular spaces contain, are likely to become an ever more prominent feature of political life. Linked to this explanation are ancillary arguments about state and class formation and their central role in these processes.

This chapter thus lays the theoretical foundations for explaining the changing scalar organization of the world economy since the 1970s. That organization is viewed from a macrostructural perspective, with an analysis of how it affected the space of Latin America, as well as state formation in the region (see chapter 2) and the changing historical sociology of the state form in Mexico (chapter 3). Finally, the chapter provides the basis to understand processes of geopolitical conflict and class struggle around particular subnational spaces that are currently being targeted as sites for increased capital accumulation (chapters 4 and 5). As was set out in the introduction, the first task is to make the theoretical argument in the abstract before putting flesh on these bones through empirical investigation and the appreciation of wider nuances. Neil Brenner (2004: 18) has stated in relation to this that "consideration of the abstract level enables scholars to examine the general, systemic features of a given historical system." Noel Castree (2000: 10) usefully illustrates how it is in the realm of abstract argumentation that we organize our worldviews and then come to act out our everyday practices. Our conceptions of the world thus clearly matter, and they motivate us toward action (Gramsci 1971: 323–25, Q 11, §12; Harvey 2010: 38). This chapter, while providing the beginnings of a theoretical framework, deliberately does not close that framework, as I am cognizant of the fact that theory is always modified and informed by the manner in which it works itself out in the real world, including processes of struggle. The concept and the lived experience, in other words, remain inseparable, and we cannot do without either (Lefebvre 1976: 20). It should also be noted that this theorizing is itself not ahistorical in nature but in fact derives from the historical materialist tradition of seeing "theory as history" (Banaji 2011). In other words, it builds on already-accumulated historical knowledge, as opposed to constructing pure, ideal types (Rioux 2013).

An overarching focus on issues of "space" can seem at first appearance to be something of an abstract concern. However, a "politics of space" occupies a central part of our daily lives and promises to have profound effects on our future. One may think here of the peculiarly modern phenomenon of urban slum proliferation, the tragic plight of those who, each year, fleeing political or economic persecution, mortgage their lives in the backs of trucks or other precarious means of transportation, only to be turned back at demarcated and fortified borders, or the relocation of corporations to far-flung parts of the globe, to highlight just a few examples of how the politics of the spatial permeates conflicts and struggles throughout the world. Since the 1980s we have also seen a rise in claims for spatial exclusiveness in terms of nationalism, or regional and localist identity (Massey 1994: 4). In light of this, a prominent, yet spurious, spatial discourse stressing a "clash of civilizations" has gained credence. This maps the world according to key cultural characteristics and claims that the "fault lines between civilisations will be the battle lines of the future" (Huntington 1993: 22). After the events of September 11, 2001, this thesis has risen to prominence, notably among those whom John Agnew and Gearóid Ó Tuathail (1992) term "intellectuals of statecraft." With the recent upsurge in indigenous activism across Latin America against the privatization of natural resources, U.S. intelligence agencies have wondered aloud whether this is to be the new backdrop for a renewed civilizational clash (Grandin 2007: 213–14). A similar thesis (albeit with a different political rationale) is to be found in one of the most famed books on Mexican history. In his celebrated text *México profundo*, Guillermo Bonfil Batalla (1996) argued that the last five hundred years of Mexican history can best be understood as a clash of civilizations between a native Mesoamerican culture, on the one hand, and an exogenous Western culture, on the other. According to Bonfil Batalla (1996: xvi), from the time of colonialization onward, Mexico has been organized on "the norms, aspirations, and goals of western civilisation." The alternative, he argues, is to return Mexico to its basis in Meso-

american culture (which has retained its presence, albeit in a marginalized fashion). This argument obviously has had wider purchase for Latin American societies that have shared experiences of colonization. However, while we cannot
deny the huge importance of cultural negation that colonialism implied (and
continues to imply), if we do not want to essentialize location and culture and
are serious about examining the possibilities for emancipatory transformation
that extend beyond the borders of Mexico or Latin America (thus avoiding
parochialism), we should perceive this scenario not as a clash between civilizations but rather as a clash between spatial class projects that were, by their
nature, culturally loaded.[1] This involves a dialectical process of defetishizing
fixed categories, leading to further fundamental questions about the processes
and interactions that serve to constitute social reality (Ollman 2003). For example, once we come to investigate the spatial transformations that occurred
during colonialism, we are also forced to explore questions of territorial control,
as well as the resources within that territory, including the population's labor.
This then leads us to inquire into the motivations driving the process of colonization. Here, appeals to essential cultural characteristics become something
of a misnomer. It is, after all, doubtful that we could identify anything inherent
to Western civilisation that made it seek to conquer other areas and peoples
of the world. If these conquests were contingent rather than linked to reified
characteristics of human nature, then we must explore what social processes
animate and transform cultures. It is here, as I will demonstrate, that a relational
category like class has far more utility, because it allows us to examine the power
interests involved and the contradictory dynamics of a mode of production.
This does not mean that issues of culture are unimportant. Rather, this examination entails exploring the manner in which culture itself is interwoven with
place-specific constructs of political-economic power (Harvey 1993: 21).

My research seeks to construct an alternative framework for understanding geopolitical conflict. A central issue under investigation in this chapter
is therefore the importance of the spatial in distinctly *capitalist* processes of
development. After all, capitalism is the dominant socioeconomic model for
development in our time. Since the fall of the Soviet Union and the collapse of
"actually existing Communism" in Eastern Europe, and following the market
reforms of Deng Xiaoping in China, there is little doubt that the world has
become more capitalist.[2] Indeed, Francis Fukuyama (1992) has gone as far as
to say that liberal capitalism represents the "end of history" in terms of a developmental paradigm, as it now has no ideological competitor (although he
left open the caveat that history was always open to begin again). In the wake
of the world financial crisis of 2007–8 (the latest in a wave of financial crises
that have afflicted the world with increasing frequency and intensity since the
1970s), it has become acceptable once again to discuss the term "capitalism" in
the mainstream (Nitzan and Bichler 2009: 1), and it indeed appears that people

(in certain parts of the world more than others) are beginning to question what sort of history we wish to create. It is imperative, therefore, that we understand why particular spaces are produced in the manner in which they are. Can we discern an overall logic to this process, and if so, in what general direction is this process heading? Is this purely a unilinear trajectory, or do we encounter multiple paths to modernity? Moreover, is this process free of contradiction, or can we infer general tendencies from which we can make certain assumptions about the future and uncover potential agents of change? Furthermore, what does the changing geography of capitalist production imply for a politics of resistance? This book seeks to address all these issues in empirical detail. In chapter 2 I conduct a *meso-level* analysis in relation to the global political economy and Latin America's relation to it. I discuss the *concrete level* of Mexico's incorporation into these structures in chapter 3 before going on to discuss the dialectic of incorporation and resistance in the cases of Oaxaca and Chiapas (chapters 4 and 5, respectively).

The argument proceeds as follows. First, I provide a general discussion of how to approach the problem of space, and I make an argument for considering the relevance of class struggle to it. Second, I will clarify what it means to talk about the "production of space" and why the term "mode of production" can serve as a useful heuristic device to explain spatial patterns. Third, I examine the difference between feudal and capitalist space, with reference to the different class relations that these modes of production embody and thus the different social purpose that the spatial serves in each mode. This discussion serves to illuminate key tendencies for spatial production under capitalism, tendencies that I will then analyze theoretically and empirically in terms of the transition to neoliberalism in chapters 2 and 3. Fourth, I discuss the role of resistance in shaping the production of place, space, and scale before finally drawing some conclusions. All these points underscore the key claim that struggles over space are ever more integral to the modern world.

A Crisis of Subject Matter? Why Class Matters

As noted in the introduction, within the historical-materialist geographical tradition, approaches to political economy and world order have often focused on the power of capital and issues of capital accumulation (e.g., see Harvey 2006a, 2010; Smith 2008). Although an explanation of contemporary phenomena like globalization can serve a useful function in pointing out some inherent antinomies of capital, there is the danger that such an explanation will be presented in one-sided terms that focus only on the dominant (and therefore singular) narrative, eliding the multifaceted processes of contestation and subversion that have concomitantly been taking place while also unwittingly giving intellectual coherence to such a process. J. K. Gibson-Graham (2006b: 41) refers to this as "capitalocentrism," whereby capitalism in placed at the center of all developmental narratives, thereby marginalizing the possibilities for noncapitalist social relations. While recognizing the importance of discerning a logic to the movement of capital, this book is equally concerned with highlighting the dialectically related power of those whom capital employs, seeks to employ, or else relies upon in other forms (such as the unemployed who can function as an industrial reserve army) as possible agents of change. It is also concerned with the potential of those who refuse to be dispossessed and incorporated (notably, indigenous and peasant communities). Indeed, the survival of noncapitalist spaces and how they interact with capitalist forms are an integral focus in chapters 3, 4, and 5.

In concurrence with John Holloway (2002a: 40), I argue that "what we want is not a theory of domination but a theory of the vulnerability of domination." This changes the focus somewhat of who the subject of a given piece of research is. As stated above, all too often, intellectual production is solely geared to analyzing processes of capitalist expansion. Capital, in other words, becomes the subject of study, whereas people and places affected by capital are viewed as passive objects (Lebowitz 2003; Chassen-López 2004: 17).[3] Drawing upon the crisis-ridden nature of the structure of capitalism, Holloway has offered a different type of paradigm, one in which we put "crisis" at the forefront of our thinking. This change in perspective fundamentally affects our research agenda. As Holloway (interview with the author, Cholula, 2008) explains, "Crisis is important first and foremost as a methodological approach. What interests us is not the question of how capitalism works, but rather the question of how on earth we get out of it. When we are talking about living in a crisis, we are not claiming that capitalism is about to collapse, but rather stressing that the question is one of crisis, the question is not one of domination. If you start with domination, you close the world all the time. It seems to me, if you start with domination, there is absolutely no way out."

The approach I develop here, while concurring with the spirit of Holloway's argument, demurs slightly by arguing that in fact we *do* need to understand how capital works in order to understand how to get out of it. Without an understanding of the overarching "field of force," the broader structural relations of capitalism, we are unable to understand present fault lines that are capable of being transformed into future earthquakes. Marx (1852/2000: 329) was profoundly aware of this need to explore the potential for the future from the standpoint of the present, writing: "Men [sic] make their own history, but they do not make it as they please; they do not make it under circumstances chosen by themselves, but under circumstances directly encountered, given and transmitted from the past." The spaces of capital and the spaces of resistance, in other words, cannot be separated from one another; instead, structure and agency are akin to a Gordian knot (Bieler and Morton 2001).

I argue below that appealing to Gramsci's notion of hegemony allows us both to understand the structural power that capital is able to wield and to be attentive to the manner in which this process is actively shaped by subaltern groups pressing their own claims. Hegemony is defined by Gramsci (1971: 57, Q 19, §24) as the intellectual and moral leadership that the dominant class is able to exercise over society as a whole. However, its stability is often predicated on concessions being granted to subaltern classes in order to secure their consent. Holloway (2005: 270) derides this concept, labeling it as a cop-out that crosses over to bourgeois theory. He further objects that it does not contain a theory of its own gravedigger and reinforces rather than dissolves relations of domination.[4] However, this is based on a misreading of the way in which Gramsci deployed the term "hegemony": he viewed it as a continuous process rather than a fixed accomplishment. Hegemony does not remove the contradictions inherent in capitalist society. What it illuminates is the manner in which the economy, politics, and culture are interwoven and how political power is constantly renegotiated as new social needs are produced and demands created (Lefebvre 1947/2008: 49). Capitalism can thus be viewed as an inherently unstable form of power that is modified by subaltern class struggles and has relied upon consent more than any system before it (Gramsci 1971: 52–54, Q 25, §5; Lefebvre 1991: 57; Roseberry 1994). Hegemony's chief purpose is to illustrate the nature of class struggle, but in a manner that avoids crude determinism based on historical inevitability. This brings us to the question of values. As David Harvey (1996: 10–11) has cogently argued, "Meaningful political action (and for that matter, even meaningful analysis) cannot proceed without some embedded notions of value, if only as a determination as to what is, or is not important to analyse intellectually let alone to struggle for politically." However, Harvey asks us not to conceive of values in timeless, nondialectical terms; instead, we need to look at "processes of valuation." As stated earlier, in order to do this, we need to read history backward, taking as our starting point the relative "permanences" that exist in the here and now and examining the processes and flows that make up these permanences and that are essential to sustaining them (Harvey 1996: 63). It is only through doing this that we can grasp the essential point that place, space, and scale are, in fact, social relations (Massey 1994: 2).

That place and space are products of our interrelations and are dependent upon particular social processes to sustain them can be witnessed by examining any historical city of splendor that now serves as a tourist attraction under the name of "ruins" (Massey 2005: 3). Concomitant with this is a change in the place's social function. For example, when it was the main seat of monarchical power in the Inca Empire Machu Picchu clearly had a social purpose different from the social purpose it has now as a commodified global attraction in modern-day Peru. In recent decades, the breakup of the Soviet Union and the restructuring of global capital have created profound changes in space. During this same period the decline of former Fordist heartland cities with the onset of deindustrialization in the United States and the converse surge in the development of industrial production in the emerging economies have occurred. All these events point to the contingent and thus changeable nature of space.

The question that we must therefore ask is, What are the dominant processes constructing modern forms of space? The approach I adopt here when answering this question is rooted in the historical-materialist tradition of understanding the social world through processes of class struggle. It should be noted that with the fall of the Berlin Wall and the collapse of Communism in Eastern Europe, as well as the increasing neoliberalization of China, issues of class have come to be viewed as an anachronism that the social sciences can do without. That religious-based rather than class-based groups have been raising the banner of revolution in recent decades, combined with the fact that major economic downturns have not been met with proportionate working-class responses, has led others to dismiss the significance of class (Cox 1987: 3). Indeed, if the past is a foreign country where people do things differently, as L. P. Hartley (1953) famously stated in his classic novel *The Go-Between*, then it has been conjectured that the language of class could only be understood there. However, Jean-François Lyotard's (1984) invective against metanarratives notwithstanding, I submit here that appeals to notions of class and class struggle remain vital for our understanding of the modern world. Without appeal to such concepts, our understanding of contemporary sources of concentrated power is highly blunted (Jameson 1991: 349). Likewise, without an analysis of class we are blinded to one of the most pernicious and pervasive forms of exploitation that exists today (Wood 1995). As Neil Smith (2000: 1011–16) rightly points out, the social sciences stopped using the term "class" precisely at a time when its relevance was being reasserted with a vengeance in terms of global class formation, most notably in Eastern Europe, Asia, and Latin America. Indeed, class remains the big nonissue within the global economy. For example, Thomas Piketty (2014) has usefully highlighted the issue of rising inequality since the beginning of the neoliberal period, resulting in an increasing share of wealth flowing to the top 10 percent of society. However, without any notion of class, this remains a historical process with no agency.[5]

This stress on class struggle should not be interpreted as some wistful longing for a politics of certainty but rather an imperative explanatory device able to illuminate key issues in today's often opaque world. Frederic Jameson (1991: 331) succinctly explained the connections between class politics and political mobilizations, postulating, "What is sometimes characterised as a nostalgia for class politics of some older type is generally more likely to be simply a 'nostalgia' for politics tout court: given the way in which periods of intense politicisation and withdrawal are modelled on great economic rhythms of boom and bust of the business cycle, to describe this feeling as 'nostalgia' is about as adequate as to characterise the body's hunger before food as a 'nostalgia for food.'"

Concurrent with David Harvey (2006b: 202), when we are explaining geographical processes of restructuring, "if it looks like class struggle and acts like class war then we have to name it unashamedly for what it is." I will make the case for this assertion in the rest of this chapter and in subsequent chapters. This does not mean, of course, accepting that other struggles around issues such as gender, sexuality, the environment, and so on are not important, merely that they largely predate capitalism, and thus the form they adopt within capitalist society is one dominated by an ever deepening class antagonism that is shaping society (Lebowitz 2003: 151; Ollman 2003: 162–63; Wood 1995: 246). In other words, it is hard to discuss these issues without also engaging in a discussion of class. An understanding of modern capitalism, for example, cannot proceed without a discussion of natural resource exploitation or an understanding of how class struggle has been both racialized and gendered (e.g., see Bakker 1994; Marable 2000; Wright 2006). The accent on class does not necessitate that we elide questions of cultural difference. Rather, in agreement with McNally (2013: 411–12), it means recognizing the complexity of class experience and acknowledging its spatial and temporal mediations. A focus on class also involves examining how categories such as race, gender, and sexuality are not preformed identities but coconstitutive of one another. I take up this point in detail when I consider indigenous struggles in Mexico in chapters 4 and 5. Marx (1843/2000: 766) cogently argued in relation to this point: "It is by no means sufficient to ask: who should emancipate and who should be emancipated? Criticism has to be concerned with a third question. It must ask: *What kind of emancipation is involved* and what are its underlying conditions?"

The central issue, therefore, as Michael Lebowitz (2003: 186–87) points out, is whether these new social actors take part in collective struggles against capital's role as mediator of social life and help identify new organizing centers of resistance (on the relation of this to environmental politics, see in particular O'Connor 1998). These struggles become class projects when they entail "a direct challenge to the circulation and accumulation of capital" (Harvey 1996: 401). As well as seeking to contribute to an understanding of space and class formation under capitalist social relations, this chapter also seeks to make an intervention into the debates surrounding the future of geopolitics. A concern with what the development of capitalism implies for the future of the state form and issues of interstate conflict has long played an important role in historical-materialist writings, notably, of course, in the classic debate between Vladimir Lenin (1917/ 1987a) and Karl Kautsky (1914/1970). Within Marxist circles, the future of geopolitics has once again become a central category of debate (e.g., see Anievas

2010; Harvey 2003; Robinson 2004b, 2007; Wood 2005). However, many of these debates (the protestations of the authors notwithstanding) actually view geopolitics in rather state-centric terms. That is, they continue to focus only on conflicts taking place between nation-states, thereby ignoring internal and/or subnational forms of geopolitical conflict (Callinicos 2007; Harvey 2003; Van der Pijl 2007). Others commit the opposite error, assuming processes of complete deterritorialization, and thus construct an aspatial view of globalization that assumes there is now simply one form of global society (Hardt and Negri 2000; Ohmae 1999; Robinson 2004b; for a critique of this position, see Brenner 2004: 47–56; Massey 2005: 82). These theories thus fail to engage in a substantial manner with any theory of the spatial as an ongoing site of change and instead succumb to what John Agnew (1994) has termed "the territorial trap."

In this chapter, while mindful of the key role of the state in the production of space under capitalist social relations, I have been attentive to the manner in which the scalar organization of the state is itself a contingent phenomenon that is currently being reconfigured under contemporary patterns of geographical restructuring to include both supranational and subnational articulations of hegemony (a point to be taken up in greater detail in chapters 4 and 5). Drawing from the tradition of critical geopolitics, this chapter thus aims to deploy the term "geopolitics" in the wider sense of the meaning, that is, the struggles to shape place, space, and scale for a particular social purpose. We must not only be cognizant of the role of the state in inducing particular transformations but also take seriously the historical geography of the state form as a contingent set of social relations that is subject to evolution and change (a theme to be taken up in more detail in chapters 2 and 3). I will demonstrate here that a differentiated geography remains vital to the political functioning of capitalism, and it is through the creation of this geographical difference that the politics of capitalism expresses itself most vividly. As David Harvey (2010: 161) argues in relation to this point, "Geographical diversity is a necessary condition for, rather than a barrier to, the reproduction of capital. If the geographical diversity does not already exist, then it has to be created." While this is an important point we must keep in mind, it is equally vital that we recognize the process of resistance as vital to geopolitics and the production of space. If there was no resistance, there would be no need for a political project (Ó Tuathail 1996: 12). Hegemony, defined in terms of providing intellectual and moral leadership, in which allies are sought and opponents nullified, would simply be a redundant question. Moreover, as will later be explained, resistance is itself the presupposition and major force of spatial difference. Lefebvre (1966/2009, 1979/2009) refers to this process of resistance as *autogestion*, which is defined as an antistatist collective struggle to shape social life in the interests of the subaltern classes, which attempt to overcome alienated conditions of existence under capitalism. Rather than an end condition, autogestion is theorized as a process that at the same time serves a reflexive, autopedagogical function. Thus, "each time a so-cial group . . . refuses to accept passively its conditions of existence, of life, or of survival, each time such a group forces itself not only to understand but to master its conditions of existence, autogestion is occurring" (Lefebvre 1979/2009: 135). Autogestion aims at the creation of a genuinely differential space, "which represents for capitalism an antagonistic and ruinous tendency" (Le-febvre 2003: 98). This idea of alternative spaces of resistance will be developed in detail in chapters 4 and 5.

The Production of Space

"Geography," Gearóid Ó Tuathail (1996: 1) argues, "is about power. Although often assumed to be innocent, the geography of the world is not a product of nature but a product of histories of struggle between competing authorities over the power to organise, occupy and administer space." Perhaps the figure who has done most to inspire thinking about space and its importance for every-day life is French Marxist Henri Lefebvre (see, in particular, 1947/2008, 1970/2003, 1991). In the opening pages of his classic treatise *The Production of Space*, Lefebvre (1991) highlights how "space" is a much-misunderstood concept. He seeks to make the distinction between the classic Euclidian or Cartesian con-cept of space, which views the world in terms of a fixed, timeless, and mappable essence that is somehow "out there" and simply occupied by actors, and, con-versely, social space, which is an ensemble of social relations that is produced through human agency (see also Brenner 1999: 41). The key point that Lefebvre wished to stress is that, contrary to how some philosophers have conceived space, it is not simply imagined into being, nor does it exist independently of so-cial action. Rather, spaces are created and transformed through material activ-ity. Mental spaces and social practice according to this conception can thus not be divorced (Ó Tuathail 1996: 51; see also Bieler and Morton 2008).[6] Space, in other words, is a social product and should not be conceived of as the "passive locus of social relations" (Lefebvre 1991: 26, 11). Rather, "space" needs to be seen as the embodiment of these very relations, because "the social relations of pro-duction have a social existence to the extent that they have a spatial existence: they project themselves into a space, becoming inscribed there, and in the process producing that space itself" (Lefebvre 1991: 129; see also Massey 1995, 2005: 9). The spatial is not the realm of stasis; instead, it needs to be rethought as a site of ongoing production (Massey 2005: 9–12). Space is not an empty stage onto which social relations are projected; instead, these relations themselves contribute to the changing mise-en-scène of development. Therefore, through a reading of the spatial the power relations of society can be uncovered. Once this point is recognized it is a logical step to inquire about what production processes dominate society, how social relations are organized under that particular type of production process, and how these relations in turn affect the manner in which space is produced. The central question we must therefore ask is, "If space embodies social relationships, how and why does it do so? And what relationships are they?" (Lefebvre 1991: 27). For Lefebvre (1991: 51) the important point to recognize is that all modes of production occupy particular spatial patterns; furthermore, every society or mode of production produces its own space and rhythms of life (see also Jameson 1991: 364). This is necessary for the society's reproduction. David Harvey (1990: 204), greatly influenced by the work of Lefebvre, clarifies this point: "Objective conditions of time and space are necessarily created through material practices that serve to reproduce social life."

The concept "mode of production" thus becomes a key term for our investigation, although as Lefebvre (1976: 61–63, 2003: 88) qualifies, this does not mean reducing space solely to the generic features of a mode of production, nor should the concept be "rigidified" and coherence stressed at the expense of contradiction (see also Banaji 2011). Instead, as Eric Wolf (1997: 76) has outlined, "The utility of the concept does not lie in classification but in its capacity to underlie the strategic relations involved in the deployment of social labour by organized human pluralities." The concept "mode of production" furthermore reveals "the political-economic relations that underlie, orient and constrain interaction." Wolf has captured the proper dialectical relationship between being and becoming. Understanding spatiality through an analysis of modes of production thus reveals a fundamental point: on the one hand, spaces are actively produced through human agency; on the other, once created, they can exert a powerful influence, serving to shape the rules and boundaries of our interaction (see Peck and Tickell 2002). It is in this sense that we can draw upon Gramsci's notion of hegemony: the means by which class forces are able to exercise a leading role within society. Indeed, Gramsci (1971: 30–33, Q 12, §1) is profoundly aware of how spatial forms serve to influence public opinion, from architectural forms to street layouts (see also Bieler and Morton 2008: 118; Jessop 2005).[7] Lefebvre (1991: 26) draws upon this concept to proclaim that space, "in addition to being a means of production[,] is also a means of control and hence of domination, of power." Stefan Kipfer (2002: 126) has powerfully argued that Gramsci and Lefebvre offer differing yet complementary approaches to hegemony. While Gramsci draws our attention to geographically based forms of state–civil society complexes, Lefebvre drew our attention to the contradictions in everyday life resulting from uneven development. These two figures, then, will be crucial to interpreting the production of space throughout this book.

In our need to uncover the relationships embedded in spaces, we need to move from analyzing things "in space" to analyzing the production of spaces themselves (Lefebvre 1991: 89). In Marx's (1867/1974: 76–87) analysis of commodity fetishism, he took the everyday appearance of the commodity and abstracted backward to show the social relations it concealed. Lefebvre likewise sought to uncover the relationships that lie behind the production of particular spaces. Three different, but related, elements composed the production of space for Lefebvre (1991: 33). These are spatial practices, representations of space, and representational spaces. Spatial practices refer to the spatial norms, of any given social formation, that ensure a degree of continuity and cohesion. Thus property relations, the physical layout of areas, including factors such as roads and infrastructure, and housing would be included under spatial practices, as would generalized work patterns (see also Lefebvre 2003: 84; Harvey 1990: 220–21). Spatial practices are closely associated with perceived space. In other words, they relate to our reflexive awareness of our surrounding environment. Representations of space, by contrast, are tied to ideology, signs, and codes. Representations of space are the realm of conceived space. They are thus related to the dominant ideology of society and, therefore, synonymous with class rule. Lastly there are representational spaces. Representational spaces are the realm of directly lived experience. Spatial practices and representations of space can combine to "facilitate the manipulation of representational space" (Lefebvre 1991: 59). However, this component of space is associated with subjective feelings or thought and can thus be linked to the more clandestine side of life from which resistance can begin to emerge.

This analysis calls for a dialectical method of investigation in which the properties of the totality or the social whole are sought in order to be explicitly rendered. All too often in the realm of modern academic inquiry, space is not treated as a conceptual whole; instead, particular pieces of it are examined. This is an explicitly bourgeois method of investigation that ignores the vital role of the internal relations that relate these constituent parts to one another (Lefebvre 1991: 91, 107; Ollman 2003).[8] Moreover, as Eric Wolf (1997: 18) has definitively demonstrated, it is a fallacy to believe that particular spaces have ever existed in isolation, independent from "larger encompassing relationships, unaffected by larger fields of force." This does not mean spatial differences are ignored. Rather, it requires us to be attentive to *how* spatial differences are *produced* (cf. Trotsky 1930/1962: 22–25). This methodological approach requires us to be cognizant "of processes that transcend separable cases, moving in, through, and beyond them, and transforming them as they proceed" (Wolf 1997: 17). As was set out in the introduction, this approach requires us to utilize the concept of uneven and combined development as a social theory able to grasp this phenomenon while being attentive to its particular characteristics under capitalism as a mode of production (a point to be elaborated later in the chapter).

Thus far, we have established that it makes sense and indeed it is vital to recognize that "space" is a socially produced phenomenon. The case has also been made for analyzing space in terms of a dominant mode of production. We need to move now from the abstract to the concrete and look at the very type

of social relations that predominate under the capitalist mode of production
to see what (if indeed anything) is particular to this kind of space. In order to
draw out the unique nature of capitalist spatiality, it is essential that we contrast
it with the spatial patterns of feudalism, as the transition from one mode to another ought to imply that rather different types of space are produced (because
each mode mobilizes social labor in a distinct manner and rests on different
class configurations). This step is vital to the dialectical method of inquiry, as
it helps to explain the preconditions of capitalist accumulation and in doing so
itself illuminates an essential element of capitalism's character (Ollman 2003:
149). As Marx (1867/1974: 668) writes in relation to this point, "The economic
structure of capitalist society has grown out of the economic structure of feudal
society. The dissolution of the latter set free the elements of the former." This
shift should consequently exemplify a novel articulation of spatial forms (Lefebvre 1991: 46).

Kings, Nobles, and Churches: The Holy Trinity of Feudal Space

With regard to feudalism, Lefebvre (1991: 53) was clear that "medieval society—
that is the feudal mode of production, with its variants and local peculiarities—
created its own space. . . . Manors, monasteries, cathedrals—these were the
strong points anchoring the network of lanes and main roads to a landscape
transformed by peasant communities." When discerning the logic to this spatiality, it is vital to note that under feudal and absolutist property relations "the
strategies for expanded reproduction of the ruling classes, organized in the pat-
rimonial state, remained tied to the logic of 'political accumulation'" (Teschke
2002: 11). Although they contained differences, both feudalism and absolutism
can thus be classified as variants of a tributary mode of production where extraeconomic coercion pertained as the dominant method of mobilizing social labor. This mode of production brought with it specific spatiotemporal patterns
that were relatively fixed (Poulantzas 1978: 102). As Marx outlines (1844/2007:
61), "The serf is the adjunct of the land. Likewise, the lord of an entailed estate,
the first born son, belongs to the land. It inherits him." Drawing upon this idea,
Lefebvre (1947/2008: 30–31) argues that labor and everyday life were far more
interwoven in this period, giving a particular rhythm to life, as well as providing
for a form of collectivity (e.g., access to the commons).

Another key aspect of feudal space was the preponderance of religious power,
with Jerusalem believed to be at the center of the world and representations
of divine order dominating the cities in the form of ecclesiastical property
(Ó Tuathail 1996: 3). This dominant iconography also corresponded to the organization of political power. As Lefebvre (1991: 266–67) succinctly illustrates,
"The social edifice resembled a cathedral," and indeed these imposing monu-

ments themselves helped sustain "the belief that the tops of the cities grazed the vault of Heaven and embodied the celestial virtues; the belief that those at the top of the social pyramid rubbed shoulders with divinity." This production of space inculcated with notions of the divine holds true for almost all tributary forms of society. The Aztec city of Teotihuacan and the ancient pyramids of Egypt demonstrate that this is not simply a European phenomenon. Indeed, this claiming of a divine right of power is an essential hallmark of all tributary societies in which those at the apex of political power not only seek to separate themselves from the rest of the population but "claim supernatural origins and validation" (Wolf 1997: 83). The key point to recognize is that class relations were very legible within this mode of production. This type of space was "imbued with social meaning" (Smith 2008: 107). As Lefebvre (1991: 267) concludes, this mode of production, "if not utterly transparent, certainly had a great limpidity." No one could observe the hacienda or the lordly estate and not see the social relations involved. To misquote from Marx and Engels (1845/2000: 192), everywhere the ruling space was the space of the ruling classes. Indeed, as a method of political control this was an essential feature of feudalism. One can thus discern that the social function of space was to reinforce a narrow form of class rule through the projection of fundamentally unequal social relations that had to be naturalized for the system of exploitation to function efficiently. Furthermore, space during this epoch was fallaciously viewed as an object that could be captured, rather than something that was constantly produced. This view was highly interwoven with the dominant property relations of the era that governed the form of spatial integration.[9]

Although as Eric Wolf (1997) has documented, long-distance trade routes existed prior to this era of European expansion, we can note here that outright plunder became the dominant form of spatial integration, leading to the creation of a global scale for the accumulation of wealth from the sixteenth century onward (Sassen 2006: 82; Wallerstein 1974). This was directly related to the expansion of European empires. With empire building in Europe itself proving too expensive, new "peripheral" sources of wealth were consequently sought out. In seeking to explain this production of space and spatial relations, it is helpful, following Trotsky (1930/1962: 10), to ask the question of what the "social needs" of a government are. Along with relying upon extraeconomic coercion as the primary means of obtaining surplus, the prevailing economic philosophy of this epoch was one of mercantilism, which implied a fixed limit to the world's wealth. Under this system, territorial accumulation was seen as a key source of income. With limits on the amount of tribute that could be extracted at home, new wealth had to be sought abroad. This was necessary to enhance the prestige of the dynastic states, helping to consolidate the rule of particular leaders, as continuing economic growth was essential to maintaining their support from rival claimants to power. Furthermore, this was a distinct class strategy that served to reproduce these particular social property relations (Teschke 2002: 11–12). Taken together, these "social needs" translated into aggressive geopolitical competition between proprietary kingships that fought one another for wealth and trading advantages in a perceived zero-sum game (Agnew 1994: 65; Sassen 2006: 84; Teschke 2002: 22). The Spanish and Portuguese colonization of Latin America was thus paradigmatic of feudal imperialism (Vilar 1971).

Principles of territorial exclusivity—much taken for granted today—were far more fluid in this epoch, governed as they were by multiple overlapping spatial domains of power that were occupied by various groups, including kings, lords, and church authorities (Sassen 2006: 146). However, with the increasing accumulation of wealth from the sixteenth century onward and the accompanying growth of commercial centers, previous spatial forms such as medieval towns, fiefdoms, city-states, and principalities were slowly subordinated to the space of the nation (Lefebvre 1991: 280). Highlighting the historical significance of these developments, Sassen (2007: 5) argues that, "notwithstanding different origins and starting times across the world, the history of the modern state can be read as the work of rendering national just about all the crucial features of society: authority, identity, territory, security, law and economic accumulation. Periods preceding those of the ascendance of the national state saw rather different types of scaling, with territories subject to multiple systems of rule rather than the exclusive authority of the state."

The production of national space had the corollary of constructing things such as capital, state, gender, age, and, of course, class (Ghani 1993: 56). This development not only implied the advance of a larger market and commercial relations that could draw in preexisting ones but also entailed a particular class strategy of violence, as it presupposed "a political power controlling and exploiting the resources of the market or the growth of productive forces in order to maintain and further its rule" (Lefebvre 1991: 112). A spatial division of labor was also established between the town and the countryside (Lefebvre 1991: 256, 2003: 84). The development of the space of the nation was thus tightly interwoven with the increasing accumulation of wealth. The analysis of Wolf (1997: 99–109) concurs with this point, demonstrating how the boundaries of modern European nation-states—largely unquestioned today—could and indeed were drawn very differently in the past, for example, with sea-based empires or combinations of various power alliances. However, the emergence of the nation-state as we know it today was intimately bound up with the expansion of trade and markets. This not only necessitated an organization larger than any single merchant, guild, or body of soldiers but also required an apparatus of control and coercion to maintain tributary forms of power and commit this form of social labor to a particular goal. The origin of the modern state system was therefore inseparable from the furtherance of class rule.[10] The development of national and global markets also led to the rise of new social groups such as merchants, bankers, and manufacturers who would later begin to consolidate themselves as a class opposed to the restrictive forms of property relations that inhered under feudalism (Sassen 2006: 87).

The important point to note here is that the international system of states in fact *preceded* capitalism. To borrow Hannes Lacher's (2006: 16) phrase, capitalism was "born into" a particular form of spatiality in many ways inimical to its form of social relations.[11] This point is in contrast to the received wisdom that associates the rise of nation-state spaces directly with the development of capitalism, an argument that in fact elides much of what is novel about its spatial dynamics. The fallacy of this position is to confuse the development of *wealth* with the development of *capital*. As Marx (1867/1974: 668) was at pains to point out, though, "In themselves money and commodities are no more capital than are the means of production and of subsistence." Contrary to those who therefore see a linear path from merchant wealth to modern capitalism, Wolf (1997: 85) argues that capitalism actually represents a qualitatively new form of mobilizing social labor. On this basis we must take care to distinguish between merchant wealth and capital, because a merchant of this time "did not yet buy labour power in a market in which workers compete for available jobs, and he did not yet control the actual labour process. Surplus was not extracted as surplus value but through unequal exchange within the framework of monopolistic and quasi-tributary relationships" (Wolf 1997: 87). We therefore need to recognize that capitalism came to be incubated within a spatial structure not of its own making. However, as Sassen (2006: 15) has demonstrated, it was the development of institutional capabilities in this era that would then become dislodged into a new type of organizing logic, entailing a long process of class struggle and a reconfiguring of this state form and leading to fundamentally different forms of spatial and scalar organization. The key question, therefore, is, What is the specific geography created by capitalism, and how are these forms altered as capitalism progresses (Smith 2008: 3)? Additionally, how do movements of resistance influence this trajectory?

Spaces of Capital

In delineating the core features of the spaces of capital, we must not forget that a variety of capitalisms exist (Hall and Soskice 2001; Bruff 2010) and that the institutional, regulatory, and ideational forms of capitalism can also shift (as will be demonstrated in the next chapter). However, there remain certain features that are, of necessity, to a greater or lesser degree, integral to all capitalist forms of society. Although these categories are not watertight and will overflow into one another, the key spatial features of capitalism to be delineated here are (1) the production of abstract space, (2) the role of primitive accumulation in creating and re-creating spaces of capital, (3) states as central to this process, (4) the uneven and combined nature of capitalism, and (5) spatial production as the outcome of class struggles (not simply an imposition of capital). Let us begin with the production of abstract space.

ABSTRACT SPACE

To understand how capitalist space contrasts with that of feudalism it is essential to clarify what the distinguishing features of this mode of production are. Marx (1894/1977: 879–80) identifies the hallmarks of capitalism as generalized commodity production by "formally free" wage laborers; surplus value as the "aim and determining motive of production"; and competition between individual capitals, leading to a continual investment in the means of production in order to expand profit. Although all modes of production seek to fashion space according to their own particular dictates, "under the social relations of capitalism . . . all elements assume a commodity form" (Harvey 2006a: 223). Capitalism can be thus distinguished from previous class societies to the degree that "it has integrated all major (and, increasingly most minor) life functions into a single system dominated by the law of value and the accompanying power of money, *but also in the degree to which it seeks to hide this achievement*" (Ollman 2003: 3, emphasis added). This is a point worth dwelling upon. In contrast to the space of feudalism, which explicitly sought to project relations of domination in order to achieve social control, under capitalism, which relies on the formally free exchange of equivalents on the market, this relation of class dominance must be hidden (Anderson 2010: 164). Unless denying that certain groups are in fact fully human (as occurred under slavery), formal equality of individuals before the law is integral to capitalist ideology (Wood 1995: 259).

The fact that we therefore need to uncover the social relationships inscribed in space is a phenomenon specific to the production of what Lefebvre calls the "abstract space" of capitalism. For Marx, the rise of capitalism involved the increasing domination of exchange value over use value, leading to a situation where we "fetishize commodities." This is the process whereby the specific social relations that commodities contain are obscured; instead, we come to endow them with an objective reality of their own (e.g., the idea that money exists independently of labor power). Rather than our interactions being mediated by actual human relations, they come increasingly to be mediated by "things." The key point to note is that this can only occur when labor itself is transformed into a commodity that can be bought and sold, losing its creative character and becoming an empty universal that is measurable by time (transformed thereby into abstract labor). Marx sought to show that, rather than focusing on "things" (commodities), what we really needed was a theory of the social relations that these things contained. In a similar fashion, Lefebvre (2003: 87) argued that instead of a description of space, what we need is a theory of the production of space to uncover the social relationships that construct it.

Lefebvre (1991: 49) contended that the process of fetishization also leads to a particular spatial form: "It was during this time that productive activity (labour) became no longer one with the process of reproduction which perpetuated social life; but in becoming independent of that process, labour fell prey to abstraction, whence abstract social labour—and *abstract space*." It must be stressed that the term "abstract" does not in any way imply that this space is any less real. As Andy Merrifield (2006: 133) clarifies, "Abstract space is a reality insofar as it is embedded in absolute space." The space is thus "abstract" in the sense that spaces produced under capitalism, although they may differ in appearance, are increasingly molded to the same social purpose: to produce surplus value (profit).[12] This process creates space that is both homogeneous and fractured. It is homogeneous in the sense that commodity and capital circulation require that within space, things are equivalent and interchangeable and subject to the law, and fractured in the sense of space being broken down into various forms of private property (Lefebvre 2003: 87).

The transition to capitalism, as discussed above, involved an essential change in the form of class rule. As the dominant social force within society, the landed nobility was gradually displaced by the bourgeoisie, who are able to command social labor by virtue of the fact that they own the means of production and control the flow of money power. Lefebvre (1991: 11) implores us to recognize that space did not (and does not) remain unaffected by this new organizing logic. Rather, the production of space is the sine qua non for the reproduction of capitalist social relations (Lefebvre 1976). The geography of capitalism, therefore, entails "the increasing displacement of inherited pre-capitalist landscapes with specifically capitalist sociospatial configurations" (Brenner 2004: 33–34). Thus, feudal space, dominated by monasteries, cathedrals, manor houses / haciendas, and landscapes dotted with peasant communities, gives way to a space "founded on vast networks of banks, business centres and major productive entities . . . also on motorways, airports and information centres" (Lefebvre 1991: 53).

Although we should be careful not to conflate urbanism with capitalism (Wood 2002: 74, 77), as numerous scholars have shown, the production of the built environment through fixed-capital formation is a necessary precondition for the extraction and circulation of surplus value (Harvey 2006a: 380; Smith 2008: 6; Brenner 1999: 44–45). For example, capitalist manufacturing industry necessitates the geographical form of the factory, workers who live within accessible distance to the place of work, entities that sell the goods produced, and roads and infrastructure to move commodities from one area to another. However, along with relying on a certain form of fixity, capital must also remain in motion in order for it to be able to seek productive outlets (Brenner 1998). Whereas past modes of production had an essential conservative basis to their spatial form, seeking to hold down transformation where possible and relying for their political control on an essential fixity of space, capital develops as a revolutionary mode of production that actively needs to transform space for its own survival. Thus, capital is forced to create "new objective conditions of time and space in its search for profits" (Harvey 1996: 240). Capitalism, in other words, has to constantly produce "the new." This process involves numerous contradictions between fixity and motion, between diachronic and synchronic benefits, as well as problems of how to contain this process socially (Lefebvre 1976: 11). For example, the manner in which space is transformed can profoundly alter the character of particular places, creating opportunities for some while dispossession for others. These transformations, therefore, frequently become the object of intense struggle (against deindustrialization, highway or airport construction, closure of mines, etc.).

This revolutionary and unsettling dynamic that capital brought with it was captured famously by Marx and Engels (1848/2000: 248) in *The Communist Manifesto* when they wrote with regard to this transition: "All that is solid melts into the air, all that is holy is profaned." Likewise, it was the clustering of industries that Marx and Engels saw as providing the sociological basis for unified working-class resistance. Whether this has been undermined by globalization or simply relocated remains a matter of debate (Chase-Dunn 1999: 209).

SPACES OF PRIMITIVE ACCUMULATION

However, it must be remembered that the transition to capitalism unfurled, and continues to unfurl, unevenly across space. This transition is, at times, elided by contemporary scholars who characterize the shift in Europe from absolutism to capitalism as representing the transition from political to economic accumulation (e.g., Teschke 2002: 31). While this characterization may be true as an overarching or ideal-type sociological classification (as well as a broader long-term trend), it ignores the fact that political accumulation / extraeconomic accumulation working in symbiosis with economic accumulation remained an essential precondition for capitalism, as well as an endemic contemporary feature (Luxemburg 1913/2003: 434; Rioux 2013; Tansel 2015: 83–85). Benno Teschke, in other words, relies on a far too simplistic periodization, viewing the transition from one mode of production to another in highly rigid terms. However, as was stressed earlier, the sociological term "mode of production" should not be thought of as all-encompassing, as it includes not only emergent but also residual counterforces and tendencies. Marx recognized in his mature writings that global development was not a unilinear process (Shanin 1984). Indeed, as a result of this uneven development he acknowledged the revolutionary potential of precapitalist spaces such as the Russian *mir*, a type of rural peasant village community. As Kevin Anderson (2010: 7) argues, Marx's concept of capitalism "was not an abstract universal but instead was imbued with a rich and concrete social vision in which universality and particularity interacted within dialectical totality." The dialectic between a universalizing capitalism and the particularity of noncapitalist spaces is explored in detail in chapters 4 and 5.

Ignoring the continuance of political accumulation / extraeconomic accumulation alongside purely economic accumulation thus omits an element that is essential to the production of capitalist spatiality, namely, the role of colonial and imperialist practices (see Lenin 1917/1987a; Ghani 1993: 52–53). With regard to the importance of extraeconomic conditions as a prerequisite for capitalist spatiality, we need to examine the process of what Marx refers to as "primitive accumulation." In the previous section it was discussed how feudal work contained an explicit spatial referent for serfs in the form of being tied to the land. However, such an arrangement mitigated against individuals being willing to alienate their labor to a third party (an essential requirement of capitalist accumulation). To arrive at this situation thus necessitated a form of political intervention. As Marx (1867/1974: 668) put it, "The capitalist system pre-supposes the complete separation of the labourers from all property in the means by which they can realize their labour. . . . The so-called primitive accumulation, therefore, is nothing else than the historical process of divorcing the producer from the means of production," a process that Marx reminds us is "written into the annals of mankind in letters of blood and fire." A precondition for the production of the "abstract space" of capitalism, therefore, was also the production of particular "absolute spaces"—those of private property and spatial exclusivity (Smith 2008: 116). In the context of Britain (Marx's case study of capitalism's genesis as a mode of production), the forcible expropriation of the peasantry through the Acts of Enclosure paved the way for peasant migration and the rise of urbanism and factory work a hallmark of capitalist geography. "Freed" serfs were thus transformed into wage workers for nascent manufacturing as a new type of city began to be constructed in the image of *corporate* rather than church power. In contrast to feudal space, which was dominated by personal ties to the land, capitalism is based on the reorganization of space resulting from the dispossession of direct producers (Poulantzas 1978: 54).

However, the story of primitive accumulation does not end here. As has been demonstrated by numerous scholars, primitive accumulation was not just a footnote to capitalism's genesis. Rather, it is an ongoing process, or what some have labeled "permanent primitive accumulation" (Amin 1974: 3; Bonefeld 2001). In theorizing this issue, Rosa Luxemburg postulated that noncapitalist spaces were vital to capitalism's ultimate survival in terms of providing new markets, sources of labor power, and means of production to facilitate capital's drive to expand. Hence, primitive accumulation remains an endemic feature of this mode of production. On this basis, capital accumulation is conceived as "a kind of metabolism between capitalist economy and those pre-capitalist methods of production without which it cannot go on and which, in this light, it corrodes and assimilates" (Luxemburg 1913/2003: 397). However, this brings with it a contradictory dynamic. As Luxemburg (1913/2003: 447) explains, "Capitalism is the first mode of economy with the weapon of propaganda, a mode which tends to engulf the entire globe and to stamp out all other economies, tolerating no rival at its side. Yet at the same time it is also the first mode of economy which is unable to exist by itself, which needs other economic systems as a medium and soil. Although it strives to become universal, and, indeed, on account of this its tendency, it must break down—because it is immanently incapable of becoming a universal form of production."

Drawing from but extending Luxemburg's analysis of the ongoing nature of primitive accumulation, David Harvey (2003: 145–46, 153) has termed this "accumulation by dispossession," which "entails appropriation and co-optation of pre-existing cultural and social achievements as well as confrontation and supersession" and which occurs to "any social formation or territory that is brought or inserts itself into the logic of capitalist development." This analysis accounts not only for continuing imperialist practices but also for the extension of the logic of commodification into areas previously held as collective assets.

Finally, those working within feminist international political economy have also sought to highlight the importance of ongoing primitive accumulation under capitalism (Federici 2004). This analysis draws our attention to gendered forms of exploitation in the "reproductive economy." Defined in terms of the unpaid, nonmarket, and private sphere (and thus an antonym to the "productive economy" of paid, market-oriented, and publicly visible work), this is a space through which workers' labor power is reproduced (saving capital the full costs of providing its chief input), as well as being a space that reinforces gender stereotypes and divisions of labor (Bakher 1995: 5–9; Peterson 2005: 511, 516).

Summing up these debates, Jim Glassman (2006: 622) concludes, "If we recognize among the 'extra-economic' conditions of accumulation the gendered labor of social reproduction, we can say that the accumulation process has both an extensive (geographical) and an intensive (social) frontier, and thus primitive accumulation encompasses an enormous socio-spatial range of activities."

CREATING THE STATE OF CAPITAL

The state has been and remains vital to the dispossession of primary producers (Harvey 2003: 145), a process James Scott (1998: 82) refers to as a project of "internal colonization." However, the initial dynamic for this dispossession came from the absolutist social property relations pertaining in Europe that fostered aggressive geopolitical competition. With tributary societies finding their ability to reinvest surpluses in war-making capabilities limited, the British development of capitalism provided a model for others to follow, one in which the newly developed credit system had proven to be more capable of financing war-making capacities (Teschke 2002: 32). As Marx (1867/1974: 711) noted with regard to other nations of the time in the transition to capitalism, "They all employ the power of the state, the concentrated and organized force of society, to hasten, hot-house fashion, the process of the feudal mode of production into the capitalist mode, and to shorten the transition. Force is the midwife of every old society pregnant with a new one." Institutional capabilities developed in a past era were thus dislodged into a new rationality. Thus, "key capabilities developed in earlier phases can become foundational to a subsequent phase but only as part of the new organizational logic that in fact also foundationally repositions these logics" (Sassen 2006: 92). For example, in the English context, embedded structures of authority developed into a process of state formation that in turn facilitated the passage of laws to protect the emerging bourgeoisie. However, as Marx (1867/1974: 703) reminds us, "Revolutions are not made by laws." Rather, the rise of the modern state in England needs to be viewed as the result of a process of class struggle between the old nobility and the developing bourgeoisie, who sought to establish themselves as a historical subject. In concurrence with Wolf (1997: 100), we can conclude with regard to the capitalist mode of production that "the state has a strategic role both in the genesis of the mode and its maintenance."

A key element to introduce at this stage, however, is the uneven nature of the process of development and also, therefore, the uneven nature of the process of state formation. (I will discuss this process in detail in relation to Latin America in chapter 2 and Mexico in chapter 3.) Within the context of England, for example, economic growth and accumulation had been quasi spontaneous. A compromise between the feudal nobility and the bourgeoisie in this context was reached in the process of state formation (Lefebvre 1964/2009: 57). However, this relationship was not repeated worldwide. "It is evident," Lefebvre (1964/2009: 58) consequently concluded, "that the problem of the state does not arise at all in the same way in a country where the state follows growth, where the crystallisation of the state follows economic development, and in countries where it precedes economic growth." Echoing this sentiment, Alan Knight (2002a: 197–98) cautions us against "Anglo-centric" theories of capitalist transition, as these may not be generalizable beyond this specific place and time. It is for this reason that I examine the precise instances of state formation (and subnational state formation) in concrete detail in the following chapters. Indeed, as I will later demonstrate, the fact of unevenness allows us to explore the means by which developmental trajectories become combined. I argue in the forthcoming chapters that the strategy for managing this unevenness has been one of passive revolution, whereby the state takes a leading role in transforming social relations but in such a manner as to privilege existing forms of power and to undermine the full potential of progressive change (Gramsci 1971: 105–6, Q 15, §59; Sassoon 2001: 8).

A central issue with the decline of feudal obligation to dynastic and religious authorities was that of political control (Agnew 1994: 61). Gearóid Ó Tuathail (1996: 53) argues that it was the appeal to the notion of the "state" as an entity locked in competitive struggle that was used to justify both the violence of internal repression and the violence of imperial expansion. However, unlike the feudal state, the capitalist state does not base legitimacy on its origins (birth, religion); instead, the state is based on repeated legitimation in the form of elections (Poulantzas 1978: 58). Marx (1843/2000: 53) noted that in relation to this changed state form, consciousness becomes split into public and private, and the state, although supposedly embodying the collective spirit of humanity, is used in actuality to preserve individual, egoistic rights:

> When the political state has achieved its true completion, man leads a double life, a heavenly and an earthly one, not only in thought or consciousness but in reality, in life. He has a life both in the political community, where he is valued as a communal being, and in civil society, where he is active as a private individual, treats other men as means, degrades himself to a means, and becomes the plaything of alien powers. . . . In the state . . . where man counts as a species-being, he is an imaginary participant in an imaginary sovereignty, he is robbed of his real life and filled with an unreal universality.

As an ideological force, the state takes over previous ideologies (Lefebvre 1975/2009: 99). The development of the capitalist state also became a mimetic form that others sought to emulate (Trotsky 1919/1962: 174). Again we see that the process of state formation cannot be understood without reference to the concomitant process of class domination. The key point to recognize, however, is that new relations of domination began to be constructed within the previous spatial structure of power. The nation-state was thus used as a protective shell to incubate the bourgeois classes while fomenting their hegemony on a limited spatial scale before expanding outward. This process, however, entailed the construction of a far greater degree of spatial exclusivity than had been seen hitherto as a new organizing logic built on modern notions of parliamentary sovereignty began to be constructed (Teschke 2002: 8; Brenner 1999: 47). The space of the nation-state thus needs to be firmly historicized. Rather than being a "natural phenomenon," it was in fact a space produced and transformed in line with a particular social purpose—that of furthering class rule. (I will return to this production of national space as a moment in the expansion of the rule of the bourgeoisie in chapters 2 and 3.) At the foundations of the modern state there is "the forced equivalence of non-equivalents: the (forced) equalization of

the unequal, the identification of the non-identical" (Lefebvre 1975/2009: 10).
From its inception the nation-state has had a logic of homogenization about it,
and it plays a dual role both "as a *reducer* (of diversities, autonomies, multiplic-
ities, multiplications, differences) and as the *integrator* of the so-called national
whole" (Lefebvre 1975/2009: 10). This is an especially salient point to bear in
mind when we consider the role of the state in its relation to indigenous groups
in chapters 4 and 5.

UNEVEN AND COMBINED SPACE

As was touched upon above, although in Europe, transformations in the dominant manner in which social labor was mobilized began to be consolidated with
the move toward economic accumulation, political accumulation in the form
of colonialism also remained vital to the genesis and functioning of capitalism.
Furthermore, the processes of uneven and combined development meant that
autocratic states now found themselves "armed with all the material might of
the European States," in which both parties could find mutual benefit (autocratic states in the maintenance of their power, European capitalist states with
the high rate of return on usurious interest) (Trotsky 1919/1962: 175, 182). Lenin
(1917/1987a) also highlighted the role of imperialism in the production of space,
documenting in particular the way in which capital was exported and railway
networks were expanded in order to better take control of other nations' resources, as well as industries and the more arduous productive activities being established in the colonies, where labor power was cheaper. Scholars such
as Neil Brenner (1982) and Teschke (2003), among others, are thus guilty of
writing from a highly Eurocentric viewpoint when they discuss the transition
to capitalism, as they ignore the persistence of tributary relationships in the
periphery, which were vital to the constitution of British (capitalist) power (see
also Lander 2006; Tansel 2015: 79, 81–82). For example, under the pressure of
continuing force, India was produced as an export platform for British trade
with China. This extraction of colonial tribute was vital to the construction of
the modern capitalist world system. As Wolf (1997: 261) succinctly explains,
"Indian surpluses enabled England to create and maintain a global system of
free trade. Had England been forced to ban imports from the United States
and Germany and to compete with them in foreign markets, American and
German industrialization would also have been significantly slowed. . . . Under
English domination, India became a key foundation of the emerging worldwide
capitalist edifice."

Thus far, then, we can conclude that from its inception capitalism grew
through a process of uneven and combined development in which the state
played a strategic role in both the genesis and the maintenance of the capitalist
mode of production. The expansion of the capitalist mode of production did

not, therefore, occur on a smooth terrain free of past relations but, in fact, developed in symbiosis with other modes of production (Wolf 1997: 79).[13] This is an important corrective to those such as Teschke (2002) who view the transition to capitalist modernity as an all-embracing movement. As Doreen Massey (2005: 63) argues, on this reading the very term "modernity" becomes imbibed with a spatializing character. World history and spatial differences are subsumed and simply reduced to the pressure of European expansion. (This one-sided narrative of history is indicative of certain liberal interpretations of the colonial period, e.g., Ferguson 2004.) However, the material preconditions for this very modernity were founded on distinctly premodern forms of exploitation that remained essential both to the origins of capitalism and to its contemporary history. Just as Europe helped to produce these countries, so too did these countries produce Europe. As Mallon (1995: 8) puts it, "The concept of freedom was partially recast in dialectic with the concepts and relationship of New World slavery. The idea of the nation as an 'imagined community' grew in relation to its opposite, the colony." This was a point recognized early on by Marx (1867/ 1974: 705, 711), who argued with regard to the origins of capitalism that "the treasures captured outside of Europe by undisguised looting, enslavement, and murder, floated back to the mother country and were turned into capital"; thus, "the veiled slavery of the wage workers in Europe needed, for its pedestal, slavery, pure and simple in the new world." Drawing upon Massey (1993: 61), we must remain attentive at all times to the "power geometries" of social relations across space.[14] Rather than just looking at movement and flows, we need to be attentive to the manner in which they affect particular people and places and the way in which they produce uneven and combined development within processes of world history.

SPACE AS THE OUTCOME OF CLASS STRUGGLES

Unlike the spaces of feudalism, under capitalist social relations "we do not live, act and work 'in' space so much as by living, acting and working we *produce space*" (Smith 2008: 15–16, emphasis added). This is what Lefebvre (1991: 89) meant when he characterized the shift from feudalism to capitalism as involving the transition from producing things *in* space to producing space itself. From its very beginnings, capital has had a geographically expansionary nature that was determined by both the search for profit and efforts to universalize the value-form, for which spatial integration is vital (Harvey 2006a: 375).[15] Through the capitalist mode of production, nature itself is transformed and indeed *produced* (Smith 2008; Castree 2000; Harvey 2010: 75–85). Thus, despite appeals from orthodox political economy to notions such as "comparative advantage," arguments for development based upon "natural resources" are increasingly outdated (as well as being intrinsically dubious from their origin). As Smith

(2008: 140) points out, although appeals to natural advantages in climate or resources may have been useful in explaining an initial path of development, such explanations become increasingly redundant as capitalism progresses (see also Massey 1994: 53). We may think here of industrialization in Latin America (discussed further in chapter 2) or the growth of world cities built on finance capital to empirically understand the point made by Lefebvre (1991: 49) that the development of capitalist social relations "smashed naturalness forever and upon its ruins established the space of accumulation." The import of this point is that any notion of environmental degradation must be considered in a more integral sense; furthermore, it must be related to the production of space (Lefebvre 1976: 13, 105). On this basis, problems of the environment can refer just as much to those of global warming as they can to a lack of urban housing or access to social services. This also requires us to understand the term "production" not just in terms of workers in a factory but also in a wider sense.

I mentioned earlier that space is fundamentally being transformed through the increasing search for surplus value. This restless search for profit is the historical mission of the bourgeoisie as a class. As Marx (1867/1974: 558) famously put it, "Accumulate, accumulate, that is Moses and the Prophets." The two levers that the bourgeoisie uses to enhance its profits are increases in absolute and/or an increase in relative surplus value, usefully characterized by Holloway (2002a: 208) as the extension of property and the intensification of labor. Both forms have explicitly geographical implications. In terms of the extension of property, capital's internal dynamic to grow beyond its current barriers was clearly recognized by Marx (1858/1973: 408), who wrote that "the tendency to create the world market is directly given in the concept of capital itself." The explanation of this tendency is more explicitly theorized in *The Communist Manifesto* where the spatial implications of capital accumulation are contrasted with previous modes of production. Here it is claimed that

> the bourgeoisie cannot exist without constantly revolutionizing the instruments of production, and thereby the relations of production, and with them the whole relations of society. Conservation of the old modes of production in unaltered form, was, on the contrary, the first condition of existence for all earlier industrial classes. Constant revolutionising of production, uninterrupted disturbance of all social conditions, everlasting uncertainty and agitation distinguish the bourgeois epoch from all earlier ones. . . . The need of a constantly expanding market for its products chases the bourgeoisie over the entire surface of the globe. It must nestle everywhere, settle everywhere, establish connexions everywhere. (Marx and Engels 1848/2000: 248)

To understand why this is the case we must recognize the essential class antagonism that capitalism is founded upon, between those who control the means of production and detain the commodities produced and those who are forced to sell their labor power and must buy back the commodities they themselves produce. As Bertell Ollman (2003: 149) notes, the primary contradiction Marx sees in capitalism is between the increasing capacity of social production, on the one hand, and its private appropriation, on the other. This leads to profound spatial changes, as the competition between individual capitals (another key element to capitalism) causes firms to pursue locational advantages in order to increase their profit rates (through either cheaper labor or increased turnover time). What certain spaces contain by way of their social relations thus becomes an essential component of capitalist production. Thus we can understand Harvey's (2006a: 440) point that "the production of spatial configurations is necessarily an active moment in the dynamics of accumulation." However, although capital seeks to overcome barriers in production, we must remember too that capital is also a process of *circulation*. It is here that the narrow social relations that the system is built upon create their own limits (Harvey 2006a: 426). As Michael Lebowitz (2003: 11) puts it, "The barriers capital faces in the sphere of circulation are not only external—they are inherent in its own nature." The private ownership of the means of production and the search for increasing profit thus cause the bourgeoisie to expand surplus value more than its ability to realize this surplus in circulation. In other words, the very exploitation of wage labor that is a precondition for the existence of capital is also its very limit to growth. This contradiction leads toward overaccumulation and the tendency of the rate of profit to fall. Overaccumulation is defined by David Harvey (2003: 88) as "surpluses of capital (in commodity, money or productive forms) and surpluses of labour power side by side, without there apparently being any means to bring them together profitably to accomplish socially useful tasks."

These crises of overaccumulation can be solved in two fundamental ways. The first is to invest in technologically innovative processes (to increase the turnover time of capital circulation) or in other forms of fixed capital (temporal fixes). The second is to expand the process of capital accumulation itself through investment in new regions or areas of life into which the commodity form has not been extended (spatial fixes). This is helpfully defined by William Robinson (2004b: 7) as the extensive or intensive enlargement of capitalism. Lefebvre (1976: 23) submits that it is through this dynamic that capitalism has, contrary to the predictions of the early prophets of Marxism, been able to reproduce its social relations through the process of economic growth: "We cannot calculate at what price, but we do know the means, *by occupying space, but producing a space*." Thus we can see that capital as a mode of production is "an inherently mobile form of domination" (Holloway 2002a: 190). The concrete agents of this change thus include developers, urban planners, architects, landowners, bankers, and political authorities.

However, it is essential that we recognize this mobility as itself predicated on the strength of the subaltern classes to resist exploitation in particular areas. If capital is forced to move from one area to another, this necessarily implies two things: (1) there is a limit to capital's form of exploitation in the place it seeks to move *from*, and (2) this limit is thought to not exist or to pose a lesser threat in another space. In other words, uneven development of class struggle is itself postulated as a necessary basis on which capitalism must grow, as it is the uneven terrain of social relations that allows capital to resolve crises. Indeed, it is only through a restructuring of the space economy of capitalism that new rounds of accumulation can begin (Harvey 2006a: 390; Smith 2008: 177). Recognizing this point, Lefebvre (1991: 335) states clearly that uneven development, "so far from being obsolete, is becoming worldwide in its application—or more precisely, is presiding over the globalization of the world market." Neil Smith (2008: 4) is at pains to stress that uneven development cannot be treated as a transhistorical concept but rather has to be viewed as *the* geographical expression of specifically *capitalist* development. This of course does not mean that prior to capitalism there existed even development among tributary modes of production but rather that capitalism produces a distinct type of uneven development that is integral to it as a mode of production (Smith 2008: 134). This fact necessitates that we hypothesize class struggle as being central to the ontology of space (see Massey 1994: 22).

If spaces contain different social relations, they must imply different levels of struggle in the first place. Unless we admit this fact, we must consider wage differentials between countries as somehow fixed and natural. However, as Harvey (2006a: 431) argues, these "spatial fixes" in no way overcome the contradictory tendencies of capital. This is because ultimately only one of two outcomes can occur: (1) there can be renewed accumulation, in which case crisis tendencies toward overaccumulation are exacerbated, or (2) the value invested in the physical environment becomes devalued as the investment turns out to be unproductive. In each case there is a place-specific form of devaluation. However, thus far we have assumed that capital does not encounter problems simply relocating and transforming space. Indeed, for some scholars, this fact is simply presented as a given. Smith (2008: 7, 186, 208), for example, is keen to assert that capital produces a world in its own image. However, while it is certainly true that capital "endeavours to mould the space it dominates" using "violent means to reduce obstacles and resistance it encounters there" (Lefebvre 1991: 49), it is by no means certain that it can simply impose its logic as it pleases. Indeed, Massey (1995: 7) powerfully repudiates such an approach, arguing that "shifts in spatial structures are a response to changes in the nature of class relations, economic and political, national and international. Their development is a social and conflictual process. . . . The world is not simply the product of capital's requirements." It is thus the attempt to impose a social logic that seeks to compel surplus labor and the struggles of the subaltern classes to refuse the domination of capital that form the essence of many contemporary geopolitical forms of conflict. These conflicts are likely to intensify as capitalism progresses and crises grow. Concomitantly, as we are beginning to see, bearing the costs of devaluation or dispossession in order to restart private accumulation is becoming unpalatable to a substantial part of the population. If space is always under construction, the outcome of our interactions and the result of "stories so far," then it is imperative to recognize both the "actually existing" multiplicity of spaces and the potential for other spaces to be progressively transformed (Massey 2005: 9, 130). After all, while capital may be a powerful actor, there is a broader ensemble cast in the story of societies.

Space, then, while central to the reproduction of capitalist social relations, is also the terrain on which oppositional struggles are launched. It is the site for the "revolt of the 'lived' against abstractions, of the everyday against economism, of the social and civil society against the 'high rates of growth' whose demands are upheld by the state" (Lefebvre 1975/2009: 114). Lefebvre (1996, 2003: 88, 97) argues that it is in the realm of everyday praxis that counterprojects and counterspaces can be formed that would include the right to control investment and space based on human need rather than simply on blind growth. Lefebvre (1947/2008: 92, 1966/2009: 147–50) theorizes this process as a fundamental questioning of the state as a force standing over society, a process that thus includes an overcoming of alienation. This overcoming leads us toward societal self-determination, in which users of space retake control of their own lives, and political activity is no longer solely associated with fleeting, privileged moments.

Conclusion

In this chapter I have attempted to demonstrate in theoretical terms how we could discern the logic of the spaces of capital. I did this by first highlighting that two terms integral to Marxist political economy—namely, class struggle and mode of production—are essential to understanding the production of space. I then highlighted the characteristics of a tributary mode of production in the form of feudal space while delineating the specific form of geopolitics connected to it. Lastly, I revealed the distinctiveness of capitalist spatiality. Included in the discussion here was the revolutionary nature of capitalism as a mode of production, its class basis and crisis tendencies, and its novel form of uneven and combined development. At a reasonably high level of abstraction, therefore, we have taken the first step toward understanding the spaces of capital. In the following chapter, building on the analysis developed here, I will consider in detail the production of space in the context of Latin American state formation both historically from the time of colonization through the twentieth-century experience of import substitution industrialization (ISI) to neoliberalism. Drawing on the key themes developed in this chapter, I will draw out the implications of ISI for the state form and the role of class agency. This will illuminate further the contemporary spaces of capital and allow us to make some tentative claims regarding the spaces of resistance and their changing nature.

CHAPTER TWO

Latin America and the Production of the Global Economy

Capitalism should be studied in the hope, not of finding how its history may repeat at a later date in the peripheral countries, but of learning how the relation between the peripheral and central was produced.
—Fernando Henrique Cardoso and Enzo Faletto, *Dependency and Development in Latin America*

In this chapter I seek to show how neoliberal space was forged within the Latin American context, replacing import substitution industrialization (ISI) as the region's dominant developmental paradigm. The purpose of this chapter is to further the empirical analysis of the spatial both as the terrain produced through capital accumulation and as the site of struggle of resistance movements. The chapter will help shed further light on the spaces of capital by providing a detailed examination of how geopolitical conflict takes place through the dynamics of capital accumulation leading to the establishment of new spatial divisions of labor. The chapter will also provide the background to understand the changing contours of resistance movements and how the major modalities of resistance and transformation have been altered in recent decades. It thus helps point toward an alternative theorization of what it means to engage in class struggle (a point to be taken up in detail in chapters 4 and 5).

In exploring the production of spatial relations within the Latin American context, I adopt the perspective of historical-geographical sociology (outlined in the introduction), seeking to demonstrate the key role of class struggle as the driving force of this process, as well as considering the role of the state, conceived as part of the totality of capitalist social relations (see Holloway and Picciotto 1977). I argue that the history of state formation and developmentalism within national contexts must be situated within (although not predetermined by) the wider fundamental dynamics of the international political economy (see also Morton 2007c: 599). I thus draw upon and elaborate three related themes emerging from chapter 1. The first of these is the need to understand hegemony and class struggle as taking place across a variety of spatial scales. The second relates to the contradictory nature of capitalism as a mode of production that generates crises of overaccumulation. Attempts are then made to resolve these crises by means of spatial and scalar fixes. Both of these ideas can be witnessed in the history of Latin America's development trajectory, in particular during the transition from ISI to neoliberalism. David Ruccio (2010: 307–8) has argued that explanations for this transition have predominantly focused on either the profit squeeze (a contradiction at the national mode of regulation) or crises among advanced capitalist countries feeding into the international environment (a contradiction between national modes of regulations). "An alternative," he argues, "would be to integrate the two accounts and investigate the connections between the internal and the external." This is exactly what I set out to do in this chapter. Bridging the gap between the internal and the external is the final theme: passive revolution. As previously discussed, passive revolution refers to the manner in which the state plays a vital role in instituting or expanding capital accumulation so as to continue class domination and neutralize subaltern initiatives. I will demonstrate how this has been a recurring feature of Latin American development over the last one hundred years.

I present here a broad historical narrative, the details and key themes of which will be complemented by the specific instance of Mexico in the following chapter. Whereas the previous chapter sought to provide an abstract level of analysis, the purpose of this chapter is to move to the meso level of analysis. An obvious objection to such an intellectual task is that the diversity of countries' experiences within the region makes any generalization ultimately fruitless. What happens to be the case for relatively wealthy countries such as Brazil and Chile might not be the case for a country such as Bolivia. However, while we must pay due attention to historical specificities, we must also be aware of the key points of commonality. For example, all Latin American countries share a colonial history of incorporation into two Iberian empires that put a major fetter on economic development. All underwent an analogous process of liberal reforms postindependence that involved an assault on peasant land tenure and the transfer of resources to politically connected landowners (Coatsworth 1998). Furthermore, all countries in Latin America (with the exception of Cuba) used capitalism as the engine of growth and development in the twentieth century, and all have a dominant class that represents "a numerically insignificant proportion of the economically active population" (Portes 1985: 34). Lastly, although these plate tectonics may be subject to change, all these countries have hitherto occupied a subordinate position within the global economy (Cardoso and Faletto 1979).

The chapter will proceed in the following manner. First, I will consider the production of space in Latin America in relation to both colonial and postcolonial integration into the world economy. Second, I will discuss the rise of ISI in relation to its class referents. Third, I will render the spatial characteristics of ISI. Fourth, I will explore the contradictions in those characteristics. Fifth, I will examine the rise of neoliberalism as a new spatial and scalar project. Finally, I will discuss the challenges to this project in the form of subaltern class resistance and draw conclusions.

Let us begin with a brief history of the production of spatial relations within Latin America in order to examine how they have been forged in dialectical relation to the international capitalist economy. This history will highlight the need to understand state formation and developmentalism as a process of class struggle taking place across multiple spatial scales. It will also contribute to understanding the role of the state in furthering capitalist development and help shed light on the antistatist nature of many contemporary resistance movements (to be considered in chapters 4 and 5).

Incorporating Latin America

The production of space in Latin America has, for the past five centuries, been heavily mediated by external factors. With the advent of colonialism, the "veins" of Latin America were forced open to facilitate the extraction of wealth and integrate the space of the "New World" with that of the West (Galeano 1971/ 2008). From its inception, this was both a racial and a class-based project involving the suppression of indigenous subjectivities. Class—defined through the means of appropriating surplus—was therefore inextricably tied to a racial hierarchy. Colonization fundamentally reordered native societies and led to the destruction of autonomous forms of production. Moreover, the form of Iberian colonization helped to export a feudal form of economy that chained Latin America to a retrograde form of class relations that was elsewhere in the processes of supersession by agrarian capitalism (Galeano 1971/2008; Mariátegui 1984: 172–86; Vilar 1971).

Owing to high transportation costs, new settlements were initially constructed near rivers or coastal areas. However, with the advent of the railroad, space as an object of exchange value was invested in, and agricultural production for export shifted to the interior of the continent (Coatsworth 1998: 28). Commenting upon the alteration in spatial practices that were affected by this process, Phillip Oxhorn (1995: 254) argues that "patterns of colonial trade and administration were highly centralizing influences, concentrating economic, political and social resources in a few major cities and ports throughout the region. After independence, these same cities came to dominate the national political, economic and social scenes in most countries."

One of the key insights into the effects of colonization provided by dependency theorists was to reject the idea that Latin America was somehow an undeveloped region as a result of not forging closer links with the global market. Such analysis also therefore rejected the idea that some areas of the region were modernized while others remained backward. Rather, these theorists charged, this appearance of backwardness was the direct result of interaction with global capitalism, which had systematically underdeveloped the region by destroying manufacturing and concentrating land into export-oriented latifundia (Gunder Frank 1966).

Postindependence, Latin America became integrated into the world economy through a strategy of export-led development fueled by primary commodities. Politically, this strategy corresponded to the dominance of the rural oligarchy (Cardoso and Faletto 1979: 14; Kaufman 1990: 127). The very same cities that had served as colonial capitals now, as national capitals, came to act as primary nodal points for Latin America's integration into the world economy, serving as "a conduit for the export of primary products and the importation of manufactured goods and capital" (Oxhorn 1995: 254). One can highlight the role of internal class forces in helping to produce this early state form as the rural oligarchy and the urban elite came to share similar interests, contributing to "a further concentration of resources and power" (Oxhorn 1995: 254). However, these internal class forces were heavily mediated by the international capitalist economy and essentially remained subordinate to foreign interests. Between 1870 and 1914 conditions within the "international" can be seen to have influenced Latin American state formation and developmentalism in two key ways.

First, Latin America's insertion into the world trading system "and the corresponding ease of borrowing from abroad helped to stifle whatever potential for a local production of technology might have survived the Spanish crown's attempt at modernisation in the closing decades of the colonial era" (Glade 1986: 2). During the latter part of the nineteenth century, British investment was particularly decisive. By the end of 1880 British investment in Latin America totaled £179 million, and by 1890 the figure was £425 million. Between 1890 and 1913 Latin America received one-quarter of all British capital flows (Inter-American Development Bank 2007: 68). These funds were primarily for infrastructural development. This exportation of capital from the center to the periphery can be explained by what David Harvey (2006a: 427) refers to as the inner and outer dialectics of capitalist transformation. As we explored in chapter 1, it is the inherent problem of overaccumulation that impels capitalists "to explore geographical frontiers or look to the production of use values that will pay off further and further into the future" (Harvey 2006a: 410). Thus, owing to overaccumulation in one particular place (in this case, the United States and Western Europe), the "inner dialectic" of capitalism causes it to expand beyond its current frontiers to forge new relations across space. Although the persistent problem of overaccumulation is not resolved by this action, it is displaced by means of a spatial fix, for example, a new round of accumulation or an "outer transformation" of the periphery. This process is of course imbibed with what Doreen Massey (1993) refers to as a power geometry: who gets to instigate flows and movements versus who receives and often remains trapped by them. As Lenin (1917/1987a: 208) summarized, "Naturally, the country which exports the capital skims the cream."

The second key factor located within the "international" was the fact that industrial production in the core capitalist countries determined the level of demand for the region's primary products (Bulmer-Thomas 1994: 57; Glade 1986: 7). In this manner, Latin American state formation and developmentalism were framed in an "overarching structure of articulation provided by the world market system" (Glade 1986: 8). During this period, although precapitalist so-cial relations persisted, "capitalism came to be installed as the hegemonic mode of production among the several co-existing types" (Glade 1986: 49; see also Mariátegui 1984). The capitalist world market was therefore providing the "law of motion," to which Latin America was subject (Banaji 2011: 60–62). The ex-pansion of the export sector had promoted urbanization and "contributed to the growth of a wage earning working class and a salaried middle class" (Bulmer-Thomas 1994: 130). This would provide the stimulus for the emergence of a domestic manufacturing sector, although at this stage agriculture was still the dominant mode of employment, and thus oligarchic power still remained both economically and politically superior to that of the bourgeoisie (who remained very much a minority). However, the absorption by industry of a new class of workers in the cities demonstrates a key point made by Antonio Gramsci (1971: 59, Q 19, §24), namely, that embryonic hegemonic activity needs to begin *before* the rise to power of a particular class. These themes demonstrate that while new sites for the recomposition of capital were created, new sites for class antago-nism were also generated (Silver 2003: 64).

The Rise of Import Substitution Industrialization

The outbreak of World War I was an important milestone as the beginning of the end both for the export-led strategies of development and (as a corollary) for oligarchic power. The war served to boost nationalism and increase accep-tance of the necessity for state intervention in the economy (Thorp 1986: 71). More importantly for the war's effect on Latin American developmentalism was the fact that the war destroyed the integrated markets for goods, capital, and labor. Due to the reimposition of capital controls that the European countries introduced to aid their financing of the war, they were no longer in a position to export surplus capital to developing countries (Inter-American Development Bank 2007: 74–75). The dominant developmental strategy that began to emerge in Latin America was that of import substitution industrialization (ISI). As will be explained, ISI was linked to a highly different set of spatial practices and ideological representation of space.

To understand the rise of ISI, it is imperative that we once again recognize how domestic class forces within national state forms reacted to conditions within the international economy in forging this new developmental matrix. From the late nineteenth century to World War II, capital exports by the United States and Europe had mainly been focused in the primary sector and public utilities. However, this focus created tension between governments and business over the amount of capital that was reinvested back into the domestic economy, contributing further to the rise of nationalism (Varas 1995: 275). Moreover, there was growing class conflict in Latin America between the old elites tied to the agrarian export economy and those linked to the newly emerging industries. Due to levels of foreign investment, "a nascent group of industrialists developed under the auspices of the state. In trying to promote their own interests, these new industrialists had to challenge the traditional oligarchic rule, producing tension and clashes with the powerful landowning class" (Varas 1995: 275). The fact that manufacturing growth, although numerically small, began to lead the expansion of GDP for the first time can be cited as evidence for the growing importance of the bourgeoisie as a historical subject (Kaufman 1990: 113). Ronaldo Munck (2013: 73) notes that from 1910 onward ideas of anarchism, syndicalism, and socialism became powerful oppositional ideologies. Adding to this atmosphere of class conflict was the fact that urban labor began to try to assert itself as a social force in the 1930s, leading to tensions within the old development structure (Skidmore and Smith 1992: 54).

It is worth observing at this point the importance of the changing character of hegemony within the international sphere and the impact this had upon Latin American state formation and developmentalism. As previously mentioned, British hegemony (the so-called Pax Britannica is usually dated between 1815 and 1914) in the international political economy helped reinforce the oligarchic export-led development strategy in its demand for Latin American primary products (as the driver of its own domestic industrialization). Furthermore, Latin America would then serve as a key destination for the exportation of British manufactured products. This corresponded to the laissez-faire era of global capitalism. The emerging American hegemony after World War II, however, would presage the rise of worldwide industrial productive relations linked to Fordism, which entailed a much stronger role for state intervention in managing the economy (Gramsci 1971: 277–318, Q 22, §1–15; Cardoso and Faletto 1979: 24–26; Glyn et al. 2000: 56). These emerging economic ideas would be used to enhance the power of nascent elites in Latin America and provide an atmosphere convivial to their further expansion. Gramsci (1971: 116–17, Q 10ii, §61, emphasis added) was attentive to the manner in which geographical interlinkages such as these were formed via passive revolutionary processes, highlighting how, in many cases, "the impetus of progress is not tightly linked to a vast local economic development . . . but is instead the reflection of *international developments* which transmit their ideological currents to the periphery—currents born of the productive development of the advanced countries." In other words, the changing character of hegemony in the international political economy laid the foundations that were conducive to change in the character of hegemony at other spatial scales such as the regional and the national levels. This is not to say that the outcome of social struggle over the state form was predetermined by the international sphere, merely that the terrain was created in which certain modes of development could be more favorably articulated. It should be noted that this emphasis on passive revolutionary transition in Latin America sits at odds with mainstream scholarship on ISI, which sees this transition as an autochthonous developmental paradigm (e.g., Love 1994).

This developmental transition had been reinforced with the onset of the Great Depression. In this period, demand for Latin America's primary products severely contracted, as did the availability of capital to the region. Duncan Green (1995: 15) describes the situation of the region in the 1930s as one of "growing poverty, social unrest, repression, economic recession and defaults over foreign debt. Latin American export markets disappeared, and economies starved of hard currency had to drastically curtail imports." This situation led to a climate of export pessimism in which ISI emerged not so much as a coherent developmental paradigm but rather as an emergency measure to "stave off the balance of payments crisis, [to] maintain employment and to defend the interests of politically important constituencies" (Kaufman 1990: 114). As will later be demonstrated, this would not be the last time the issue of debt was used to presage a restructuring of the state and the direction of development. World War II further contributed to the change in developmental policy. The scarcity of imports led to a stimulation of domestic manufacturing so that postwar industrial production expanded more than 33 percent above prewar levels (United Nations 1949: 1). The end of World War II, furthermore, was not a positive experience for the region's economy, as wartime cooperation with the United States ceased. Moreover, with the new geopolitical dynamics of the Cold War, the reconstruction of Europe was prioritized over investment in Latin America, thus limiting the exogenous capital available for development (Bulmer-Thomas 1994: 257). After the war, the region had a reasonably healthy level of foreign reserves. However, a combination of debt resettlement, nationalizations (and subsequent compensation paid), and the massive rise of imports (an increase of 75 percent in three years) meant that these reserves were quickly diminished (Bulmer-Thomas 1994: 262). In this international climate of changing hegemonic structure, scarce capital flows, a rising domestic bourgeoisie who sought to insulate itself from foreign competition, and an increasingly aware working class, ISI emerged in Latin America as the dominant developmental paradigm. Drawing upon Adam Morton (2007c:

612–13), it can be highlighted how transitions to capitalist modernity unfolded "in a world-historical context of uneven and combined development," as it was the desire for economic development from all classes within Latin America, coupled with particular conditions within the "international," that led to the decline of the old model of accumulation and its replacement with ISI.

By the 1960s every republic had an ISI policy of sorts (Bulmer-Thomas 1994: 262). As Ricardo Ffrench-Davis (1994: 188) summarizes, although the specific policy content differed, "most Latin American countries from the 1950s to the 1980s have in common the basic features of relying upon the manufacturing sector as the main engine of growth. It is therefore possible to speak of a common Latin American experience of ISI." This experience was reinforced by institutions such as the Comisión Económica para América Latina y el Caribe (CEPAL, Economic Commission for Latin America and the Caribbean) that helped lay the intellectual foundations for the model. Of particular importance were the economists Raúl Prebisch and Hans Singer, who, in Gramsci's (1971: 10–15, Q 12, §1) terms, acted as key "organic intellectuals," providing homogeneity and awareness to the emerging bourgeois class and providing the theoretical terrain on which they could establish their hegemony. Drawing upon the theoretical basis that was laid out in the previous chapter, we can see once again how ideology (the manner in which space is represented) can intervene in spatial production. In particular here, the idea of the nation and nation building was reinforced as the locus for capital accumulation. Likewise, these ideas were crucial points of framing for the spaces of resistance.

The State Mode of Production in Latin America

ISI sought to build on the prevailing Keynesian ideas with regard to the central role that the state had to play in the direction of economic activity (although the term 'Keynesian' will require some qualification). The overarching purpose of ISI was to facilitate a development strategy for the countries of the region that had been denied to them due to the experience of colonialism (Kiely 2007: 53). The adoption of ISI thus represented a new epoch in state formation in Latin America. Previously, the state had sought to promote the interests of the exporting sector while also acting as a conduit for foreign investment and thus had taken a subordinate role to the private sphere (Cardoso and Faletto 1979: 129). As was explained earlier, this process corresponded to the dominance of the domestic oligarchy and the particular mode of integration with the international political economy. With the newly emerging model, the state's function changed to providing the infrastructure necessary to create the conditions propitious for industrialization and domestic capital accumulation. The state intervened to regulate prices and provide credit and subsidies, as well as to control the labor market and establish state-owned enterprises (SOEs). Concurrently, tariff barriers were erected and/or quotas installed to protect domestic industry from competition.

Lastly, in congruence with the received wisdom of the time, the state imposed strict financial controls on capital movements (Stallings 2005: 3–4). ISI thus came to be based around three key ideas: the promotion of the domestic industry that should produce goods for the domestic market, the reduction of dependence on both foreign manufactured imports and the exportation of primary products, and protection for these domestic industries (Kiely 2007: 50).

In terms of the spatial relations that were produced, ISI formed a contrast to the previous era of export-led growth. Instead of looking outward and seeking to generate growth through integration with the world market, ISI can be thought of as an inward-looking development strategy in which the countries of the region based their economic dynamism on the growth of their own domestic industrial sector. The nation, as opposed to the global market, came to be prioritized by intellectuals of statecraft. The results of this prioritization can be empirically witnessed by examining developments in world trade and Latin America's role in that trade. Between 1948 and 1973 the value of international trade rose at an annual rate of 9.7 percent. However, this growth was mainly concentrated in the developed countries. In this same period Latin America's share of world exports declined, so that "by 1965 the region's share of world exports had fallen below its share of population, perhaps for the first time since independence" (Bulmer-Thomas 1994: 270). Imports also declined substantially as a percentage of GDP (Furtado 1970: 111). It is important to stress at this point that the institution of ISI was not an autocentric process but rather the confluence of national and international class dynamics. Due to the collapse of the export-led growth model, the economic hegemony of the oligarchs receded; concomitantly, there was a shift in power toward "foreign and domestic industrial capitalists interested in preserving or gaining access to protected markets" (Kaufman 1990: 121). We can demonstrate this point regarding the relative power of class forces in Latin America if we compare the contributions of agriculture and manufacturing production to GDP. During the 1950s primary products fell from 17.2 percent of GDP to 8.9 percent. Conversely, manufactures rose from 18 percent of GDP to 21 percent (Ffrench-Davis 1994: 172).

Following the demise of agroexportation as a model of development, the industrial bourgeoisie tied to the state was the only group capable of establishing a viable hegemonic project, defined as "the mobilization of support behind a concrete, national-popular program of action which asserts a general interest in the pursuit of objectives that explicitly or implicitly advance the long term interests of the hegemonic class" (Jessop 1990: 208). As mentioned above, since the 1930s (and continuing with the growth of industrialization) the working class had increasingly been constituting itself as an important political constituency. Migration from the countryside to the cities in search of employment threatened to create urban unrest and necessitated job creation. Thus, as Fernando Henrique Cardoso and Enzo Faletto (1979: 26) explain, the industrial group was—despite its apparent marginal situation—the "only group in the new urban sectors that possessed a real economic base. As the one group that could actually absorb urban popular sectors in a productive way [they were] strategically situated to establish terms of alliance or compromise with the rest of the social system." This conforms to Gramsci's (1971: 116, Q 10ii, §61) view of how hegemony is established, as what is important is not necessarily the numerical size of a class but its ability to represent (or potentially represent) the wider interests of society at a particular juncture. Bob Jessop (1990: 99) elaborates upon this point, highlighting how economic hegemony is established "through general acceptance of an accumulation strategy. Such a strategy must advance the immediate interests of other fractions by integrating the circuit of capital in which they are implicated at the same time as it secures the long term interests of the hegemonic fraction."

When examining the constitution of ISI's economic hegemony it is imperative to note that the power of the landowners was not completely eroded. This was because, instead of a bloody revolution (the case of Mexico notwithstanding), there were "sufficiently elastic frameworks to allow the bourgeoisie to gain power without dramatic upheavals," and while not eliminated, the old oligarchic classes were "demoted from their dominant position" (Gramsci 1971: 115, Q 10ii, §61). Instead, new class alliances were formed under the new accumulation strategy. In order to industrialize, the region needed to purchase the necessary capital goods from abroad. This necessitated foreign exchange raised through the continuing exportation of primary products. ISI thus provided a "framework of tense interdependence between industrial and agro-exporting sectors; a growing power for state elites emerging within this framework; and an increasing use of the state's regulatory apparatus to protect organized interests" (Kaufman 1990: 112). In this manner the emergence of ISI can clearly be thought of as a Latin American variant of the "state mode of production." In other words, the capitalist growth was one clearly managed and controlled by the state (Lefebvre 1975/2009: 107–11). This state power was enhanced by the control of exports (Pearce 2004: 493). The process of state formation in Latin America can clearly, therefore, be related to Gramsci's twin concepts of passive revolution and *trasformismo*. As discussed in the introduction, passive revolution refers to a situation whereby the state plays the leading role in the process of transforming social relations while also absorbing subaltern class pressure for more radical change. Rather than being literally passive, the social compromise that was ISI can be seen as a response to activated subaltern classes, but one in which these subaltern classes did not fully come to author the process themselves (Munck 2013: 87). The associated concept, *trasformismo*, describes the "establishment of an ever more extensive ruling class" within the framework of the established order (Gramsci 1971: 58, Q 19, §24). As Robert Cox (1983: 167) has noted, these concepts have particular purchase when applied to peripheral industrializing countries.

The emerging form of the state in Latin America after the 1930s is generally characterized as being of the "national-popular" variety (Munck 2013: 79). Another way of analyzing this project would be through the lens of populism. As James Malloy (1977) notes, populism combined nationalism with developmentalism in its rejection of the previous liberal, oligarchic model. However, populism was statist as opposed to socialist. Reformist, not revolutionary, and as a political project, it appealed to the idea of social harmony rather than stressing class differences (for which appeals to nationalism helped provide the mediating ideology). Ernesto Laclau clarifies how populism links with class rule, as it is able to transform class discourse into nonclass contradictions and offer forms of compromise. Therefore, "a class is hegemonic not so much to the extent that it is able to impose a uniform conception of the world on the rest of society but to the extent that it can articulate different visions of the world in such a way that their potential antagonism is neutralised" (Laclau 1977: 161). ISI was able to do this via passive revolutionary tactics that resulted in a populist and (relatively) inclusive historical bloc of class forces.

Recalling the triad of spatial practices, spaces of representation, and representational spaces (the perceived, the conceived, and the lived), we can see how ISI maps onto each level. With regard to spatial practices, the focus on the growth of internal markets clearly represented a break from the previous model of integration based on agricultural exports. In relation to spaces of representation, we can examine how nationalism and the representation of national space came to be utilized as an elite class strategy for capital accumulation. There was, however, a limited degree of incorporation of the demands of the popular classes, such as spending on social services, subsidized consumption, increasing employment opportunities, and rising real wages (Robinson 2004a: 137). These reforms were achieved through the process of strong unionization, often linked closely with the state in the method of corporatism (see O'Donnell 1977). In terms of the representational spaces of ISI, the previous two elements were able to exert a powerful influence in creating a model for incorporation and mediating everyday spatial practices. In this manner, ISI as a hegemonic project can usefully be defined as one of "controlled inclusion" (Oxhorn 1995). In other words, it was very much a process of inclusion from above in which the electorate were viewed as clients rather than citizens (Pearce 2004: 494–96). Co-optive democracy and populism were to become key traits of Latin American states during this era (Skidmore and Smith 1992: 55).

Deborah Yashar (2005: 46) highlights how citizenship is articulated through a combination of civil rights (freedom of speech, freedom of association), political rights (participation in electoral processes, the right to form trade unions), and social rights (health, education, housing, welfare). Under ISI it was the advance of certain social rights that was vital to the state's legitimacy, with civil rights and political rights often fluctuating (notably with the turn to authoritarianism in Southern Cone countries). Furthermore, the project of state building was one of assimilation. This meant that indigenous subjectivities were reclassified as peasants so that they could gain access to state funds. Often, however, de facto autonomy remained for many indigenous communities, "one in which ethnic identities remained salient, local authority structures evolved, and actors learned to maneuver between local ethnicities and national identities" (Yashar 2005: 7). As will later be discussed, this relationship could be maintained only while state formation effectively remained weak and continued to grant communities either autonomy or material concessions. In the neoliberal period, however, ethnic conflict has openly reemerged as a crucial battleground in Latin America.

As a strategy for national development, ISI had some degree of success. Between 1950 and 1981 there was a large increase in economic growth at almost 5.5 percent per annum, with output per capita concomitantly increasing by 2.8 percent (Ffrench-Davis 1994: 169). The region also made significant progress in industrializing. Between 1950 and 1978 manufacturing increased its contribution to GDP from $9.3 to 57.9 billion. However, it should be stressed that this impressive growth sat alongside the continuation of vast inequalities. Critically, despite the inward-looking nature of the developmental model, Latin America never managed to create a development strategy that was not reliant upon both foreign technology and capital to sustain its accumulation process. In what follows I will highlight how ISI as a hegemonic project collapsed not only as a result of the accumulation strategy underpinning it, exhausting its potentialities and thus creating the terrain for new social struggles, but also because worldwide there was a restructuring of capitalist social relations that the region was not immune to. After all, it should be remembered that "the history of central capitalism is, at the same time, the history of peripheral capitalism" (Cardoso and Faletto 1979: 23). This contention will be explored in relation to the debt crisis that swept through Latin America in the 1980s. However, as I will demonstrate with regard to this crisis, the history of peripheral capitalism is equally the history of central capitalism. This contention serves to underscore the key points made in the previous chapter with regard to the mutual construction of various spatial scales for capital accumulation and the vital role that uneven and combined development plays within this process.

ISI: Failed Incorporation or Successful Class Project?

What were the principal contradictions of ISI as both an economic and a political project? A key difficulty Latin America faced was trying to develop a self-sustaining manufacturing sector. Other nations that had managed this, such as New Zealand, South Africa, and Canada, had industrialized alongside their integration into the world economy (United Nations 1949: 53). Latin America, by contrast, was inserted into the global trading system prior to these countries and thus came to rely on the transfer of resources generated from the sale of primary commodities to fuel the domestic industrial sector. As mentioned previously, this process was essential to generate the foreign exchange revenue necessary to buy the components needed for domestic industrialization, as there were only limited indigenous capital goods industries in most Latin American countries. However, it is always difficult to increase the inputs necessary for industrialization while relying on primary products, as historically they have a relatively low elasticity in terms of demand. Compounding this problem was the fact that the net barter terms of trade (the ratio of export prices to import prices) for primary products had declined significantly following the Korean War, so that by 1967 they were 30 percent below the level of 1950 (Ffrench-Davis 1994: 180). Thus, despite the attempt to create endogenous growth conditions, ISI failed to move the region away from exogenous shocks. Although ISI did manage to reduce Latin American dependence on consumer goods, this was only achieved through a new relation of dependency on capital goods (Kiely 2007: 54; Skidmore and Smith 1992: 56). We must at this juncture take heed of Doreen Massey's (1994: 59) point, namely, that in analyzing space and spatial changes in one area, we must also remain mindful of the fact that the rest of the world does not remain static and that, furthermore, the requirements of production are constantly evolving. Indeed, during the period 1965–73 the world economy began to move away from internal growth to growing internationalization of trade (Glyn et al. 2000: 87). The prevailing climate of "export pessimism" in Latin America, however, meant that the region was slow to adopt to the openness of the international political economy, and unlike the newly industrialized countries (NICs) in East Asia, Latin America failed to see the potential of exporting manufactured products as a strategy for growth. When this situation was recognized in the 1960s, years of high tariff barriers meant that Latin American manufactured products were uncompetitive and often of a low standard. These problems, coupled with the overvaluation of most Latin American currencies, meant manufacturers struggled to break into world markets (Baer 1972; Bulmer-Thomas 1994: 283–84).

The region also remained heavily dependent on foreign capital to expand the accumulation process. This led to attempts to encourage foreign direct investment (FDI) in a bid to facilitate technology transfer and provide much-needed capital.[1] An alliance thus developed between foreign capitalists and the domestic bourgeoisie connected to state power (O'Donnell 1977: 62). Investment in Latin America provided foreign companies a region with new fertile markets, cheap labor, and a highly protected environment that they could invest inside

(Twomey 1998: 181; Varas 1995: 276). However, foreign firms often sought to re-patriate profits, creating tension with an inward-looking model of development that relied upon the reinvestment of this capital in order to expand domestic production. Therefore, we have to be cognizant of the place of Latin America within the emergence of a new spatial division of labor. As Massey (1994: 59) has argued, the production of spatial inequality is inherent to this very con-cept. In order to pay the dividends accruing to foreign investors while retain-ing their productive capital and expertise, governments of the region began to seek new loans (Martínez 1993: 67). As we shall later see, this situation co-incided with an international environment in which surplus capital was actively seeking new markets. This fact, however, makes any claim of ISI representing a purely nation-state phase of capitalist development (e.g., Robinson 2003, 2004a, 2004b, 2008) problematic, due to the fact that global forces, as we have seen, were partly constitutive of this model from the outset. Full sovereignty within each country over economic development was never achieved, leading Alain Lipietz (1984: 76–77, emphasis added) to conclude that ISI as a model of accumulation was "immediately and durably *international in character.*" The portrayal of ISI as simply a "region-specific version of Fordist-Keynesian na-tional capitalism" (Robinson 2008: 51) therefore becomes slightly problematic, as that portrayal elides the very different power geometries involved. Whereas Fordist-Keynesian regimes generated their own surpluses (and indeed suffered from a lack of avenues for profitable investment), Latin America was reliant upon the importation of this surplus capital and therefore occupied a structur-ally subservient position within the global economy. As a result, Lipietz's (1984: 74) concept of "peripheral Fordism" is more accurate, as it also denotes the fact that skilled production remained in the core countries and that accumulation in Latin America was based not on mass consumption but on middle-class con-sumption and limited export to the core.

Another long-term structural problem with ISI was its inherent class divide. As Oxhorn (1995: 258) powerfully argues, "The viability of the industrializa-tion model required growing domestic markets. Ultimately this led to growing demands by the working classes which Latin American economies strained to meet." Few workers could afford to buy the products they manufactured (Green 1995: 18), highlighting the alienating conditions under which capitalist production was taking place and its internal contradictions as an accumulation strategy. Moreover, under ISI the income in real terms going to the poorest ele-ments in society actually shrank (Portes 1985: 24). Unlike Fordism in the West, a consensus about the merits of large-scale redistribution was not reached in Latin America. While those elites tied to the basic consumer goods industries favored a more progressive income distribution to expand their sales base, this was opposed by those linked with consumer durables and intermediate goods (Varas 1995: 277). Some attempts to overcome this limited scope for capital accumulation were attempted by means of a "spatial fix" of regional integration in order to achieve economies of scale. However, despite some increases in interregional manufacturing exports, this new scalar arrangement did not fulfill expectations, and the lack of domestic demand remained a key contradiction of the accumulation strategy.

Adding to this difficulty was the fact that unemployment was an increasing problem in Latin America. Despite the success of ISI in stimulating economic growth, it suffered from the fact that its model of industrialization was highly mimetic of patterns found in the developed countries. This meant that it tended to be technology intensive and thus had a limited potential for job creation, as it failed to absorb workers into formal productive structures (again highlighting the importance of recognizing Latin America's place within a global spatial division of labor). Unemployment thus became a structural condition of ISI due to the fact that technology was imported in an effort to "catch up" with the West (Duménil and Lévy 2004: 37–42). Therefore, as Alejandro Portes (1985: 29) illustrates, "Despite accumulated industrial growth during the period following World War II, the relative size of the informal proletariat declined by only 4 percent between 1950 and 1980." This would lead to increasing social tension and conflict, heightened by the fact that "the capacity of education to provide avenues for social mobility was nearing exhaustion as the creation of high paying employment failed to keep pace with the expansion of education levels in the workforce" (Oxhorn 1995: 258). The frustration of the popular classes led to increasing demands to maintain their limited political and economic inclusion. These mobilizations from below were often met with highly authoritarian responses by elite classes in which "coerced marginalization" emerged as a key state policy to replace the former model of "controlled inclusion" (Oxhorn 1995: 257–58).[2] As Beverley Silver (2003: 165) explains, a key contradiction of the developmentalist state was that increased labor militancy led to a loss of state legitimacy. However, to overcome this loss through increased social spending would threaten profit rates and therefore reduce foreign investment.

Ultimately, ISI as a hegemonic project withered as the accumulation strategy that underpinned it came into crisis. Just as the oligarchs had sought foreign investment as a means of helping to secure their own power, so a similar strategy was now pursued by the bourgeoisie. Within all the Latin American states, infrastructural development, SOEs, and social welfare provisions were consuming a vast amount of resources. This expenditure helped precipitate a shift in class power away from manufacturing and toward the financial sector. Such a shift has been identified as one of the hallmarks of neoliberalism worldwide (Duménil and Lévy 2004). David Harvey (2006a: 303) synthesizes the changing relationship as follows: "The capacity of industrial capitalists to finance their own investments and extend credit to each other is exhausted as they reach the limit of their cash reserves. They are forced to turn to the banks and the financiers who strengthen their power vis-à-vis industrial capital as a consequence." This was exactly what occurred in Latin America, but, crucially, the financiers were external forces in the shape of international banks. Thus, the rapid expansion of debt-led growth should be viewed as "a concrete and costly manifestation of the continuing and deeply retrograde nature of Latin America's class structure, a structure that profoundly affects the nature and completeness of the region's productive apparatus and its mode of development. Lacking the internal basis for expanded development, Latin American elites, very often via the state and state investment, turned outwards in the 1960s for loans to fuel capital accumulation and growth" (Dietz 1989: 21).

Developments within the international political economy crucially helped to shape this trajectory, however, confirming the point that class strategies have to be understood in relation to wider spatial scales and not viewed merely within a national context. The creation of the Eurodollar market and breakdown of the Bretton Woods financial system had led to the rise of transnational capital flows.[3] The oil shocks of the 1970s not only generated vast excess liquidity in international markets but also created a foreign exchange crisis for the oil-importing countries of Latin America, while oil-producing countries such as Venezuela, Ecuador, and Mexico sought to borrow in order to expand their production capabilities.[4] These "petrodollars" thus not only presented an opportunity for Latin American elites to offset the contradictions of ISI's weak domestic capital markets by borrowing abroad (while also generating surpluses for a degree of social redistribution to offset rising labor militancy) but at the same time provided a "spatial fix" for overaccumulated capital in Western banks, as opportunities for investment there were limited due to the onset of stagflation (a combination of stagnating production and inflation). Capital, after all, "is defined as a process—as value 'in motion' undergoing a continuous expansion through the production of surplus value" (Harvey 2006a: 83). Recycling "petrodollars" into Latin America thus became a way to productively put this capital to work and stave off domestic inflation and devalorization (Lipietz 1984: 80). The accumulation of debt within Latin America thus needs to be firmly situated within the context of uneven and combined development and the very different sociospatial relations contained within different geographical regions of the world.

Debt helped to further the process of expanded capital accumulation through deficit spending based on "fictitious capital," defined as "a flow of money-capital not backed by any commodity transaction" and based upon "future labour as a counter-value" (Harvey 2006a: 265–66). The assumption was that loans could be repaid through increased export earnings, the creation of profitable new markets, and the further recycling of loans back to the center to purchase capital goods, thus helping to stimulate Western economies (Lipietz 1984: 77). Latin America, in other words, became a vital site for the reproduction and stabilization of global capitalism. This integration of spatial relations through overaccumulation is consistent with the inner logic of capital identified by Marx (1863/1972: 172): "Over-production, the credit system, etc. . . . are the means by which capitalist production seeks to break through its own barriers and to produce over and above its own *limits*. Capitalist production, on the one hand, has this driving force; on the other hand, it only tolerates production commensurate with the profitable employment of existing capital. Hence crises arise, which simultaneously drive it onward and beyond its own limits."

Crisis, then, should be viewed as an essential moment in the dynamics of capitalist production, becoming a tool to restructure economies so as to extend and deepen the value-form. This is vital to understanding the rise of neoliberalism in Latin America, as it highlights that we cannot conceive of modes of capitalist production in isolation but rather always have to examine capitalism as an integrated whole. Realizing this allows us once again to empirically grasp the point made by Lefebvre (1991: 55) that class struggle is increasingly waged through the production of space. Let us explore, then, the specific class content of the debt crisis to demonstrate how this is the case.

The (Neoliberal) Road to Serfdom

In the postwar period, capital flows to Latin America had predominantly taken the form of bilateral or multilateral lending, with some FDI also proving crucial. However, with the emergence of the Eurodollar market the nature of capital flows was altered, and syndicated bank loans emerged as the dominant form of investment (United Nations Conference on Trade and Development 2003: 33). By 1980 80 percent of the region's debt was held by private banks (Ffrench-Davis 1994: 235). Financial capital thus came to displace productive capital (Martínez 1993: 67). This put the region in a precarious situation, as integration into the world economy through this means was an even more unstable link than the previous one through commodities (Ffrench-Davis 1994: 185). We can witness the increasing vulnerability of the region to the influx of foreign capital if we examine the debt ratios compared with the value of exports. In 1950 foreign debt amounted to one-third of the value of all exports. However, by 1960 the external debt was almost a third more than the region's total exports, and in 1973, prior to the first oil shock, it was almost twice as much. From this we can see that the structural conditions for the debt crisis were already firmly in place and that the oil shocks merely served to exacerbate the problem (Martínez 1993: 65). In real terms, the average capital flow to Latin America increased four times from 1966–70 to 1974–81, so that by the beginning of the 1980s the region had accumulated the largest debt stock in the world (Ffrench-Davis 1994: 226–27). The viability of debt-led growth in Latin America was conditional, though, upon the persistence of three factors: (1) the continuing availability of foreign capital, (2) the maintenance of low interest rates, and (3) rising commodity prices to help service accrued debt. However, the election of Paul Volcker as chairman of the Federal Reserve in 1979 precipitated a new monetarist policy in the United States in response to domestic fears of inflation. This canceled out all of the above three premises. First, the unilateral raising of interest rates markedly increased the value of Latin American debt. Second, at the same time, the raising of interest rates caused a contraction in international liquidity, leading, third, to declining demands for primary products as recession became a feature of the central economies. Financial markets also became aware that Latin America could not repay its vast loans, and thus foreign capital began to dry up. All of these elements helped precipitate the debt crisis in Latin America that erupted in 1982. This provides empirical detail to Harvey's (2006a: 431) assertion that "general crises arise out of the chaos and confusion of local, particular events. They build upwards on the basis of concrete individual labour processes and market exchanges into global crises in the qualities of abstract labour and in the value form. . . . Crises build, therefore, through uneven geographical development."

The crisis of overaccumulation within Western economies was thus successfully switched to Latin America, which was forced to bear the major costs of the restructuring process. The debt crisis marked a watershed in Latin American state formation and developmentalism. Gramsci (1971: 184, Q 13, §17) remarks with regard to the political significance of economic crises: "[They] create a terrain more favourable to the dissemination of certain modes of thought, and certain ways of posing and resolving questions involving the entire subsequent development of national life." This was certainly the case in Latin America, where the debt crisis would be used to redefine the trajectory of development, with an outward-looking neoliberal economic model emerging to replace the inward-looking one of ISI. As Merilee Grindle (1996: 4) counsels, the debt crisis "opened up increased space for deliberative efforts to craft new relationships of power and accountability within society." International financial institutions such as the International Monetary Fund (IMF), the World Bank, and the Inter-American Development Bank were key levers of power in this regard. Although external forces had never ceased to influence Latin America's state formation and development, this tendency became ever more pronounced after the debt crisis. As countries in the region could no longer service their debts and sources of private lending had ceased, they had to look to international financial institutions as a means of obtaining much-needed foreign exchange. However, these loans came with key conditionalities attached to them, including the reduction of public spending, exchange rate stability, import liberalization, privatization, deregulation, and the opening of their economies to FDI (United Nations Conference on Trade and Development 2006: 43–44). This was in line with the newly emerging "Washington Consensus," which sought to reduce (or, in reality, alter) the role of governments in the economic affairs of developing countries and move them more generally to export-oriented models of growth (Williamson 1990: 1). Duncan Green (1995: 64) captures the essential policy dilemma that Latin American countries faced with no loans forthcoming: they could "either declare a moratorium on the debt and become an international pariah, or generate a trade surplus and use the excess hard currency to pay the banks. They chose trade." Commenting upon the new discourse of development, Thomas Biersteker (1995: 180) writes that despite the unevenness of the shift to neoliberalism, "the change in development ideas has been profound."

Table 1 highlights the huge impact and continuing problem of debt for Latin America. The levels of most countries' indebtedness continued to expand rapidly up to 1995 (and in some cases beyond this) due to both inflation on existing obligations and new debts accrued. Owing to this, Latin American governments' policies became directed toward "ensuring significant flows of external funding rather than encouraging domestic capital formation and productivity growth" (United Nations Conference on Trade and Development 2003: 144). As we shall see later, these policies have had huge implications for the region's development path.

The huge debt burden also meant that countries were forced to create the conditions necessary to service this debt. Practically, this entailed increasing exports while trying to reduce domestic demand, which quickly led to a disastrous recession. The rapid opening of these countries' economies to foreign competition helped destroy local research and development (United Nations Conference on Trade and Development 2003: 140), which meant that the products of Latin American industries would remain dependent upon a high import content, exacerbating the balance-of-payments crisis (United Nations Conference on Trade and Development 2006: 48).

As a method for dealing with the debt crisis, economies were restructured (in line with World Bank recommendations) to become more "investor friendly." Tariffs on foreign trade, for example, dropped from 42 percent in 1985 to just 14 percent in 1995 (Robinson 2008: 54). This decrease led to FDI replacing portfolio investment and commercial bank loans as the most important form of investment (United Nations Conference on Trade and Development 2004: 8).

Tables 2 and 3 highlight the massive expansion of FDI that has taken place in Latin America since the 1990s. A significant proportion of this expansion has been in mergers and acquisitions and the takeover of privatized state enterprises (United Nations Conference on Trade and Development 2000: xvii). By 2005 FDI stock accounted for 32.7 percent of Latin America's gross fixed capital formation, expanding at a much faster rate than that of North America or the European Union. The transformation of the role of the state in economic development has had important ramifications for the region. The neoliberal

TABLE 1. Total External Debt (Thousands of U.S. Dollars) of Various Latin American Countries, 1970–2000

Country	1970	1975	1980	1985	1990	1995	2000
Argentina	5,809,759	7,722,484	27,157	50,946	62,232	98,482,300	147,402,500
Bolivia	588,300	1,012,794	2,702,381	4,804,566	4,274,968	5,272,147	5,785,173
Brazil	5,734,466	27,331,380	71,526,930	103,611,700	119,964,200	160,515,300	243,668,500
Chile	2,977,238	5,518,637	12,081,260	20,383,880	19,225,820	22,038,220	37,288,690
Colombia	2,236,453	3,757,762	6,940,527	14,248,250	17,222,120	25,044,290	33,929,830
Ecuador	364,311	908,754	5,997,483	8,702,830	12,107,260	13,993,570	13,717,070
Mexico	6,968,569	18,230,540	57,377,670	96,867,300	104,442,000	165,378,600	150,313,500
Nicaragua	6,968,569	800,688	2,192,851	5,772,308	10,744,680	10,389,700	6,853,055
Peru	3,211,338	6,117,777	9,385,848	12,883,950	20,043,570	30,833,180	28,660,980
Uruguay	363,012	904,235	1,659,824	3,919,448	20,043,570	30,833,180	8,113,318
Venezuela	1,422,233	2,233,282	29,355,700	35,339,580	33,170,910	35,537,940	41,953,410

Source: World Bank: World Development Indicators.

TABLE 2. FDI Inflows (Millions of U.S. Dollars) to Latin America, 1970–2005

Region/Economy	1970	1975	1980	1985	1990	1995	2000	2005
Latin America and the Caribbean	1,599	3,514	6,483	6,242	9,748	29,610	97,803	75,541
Argentina	90	56	678	919	1,836	5,609	10,418	5,008
Brazil	392	1,203	1,910	1,418	989	4,405	32,779	15,066
Chile	12	37	287	165	1,315	3041	4,860	6,960
Columbia	43	37	157	1,023	500	968	2,395	10,255
Ecuador	89	95	70	62	126	452	720	1,646
Peru	−14	81	27	1	41	2,557	810	2,579
Costa Rica	26	69	53	70	162	337	409	861
Mexico	312	458	2,090	1,984	2,633	9,526	17,789	19,736
Venezuela	−23	418	80	99	778	985	4,701	2,583

Source: UNCTAD 2007.

TABLE 3. Inward FDI Stock as a Percentage of Gross Domestic Product, by Host and Regional Economy, 1980–2005

Region/Economy	1980	1985	1990	1995	2000	2005
World	5.2	6.8	8.4	9.3	18.3	22.6
European Union	6.1	9.1	10.5	12.6	26.0	33.1
North America	4.5	5.5	8.0	8.3	13.9	14.2
Latin America and the Caribbean	4.6	8.2	9.3	10.0	23.9	32.7

Source: UNCTAD 2007.

accumulation regime established in Latin America on average now only commits around 20 percent of national income to capital formation, "well below the level thought to be necessary to allow the region to catch up rates of economic growth" (United Nations Conference on Trade and Development 2003: 65). Whereas under ISI, state banks were the key providers of credit (in keeping with the national spatial strategy of development), now FDI is "to an increasing extent intended to serve global and regional markets often in the context of international production networks" (United Nations Conference on Trade and Development 2006: 10). Thus, Latin America has further become integrated into what Gary Gereffi (1995) refers to as "global commodity chain" production. Not only have exports increased, they have also become more diversified, for example, in terms of nontraditional agricultural exports (Robinson 2008: 56).

We need to be cautious, however, about viewing changes in Latin American developmentalism solely as an external imposition. As Alejandro Colás (2005: 70) argues, neoliberal globalization is a process "heavily mediated, when it is not actually authored by states." While external factors were important influences in setting the terms of the debate and transmitting these new discourses of development, the furtherance of neoliberalism in the region would not have been possible without the support of local elites, as well as the crisis of the existing model and the seeming lack of alternatives (Green 1995: 23; Morton 2003). Michael Burawoy (1998: 20–21) has highlighted that blaming shifts in development trajectories solely on exogenous forces is often used as a strategy to mask the establishment of new domestic classes. Class struggles around the state form have thus proved to be essential, as its regulatory capacity has been used to craft these new relationships with external capital. An example of this would be the manner in which states seek to valorize their cheap sources of labor to attract FDI (Lipietz 1984: 74). It should also be noted how particular elite factions in Latin America saw their positions augmented and enhanced by the transition to neoliberalism and the restructuring of the region's economies (Dietz 1989: 13–15). All in all, the transition to neoliberalism saw the consolidation rather than the destruction of a capitalist class within Latin America, highlighting a new phase of *trasformismo*. Although ISI therefore can be viewed as a failure both as a viable (long-term) accumulation strategy and as a project to incorporate the subaltern classes, when viewed from a class-theoretical perspective it has been enormously successful in fostering the consolidation and dominance of the bourgeoisie. Therefore, as David Ruccio (1991: 1329) explains, "What are often seen as development failures may, in fact, be part of a more general process of the successful emergence and strengthening of capitalist class processes in Latin America and the rest of the world."

It is also important to view the debt crisis not simply as a crisis of Latin American capitalism but rather as a potential crisis of capitalism seen as a totality. Following the Mexican default in 1982, thirteen American banks were owed $16.5 billion. Had other countries followed suit in defaulting, the financial system of world capitalism could well have collapsed, as it did in 1930, precipitating a global depression (Green 1995: 61). As Duménil and Lévy (2004: 87) note, by 1983 twenty-three other countries had to reschedule debt repayments, and the four most indebted nations in the world (Mexico, Brazil, Venezuela, and Argentina) owed 74 percent of the debt held by developing countries. However, rather than becoming a crisis of capitalism and threatening the social relations upon which the system is based, the debt crisis simply became a crisis within capitalism, thus acting as a necessary precondition to drive the system forward and begin a new round of accumulation (Lebowitz 2003: 165). This new round of accumulation, however, involved a process of highly spatialized class struggle (or geopolitical conflict). With regard to this process, Harvey (2003: 151, emphasis added) states: "Regional crisis and highly localized *place-based devaluations* emerge as a primary means by which capitalism perpetually creates its other to feed on." As mentioned above, the new round of accumulation was achieved through a massive privatization of Latin American public resources and SOEs, as well as large-scale reductions in social welfare provisions. This is a classic example of what Harvey (2003: 145) theorizes as "accumulation by dispossession," as resources went from being state owned and geared toward national development to exclusive private property rights devoted solely to surplus value extraction. As discussed in chapter 1, this form of primitive accumulation also results in highly gendered forms of exploitation. IMF-mandated structural adjustment programs were largely constructed with scant consideration of their gendered impacts. However, as Isabella Bakker (1995) notes, state rollback in the form of public expenditure cuts disproportionately tend to affect women as they obtain more and better-paying jobs in the public sector. Furthermore, owing to the sexual division of labor, such cutbacks served as a double burden as household incomes came under attack. This meant those responsible for administering household budgets were under increased pressure both in their role within the reproductive economy (making meagre ends meet) and (often) in having to seek paid employment.

Surveying the change in development discourse, Biersteker (1995: 178) highlights how development came to be redefined solely in terms of growth of productive capacities while "concerns about the provisions of basic needs were shunted to the side." Latin America's transition to neoliberalism thus seems to support the view expressed by Duménil and Lévy (2004) that it is a class project designed to reconstitute the wealth of the upper factions of capital at the expense of the subaltern classes (see also Harvey 2005). Evidence for this can be highlighted by the fact that average urban incomes in all Latin American countries (with the exception of Chile) stagnated or declined with the onset of neoliberal reforms. This decline was especially pronounced in Uruguay and Venezuela, where income declined by 30 percent and 50 percent, respectively. The dominant classes, meanwhile, have increased their income faster than average (Portes and Hoffman 2003: 63–65). Business also came to be highly privileged over labor (Phillips 1999: 85; Veltmeyer 1997: 210). Jean Grugel (1998: 226) elucidates this matter further, highlighting how businesses became favored due to "their organization capacity, their familial and social contacts with government elites, their external linkages, and their growing importance in terms of production and export performance." Evaluating the success or failures of neoliberalism is therefore essentially a class-loaded question.

The shift to neoliberalism meant that as a region Latin America has undergone a dramatic deterioration in terms of its position within the world economy. This deterioration can be starkly observed if we look at the difference in GDP growth and GDP per-capita growth between Latin America and the NICS of East Asia, expressed in tables 4 and 5.

Further social costs of the neoliberal economic model in Latin America can also be witnessed from the huge increase in poverty. During the 1980s, the number of people living in poverty increased by sixty million. Concomitantly, there was a massive growth in unemployment and underemployment, with new jobs largely being created in the informal sector (Veltmeyer 1997: 220–23). The region's integration into the new social geography of neoliberalism has made its

TABLE 4. GDP Growth (Annual Average Percentage Change) in Latin America and East Asia, 1960–2005

Region	1960–65	1965–70	1970–75	1975–80	1980–85	1985–90	1990–95	1995–2000	2000–2005
Latin America	4.6	5.8	6.6	5.1	0.5	1.8	3.6	2.8	1.5
East Asia	5.0	7.5	6.8	7.6	7.1	8.2	8.8	4.9	6.2

Source: UNCTAD 2006.

TABLE 5. GDP Per Capita Growth Rates in Latin America and East Asia, 1960–2005

Region	1960–65	1965–70	1970–75	1975–80	1980–85	1985–90	1990–95	1995–2000	2000–2005
Latin America	1.7	3.1	4.0	2.7	−1.6	−0.2	1.9	1.2	0.1
East Asia	3.0	4.7	4.4	5.9	5.4	6.4	7.5	3.8	5.3

Source: UNCTAD 2006.

dependency on external finance and technology more acute than ever. This has meant that it has become increasingly hard to generate a divergent trade profile. FDI remains concentrated either in low-wage, low-skill industries serving as a cheap export platform for transnational corporations' commodity production (with highly gendered forms of exploitation) or in the extraction and exploitation of primary commodities with little labor employed, neither of which creates strong backward linkages with the host societies (Gereffi 1995: 134; United Nations Conference on Trade and Development 2006: 111). Surveying the period from the early 1980s to 1995, Duncan Green (1995: 111) comments, "Although the rich have had a vintage decade, most of the region's people are poorer and more insecure; their homes, communities, schools and hospitals are collapsing around them, while their cities, towns and villages are increasingly polluted."

The neoliberalization of Latin America has also involved a return to the Ricardian economic theories of "comparative advantage," the very theories that proved so disastrous for the region in the past and that, as chapter 1 highlighted, were erroneous for thinking about development in the modern world. With this transition the very term "development" was redefined. Rather than being concerned with the transformation of the productive structure as it was in the past, "development" came to be focused on issues such as poverty reduction, the provision of minimal needs, and individual advancement (Chang 2010). Development on this basis can only be a palliative and not a cure for the alienation inherent in capitalist social relations (in other words, it recognizes the permanence of structural inequality). Duménil and Lévy (2004: 82, emphasis added) are therefore surely correct when they conclude: "That it was necessary to manage the crisis was an undeniable fact. *That the neoliberal strategy was particularly harmful is another one."*

Resistance: A Tale of Two Lefts?

The above factors have meant that the viability of neoliberalism in Latin America as a new incorporation strategy was always inherently fragile, as there has been a growing tension with the social polarization that the accumulation strategy has caused, as well as a distrust of traditional political parties and elites (Luna and Filgueira 2009: 371). The long-term viability of neoliberalism was therefore reliant upon generating a wide base of political support beyond the privileged few who have benefited from privatization, deregulation, and the move to export-oriented growth (Cameron 2009: 338). In fact, the opposite has occurred. Latin America has been at the epicenter of resistance to neoliberalism worldwide since the twilight of the twentieth century and the beginning of the twenty-first, prompting William Robinson (2008: 237) to proclaim that the neoliberal model is now moribund in the region.

This perspective obviously necessitates new thinking about how this resistance is best theorized and articulated. I submit that to postulate resistance simply in terms of a transnational working class, as does Robinson (2003, 2004b, 2008), is highly problematic, not least because the transition to neoliberalism actually witnessed a decline in the formal proletariat. This decline means that "the numerically most important segment of the employed population in Latin America is that excluded from modern capitalist relations and which must survive through unregulated work and direct subsistence activities" (Portes and Hoffman 2003: 53). This evidence would seem to directly contradict the thesis put forward by Robinson (2004b: 7) that "capitalist productive relations are replacing what remains of pre-capitalist relations around the globe." The rise of the informal sector, therefore, has important implications for how we view class struggle and resistance to neoliberalism, because "the interests around which informal workers coalesce have to do less with control over the means of production than with minimal access to the means of collective reproduction, such as transport, water and basic services" (Portes 1985: 31). It was, in fact, the rise in bus fares that provoked the Caracazo riots in Venezuela in 1989, spelling the beginning of the end of the Punto Fijo regime and the rise of Hugo Chávez. These events are sometimes dated as the beginning of Latin America's formal rejection of neoliberalism. Similarly, struggles over access to land have been a prime factor motivating an array of movements such as the EZLN in Mexico (to be analyzed in chapter 5), the MST in Brazil, and the Confederación de Nacionalidades Indígenas del Ecuador (CONAIE, Confederation of Indigenous Nationalities of Ecuador). Other recent examples of everyday life struggles include mass mobilizations in Cochabamba and El Alto, Bolivia, against the privatization of water and gas, neighborhood assemblies linked to the unemployed workers' movement in Argentina, and the social tensions that have arisen from the implementation of the Transantiago public transportation system in the Chilean capital, to mention just a few. What these examples make clear is that the notion of class struggle must be extended beyond the workplace to include notions of everyday life. This (as was theorized in chapter 1) means that class struggles essentially revolve around the production of space and the social relations that spaces contain. Raúl Zibechi (2012) has noted that one of the major new trends among social movements in Latin America is their territorialization. That is to say, these social movements have roots in spaces that have been recuperated or secured through political action. As Lefebvre (1976: 85) summarizes, "If space as a whole has become the place where the reproduction of the relations of production is located, it has also become the terrain for a vast confrontation which creates its centre now here, now there, and therefore which cannot be localised or diffused." We can thus observe a key dialectical relation to class struggles inscribed in space. Neoliberal globalization seeks to deterritorialize space before reterritorializing in order to forge new global spatial divisions of labor for the increasing accumulation of capital. However, at the same time, subaltern movements are also seeking to reterritorialize space, making control over it a key aspect of social struggle (Dirlik 1999; Escobar 2001; Zibechi 2012). Attempts are then made to reorient spatial production toward social needs. Rather than a simple normative statement of how, theoretically, class struggles have to be transnationalized in order to challenge neoliberalism, the difficult task of integrating these place-based movements of resistance with national and transnational spatial scales must be undertaken. This challenge will be discussed in detail in chapters 4 and 5.

Another new trend that can be observed in Latin America is the rise to prominence of indigenous activism and resistance. Notably since the quincentennial remembrance of the Spanish conquest, indigenous groups—often fusing with class-based politics—are now among the leading social forces of popular mobilization in the region (Nash 2003; Robinson 2008: 298–304; Webber 2011; Yashar 2005). This mobilization must be understood with reference to processes of changing state formation that have also altered the spaces of capital. As was mentioned earlier, ISI functioned as both a broadly assimilationist project and one in which indigenous communities were granted de facto autonomy (essentially owing to the weakness of state control over territory). However, under neoliberalism the relationship between indigenous communities and the state altered considerably. The transition to neoliberalism slowed or ended policies of land redistribution (explored in more detail in the forthcoming chapters). It also undercut state support for agriculture, as well as opening up land to global capital. All of this threatened the communal basis of indigenous life (Yashar 2005: 68). As June Nash (1994) highlights, for indigenous communities the neo-liberal period has frequently entailed a crisis defined by three crucial factors distinguishing it from previous eras. These are (1) the global integration of the economy, (2) the shift from industrial to finance capital, and (3) the shrinking possibilities for subsistence activities. All of these factors have helped to propel indigenous actors to the forefront of the political scene in many (but not all) Latin American countries.

A key question will be how an alternative political project that seeks to overcome alienation and that aims at genuine inclusivity of subaltern classes can be formed that challenges established hegemonic practices. Here the issue of state power looms large. Jorge Castañeda (1994) acknowledges that the very things that give rise to the Left, such as poverty, discrimination, inequality, and so on, have not disappeared, and thus Left-oriented governments are likely to remain a feature of Latin America. However, he also argues that it is clear that the Left has historically failed to change any of these issues in a meaningful way, especially through armed revolution. He therefore advocates an approach to political transformation that seeks to combine free-market economic principles with social redistribution as the best means for taking the continent forward. Surveying recent political developments, Castañeda (2006) has sought to identify both a "right" Left and a "wrong" Left. The "good," or right, Left is defined by a market-oriented "third way" approach and is associated with countries such as Brazil, Uruguay, and Chile (under the Concertación, a coalition of left-of-center parties founded in 1988). The "bad," or wrong, Left, by contrast, is characterized as "nationalist, populist, and strident" and is said to represent a threat to the region's future. This version of the Left is associated with the model of change in Venezuela and Bolivia and the whole legacy of the Cuban Revolution. The problem with such an analysis, however, is precisely the fact that it ignores the different conditions in which these movements have emerged and grown. First, classifying as a good Left those countries that accept market-oriented policies is precisely to ignore the lessons of why neoliberalism failed as a project of incorporation (Cameron 2009: 336–37; Luna and Filgueira 2009). Second, this analysis (shared but inverted by Robinson 2008: 293–94) actually closes the world and fails to imagine that other institutional arrangements and political practices could exist beyond the nation-state. Here the concept of passive revolution looms large. As numerous interpretations have sought to highlight, so-called progressive governments of the region have largely been reformist rather than revolutionary thus far and have often served to demobilize social movement activism (Hesketh and Morton 2014; Modonesi 2013; Tapia 2011; Webber 2011; Zibechi 2015). A tension thus exists between social movements seeking greater autonomy and the absorptive capacity of state power (Gutiérrez Aguilar 2008: 319). This relationship between social movements and the state has been further strained by the model of neo-extractivism that has been pursued in large parts of Latin America. This model has functioned as a new development paradigm focusing on natural resources extraction and primary commodity exports as the major means of growth (Burchardt and Dietz 2014; Gudynas 2009; Velt-meyer 2012).

Chapter 1 highlighted the historical constitution of the nation-state and its intimate relation to class rule, yet in the analysis of the "two Lefts" the state becomes reified and defines the limit of political action (Luna and Filgueira 2009: 275; Motta 2006). This analysis also ignores a hugely important feature of contemporary Latin American resistance. Rather than formulating just "two Lefts" in Latin America, we must in fact postulate a "third Left" in the form of the antistatist social movements that seek to effect change through the very processes of *autogestion* theorized in chapter 1. As opposed to a centralization of forces concentrated on the state, Zibechi (2010) refers to these movements as being about the dispersal of political power.

Conclusion

This chapter has contributed further to our understanding of the spaces of capital by offering a detailed historical-geographical sociology of spatial production and state formation in Latin America. In it I have explored the manner in which Latin America became inserted into the global economy, noting the important developments in class relationships that followed. I then connected the rise of ISI to the dialectical movements between domestic class formation and the global economy and explained them as a process of passive revolution. I explored the contradictions of ISI in relation to both the inward-looking spatial practices that ISI was built on as a regime of capital accumulation and the manner in which it became produced as a site for a spatial fix for overaccumulated capital in Western countries. ISI, I concluded, served as neither a long-term viable hegemonic project or an accumulation strategy. Thus, while it may well have proved to be successful in other instances, such as forging capitalist class formation, it failed as a model of incorporation of the subaltern classes.

Likewise, neoliberalism has proved incapable of offering any solution to this incorporation crisis. Instead, the region became the central battleground for a new politics of resistance as class struggles proliferated over the attempted dispossessions upon which this model of development was based. In many countries neoliberalism has led to the rise of Left-oriented governments (although with significant differences between them in terms of their commitment to the market, social redistribution, etc.). However, even the ostensibly Left-oriented governments can be charged with furthering the process of *trasform-ismo* as opposed to fundamentally reorienting political and economic power.

Concomitant with this process, however, has been the rise of social movements, notably indigenous movements, that have frequently questioned the efficacy of taking state power as a means of effecting real change and have instead sought to construct alternative geographical projects of their own. To understand these movements it is necessary once again to combine the theoretical with the lived. This will now be done through an examination of the specific case of Mexican development in the twentieth century via the key concept of passive revolution alluded to above. This examination will sharpen our level of analysis and clear the way to understanding processes of resistance in greater detail.

CHAPTER THREE

From Passive Revolution
to Silent Revolution

The Politics of State, Space, and Class
Formation in Modern Mexico

> As the national becomes a more complex site for the global, the specific and deep
> histories of a country become more, rather than less significant.
> —**Saskia Sassen, *Territory, Authority, Rights: From Medieval to Global Assemblages***

This chapter now seeks to move from the meso to the concrete level, using a case study of Mexico to demonstrate in a more empirically detailed fashion the generalizations drawn out in previous chapters. Themes from the previous chapters such as passive revolution, the construction of hegemonic projects alongside accumulation strategies, and the dialectical relationship between the national and global in mutually constituting one another are examined to highlight the role of state and class formation as a process of social struggle that produced the space of modern Mexico. This chapter therefore helps us understand how spatial configurations have been historically produced through the unfolding of capitalist social relations of production, offering an insight into the contradictory character of this accumulation process while emphasizing the role of the subaltern within this overall development trajectory. In order to make this argument, evolving processes of state formation and particular state "spatialization strategies" linked to it are examined in detail. This chapter will also help us to situate and understand current resistance movements to the deepening of the capital relation, movements that have implications not only for Mexico but also worldwide, as this case study is but a national manifestation of the global contradictions of capitalist accumulation.

Drawing on Gramsci's key concepts of passive revolution and hegemony, this chapter seeks to provide an insight into how specific spatial configurations have been historically produced in Mexico within the conditions of worldwide capitalist development. It aims to offer an explanation of the contradictory character of this accumulation process, highlighting the class strategies involved while giving due attention to the process of contestation and the potential for change. Passive revolution has, in recent years, become an increasingly important concept to analyze the global political economy (Hart 2014: 219–42; Morton 2007b), as well as Latin America more specifically (Coutinho 2012; Kanoussi and Mena 1985; Modonesi 2013; Morton 2013; Roberts 2015; Del Roio 2012). We should rightly be wary of using political theory indiscriminately across disparate cases. However, as Gramsci (1971: 108–9, Q 15, §11) argues, "Since similar situations almost always arise in every historical development, one should see if it is not possible to draw from this some general principle of political science."

In contrast to the position of Alex Callinicos (2010), I argue that the concept of passive revolution—understood as the state-led reorganization and restoration of class power—has particular utility as a *recurring* theme of Mexican history in the twentieth century. The reason for this recurrence lies within the very unresolved class contradictions inscribed in capitalist development, which result in periodic crises and restructuring of the social basis of the state. Passive revolution, although an important class stratagem for the maintenance of control, thus remains ultimately a strategy that does not overcome the fundamental contradictions within capitalist society. As Gramsci (1971: 114, Q 15, §62) puts it, "The concept remains a dialectical one—in other words, presupposes, indeed postulates as necessary a vigorous anti-thesis which can present intransigently all its potentialities for development." The scope for the reappearance of passive revolution thus is implicit within the very conceptual framework, as is the open-ended nature of subaltern struggles to overcome it. This is essential to understanding how current resistance movements have organized and also contributes to the debate on how we need to problematize and understand the role of the state in processes of transformation.

At first appearance this argument would seem to accord with the broader thesis put forward by Enrique Semo (2012: 443–75) regarding what he refers to as the "cycle of Mexican revolutions" (a thesis that indeed makes reference to the concept of passive revolution). However, the argument constructed here departs from his in crucial respects. In Semo's periodization, these revolutionary cycles took place during the era of Bourbon reform (1780–1810), at the end of the Porfiriato (1890–1910), and during the neoliberal era (1982–present). Semo's (2012: 443) preferred terms for describing these processes are "modernization from above" and "passive modernization." However, his terms betray a limited reading of Gramsci, as passive revolution has a wider significance as a mode of statecraft that is capable of responding (partially) to subaltern discontent (as will be set out below). This vital element of statecraft is absent from Semo's conception, which instead views the process of modernization purely as a repressive imposition, eliding the subtlety of Gramsci's concept.[1]

My argument will be set out as follows. First, I situate Mexico historically within the global economy in order to understand the antecedents of the revolution. Second, I explicate an understanding of the Mexican Revolution as an instance of passive revolution and make clear the importance of the bourgeois state form. Third, I outline Mexico's development trajectory with reference to the particular scales and spaces upon which it was founded, before, fourth, elaborating the fundamental contradictions of Mexico's developmental paradigm. Fifth, I explain the rise of neoliberalism as a political and economic response to these contradictions as a second instance of passive revolution. Finally, I briefly discuss the unresolved antagonisms of this transition from ISI to neoliberalism. I intend to provide the framework that we can then use to move our analytical lens to the subnational level to consider the cases of Oaxaca and Chiapas in chapters 4 and 5.

Situating Mexico within the World Economy

How, then, should we approach the problematic of state, space, and scalar development? Adam Morton (2007a: 599) has argued that Gramscian theory offers us a "history of state formation and thus social development within the 'national' that are linked internally to the casual conditioning and wider geopolitical dynamics of 'the international.'" Womack (1978: 97) takes this argument further, claiming that explanations for Mexico's development trajectory need to be located within the global economy rather than in Mexico itself. However, we need to be wary of reifying and dehistoricizing the world system (Cox 1981). A more fruitful approach is found in Philip McMichael's (1990: 391) method of "incorporated comparison," within which "totality" is viewed as "a conceptual *procedure* rather than an empirical premise. It is an imminent rather than *prima facie* property in which the whole is discovered through an analysis of the mutually conditioning parts" (see also Morton 2010).

Mexico, like the rest of Latin America, had its identity indelibly stamped by the experience of colonialism (see the previous chapter). Spatial production was thus from the outset heavily conditioned by international forces. As Nora Hamilton (1982: 18) states, "Between the sixteenth and nineteenth century, through the world market, as well as through more direct means of colonisation and conquest, the core states succeeded in imposing on the rest of the world a division of labour in which the latter functioned to provide certain types of commodities, as well as markets needed by the core."

The *social function* of the space of Mexico is thus an important point and one that needs to be borne in mind when we consider the changing dynamics of capital accumulation. Mexico's spatial production was inextricably tied to questions of class and race, largely dispossessing the indigenous population and reorienting social life to meet the interests of the colonizers (see Bonfil Batalla 1996). As Mexico became unevenly inserted into the world economy, the model of "development" adopted was based on the intense exploitation of cheap labor and the extraction of natural resources. The growth of European capitalism hugely shaped the landscape of Mexico, with the construction of railroads being necessary to facilitate the exportation of mineral wealth, the growth of urban centers necessitated by the enclave economy, and the expansion of the export-oriented hacienda at the expense of the communal Indian village (Glade 1963: 14; Hansen 1971: 17; Cockcroft 1983: 30–31).[2] Nascent capitalist relations began to be developed through European colonial expansion, and Mexico evolved to become a focal point for interimperialist rivalries during the late nineteenth and early twentieth centuries (for a general description of this process, see Lenin 1917/1987a). International forces were thus instrumental in informing the *national* conditions of class struggle. As James Cockcroft (1983: 44) puts it, the colonial period "dialectically established in Mexico an embryonic dependent capitalism and the impoverishment and blocked opportunities that were to generate the repeated uprisings that ultimately broke out." Adolfo Gilly (1983: 30–36) contends that it was the construction of railroad infrastructure under Porfirio Díaz (1876–80, 1884–1911) that facilitated the expansion of capitalist social relations of production, helping reshape space and the organization of work. This, he argues, led to the proletarianization of the country and exposed the contradictions of the old political order by provoking new challenges that were to coalesce with the revolutionary upheavals beginning in 1910 (table 6).

The growth of railways, as well as facilitating the extraction of natural resources, also allowed for the beginnings of a domestic market, with commodities beginning to circulate more freely, as well as increasing the centralized power of the state (Hamilton 1982: 43–44; Katz 1986: 37). Mexico's transition to modernity therefore took place through the dialectic of national and international development. However, while there is undoubtedly some truth in the claim that productive forces were coming into conflict with old forms of property relations, we should proceed with caution in claiming that prerevolutionary Mexico was in fact a fully capitalist country. Although proletarianization of the country had no doubt increased during this period (with the amount of industrial workers estimated at 803,294 by 1900), it had done so in a highly uneven manner, with the north of the country overwhelmingly predominating (Katz 1986: 59). William Glade (1963: 53, emphasis added) thus concludes that

TABLE 6. Growth of Railroads in Mexico, 1880–1910

Year	Length of Railroad Track (km)
1880	1,086
1881	1,661
1882	3,583
1883	5,308
1890	9,558
1910	19,205

Source: Gilly (1983: 29).

"despite incipient industrialisation and the spectacular achievements of various mineral enclaves, pre-revolutionary Mexico was basically an agrarian nation, not only in terms of the overwhelming preponderance of the population in agriculture and the share of the national product originating in the agricultural sector, *but also in the tone of national life.*"

In keeping with the pattern in Latin America sketched out in the previous chapter, the agroexport oligarchy dominated both economic and political power, which was reinforced through patterns of global investment. Under Díaz, foreign influence had increased dramatically, providing resources that endogenous economic activity could not. The growth of U.S. capital was especially marked, with investment in Mexico greater than in any other area of the world. By 1911 this investment exceeded that of the domestic bourgeoisie and was more than twice as much as other foreign investors (Cockcroft 1998: 85). Furthermore, foreign capital was diversified, dominating not only mineral resources but also electrical and communications systems, furthering the growth of wage labor. By the end of the Porfiriato, over half the country's wealth was foreign owned (Glade 1963: 52).

However, despite these developments, we should not conceive of prerevolutionary Mexico as being a country grounded in an advanced state of capitalist development. As Alan Knight (1985: 2) argues, the fallacy of this position is to confuse relations of *exchange* with relations of *production*. Thus, while Mexico was indeed producing goods for the world market and had high levels of foreign investment during this time, the social relations of production that persisted were often precapitalist ones in which extraeconomic coercion inhered. However, this is where we need to pay attention to conditions pertaining within the "international." While it is true that precapitalist relations of exploitation were probably more dominant than wage labor under Díaz, "they were more subordinately articulated within the dynamic thrust of capitalist relations" (Gilly 1983: 339). The form of capitalism that would be instituted in Mexico represented not only the international social forces that exerted their influence over the territory but also the class forces tied to these influences. These class forces included the *comprador* classes, epitomized by the Científicos, a circle of technocratic advisors to Porfirio Díaz who were to gain their political power through their role as intermediaries for foreign capital or resistance movements led by workers and peasants. Cockcroft (1983: 57) neatly summarizes this point, highlighting how the nature of capitalism in Mexico was "varied and complex, reflecting the socio-economic materials out of which it has grown—from Indian communal traditions to those of the Spanish mobility; from conquest to pillage, and 'original accumulation' to the separation of labourers and artisans from the means of production for an external market and a growing home market, to labour recruitment through starvation and the 'tying' of labour through debt obligations."

Eric Wolf (1997: 79) shows how, in contrast to an even spread of capitalist social relations, symbioses were frequently formed within a world-historical context between an expansive capitalist mode of production hungry for resources and precapitalist means of mobilizing social labor. This is, of course, the process theorized by Trotsky (1919/1962: 175, 1931/1962: 24–25) in his notion of uneven and combined development and the contradictions that emerge from establishing advanced economic activity within a backward social formation (as discussed in chapter 1). It was exactly these conditions that pertained in Mexico under the Porfiriato. On the eve of the revolutionary outbreak, this model of accumulation led to the social fabric of the country unravelling. While the wealthy minority were still importing luxury goods and engaging in conspicuous consumption, there was a massive decline in real wages from 1898 to 1911, and by the time of the revolution in 1910, never had so many Mexicans been landless (Hansen 1971: 22, 27). The vast majority of cultivable land was dominated by just 835 families (Instituto Nacional de Estadística y Geografía 1994: 364). As the country was only minimally industrialized, economic opportunities were not being generated that could serve to pacify the increasing demands of the population. It was in this atmosphere that revolutionary activity was to break out. Although beginning as an attempt to reform the country from above, the Mexican Revolution quickly spread to the subaltern classes, which gave it new direction and momentum. The mobilization of the masses altered the terrain of struggle, transforming the original demands for reform into a wider struggle against dictatorship (Leal 1986: 22). This process, however, provides us with the beginnings of our central inquiry. As Nora Hamilton (1982: 3) succinctly puts it, "The problem of the Mexican state derives from the apparent contradiction between its historical origins in the Mexican Revolution and its contemporary function of maintaining peripheral capitalist development."

The Mexican Revolution as Passive Revolution

When analyzing the Mexican Revolution, it is imperative to view it as a process (or, indeed, a set of processes) "rather than a discrete event" (Knight 1985: 3). When defining the revolution's character, as well as stating what it *was*, it is just as important to examine what it was *not*. Moreover, it must be remembered that during the revolutionary upheavals there was not one struggle but rather a number of diverse and at times overlapping struggles taking place: landed versus commercial power, subaltern versus bourgeoisie, nationalist versus imperialist, constitutionalist versus federalist, and so on. As Guillermo Bonfil Batalla (1996: 111) puts it, "A single fuse blew up very different powder kegs." The revolution's outcome was in many respects an uneven synthesis of these explosions. If one thing is clear, it is that the revolution did indeed precipitate the destruction of the old oligarchic state. However, it is vital to then analyze what forms of exploitation remained, where political power was concentrated, and where the impetus for the nation's development strategy came from. In order to do this analysis, a theory of the capitalist state grounded in civil society relations (in both the state's national and international circumstances) needs to be explicated with reference to Gramsci's concept of passive revolution.

When any social order is challenged, forces of change and conservatism are naturally pitted against one another. "The problem," argues Gramsci (1971: 219, Q 13, §27) "is to see in this dialectic 'revolution/restoration' whether it is revolution or restoration that predominates." I argue that the Mexican Revolution is a classic example of what Gramsci referred to as a passive revolution (see also Morton 2010, 2013). A passive revolution, or a "'revolution' without a 'revolution'" (Gramsci 1971: 59, Q 19, §24), occurs when social relations are fundamentally reorganized (revolution), but, ultimately, popular initiatives are neutralized so that the ruling class can retain its power (restoration) (Jessop 1990: 213).

The revolutionary struggles in Mexico undoubtedly caused a crisis of authority, destroying the social base of the Porfirian state and leaving a power vacuum that the various contending factions sought to fill. However, as Gramsci (1971: 210–11, Q 13, §23) notes with regard to periods of upheaval, "The various strata of the population are not all capable of orienting themselves equally swiftly or of reorganising with the same rhythm. The traditional ruling class, which has numerous trained cadres, changes men and programmes and, with greater speed than is achieved by the subordinate classes, reabsorbs the control that was slipping from its grasp. Perhaps it may make sacrifices, and expose itself to an uncertain future by demagogic promises, but it retains power, reinforces it for the time being, and uses it to crush its adversary and disperse his leading cadres."

The assassination of Emiliano Zapata in 1919, the refocusing of an accumulation strategy based on industrialization and the commercialization of agriculture, and the concomitant incorporation of a limited amount of worker and peasant demands into the constitution of 1917, coupled most importantly with large-scale agrarian reform, give concrete historical witness to these claims. Thus, the revolution can be partly interpreted as the failure of the subaltern classes to develop their own hegemony expressed as a national-popular collective will. While the oligarchic classes had lost their political power, the "mass of peasant farmers, undoubtedly the driving force of the Revolution showed itself, time and again to be incapable of forming a government" (Leal 1986: 23). The nearest the peasants came to doing so was through the Ayala Plan of the Zapatistas, which contained specifically anticapitalist values. The plan called for the immediate expropriation of land and the nationalization of all property of enemies of the revolution while also defending villages and an agrarian orientation (Bonfil Batalla 1996: 64). However, this plan also had its limitations, intending to set up dual power alongside a bourgeois state rather than actually displacing it. Commenting upon the plan, Gilly (1983: 79) reflects that "the peasants could not rise to a nation-wide perspective nor offer a revolutionary solution for the insurgent nation" because they did not challenge fundamental existing structures of authority. The eventual co-optation of the workers and peasants into the state's corporatist structures would therefore be made easier because the peasants "lacked an ideology of their own and took up the ideological stand of the Mexican Revolution, which is after all bourgeois" (Leal 1986: 32). This ultimate weakness of the subaltern classes to create their own hegemony is a hallmark of passive revolution (Sassoon 1980: 204). However, the labeling of the revolution as a passive revolution, it should be made clear, does not imply that the subaltern classes were not engaged in struggle (to deny such a fact would be absurd). Rather, the key aspect in defining the Mexican Revolution as a passive revolution was the acceptance of the state as being "above the classes" and thus a neutral arbiter of conflict capable of implementing the revolution's goals (see Mariátegui 1930/2011: 460). As Bob Jessop (1990: 213) writes in relation to this, "The crucial element in passive revolution is the *statisation* of reorganisation or restructuring, so that popular initiatives from below are contained or destroyed and the relationship of ruler–ruled is maintained or reimposed" (cf. Gramsci 1971: 105–6, Q 15, §59).

However, the bourgeois character of the Mexican Revolution, so frequently asserted, requires some reflecting upon, as there remains a great deal of debate as to who were the leading agents of it. James Cockcroft (1998: 111), for example, contends that it was led by segments of the industrial bourgeoisie. However, this is disputed by other scholars who claim conversely that no such class as a nationally oriented bourgeoisie existed (Hamilton 1982: 22; Hansen 1971: 97; Knight 1985: 5; Morton 2010). It is useful here to turn to Trotsky (1930/1962: 60), who asserts that a revolution's character can be better defined by the historical tasks that it sets itself. In the Mexican case, these tasks included the breakup of haciendas, the widening formation of private property and industry, and the fundamental transformation of social relations from those based on prestige and extraeconomic coercion to those governed by wage labor. The Mexican Revolution can thus be identified as bourgeois "not because it was the conscious work of the bourgeoisie (still less the national bourgeoisie), nor because it instantly transmuted the base metal of feudalism into the pure gold of capitalism . . . but rather because it gave a decisive impulse to the development of Mexican capitalism and of the Mexican bourgeoisie, an impulse that the preceding regime had been unable to give" (Knight 1985: 26).

However, as Trotsky (1930/1962: 197) reminds us, "The general sociological term *bourgeois revolution* by no means solves the politico-tactical problems, contradictions and difficulties which the mechanics of a *given* bourgeois revolution throw up." In order to resolve these problems, we need to turn to Gramsci's other key notion of hegemony and the associated concept of historical bloc.

As was alluded to in the previous chapters, hegemony is not reducible to domination and is defined as the "intellectual and moral leadership" that a certain class is able to exercise due to its "position and function in the world of production" (Gramsci 1971: 12, Q 12, §1). However, when looking at the type of hegemony that was constructed in Mexico, we need to remain mindful that "state power is not suspended in mid-air" (Marx 1852/2000: 346). That is, state power is responsive—within certain form-determined limits—to demands placed upon it by subaltern classes, as it still remains grounded in civil society relations as a site of ongoing conflict. Thus, as Gilly (1983: 40) argues, despite their failure to develop an alternative national popular program, the peasants' struggle "shifted the whole logic of capitalist development. It could not block it completely or substitute a different process, but it interrupted and altered its course and changed the relationship of force between its political representatives."

The Mexican Revolution therefore needs to be interpreted as a rejection of the economic and political logic of Porfirian Mexico and the corresponding narrow social relations it was built upon for a new type of accumulation strategy that would create the conditions necessary for wider participation and redress of grievances. As Jessop (1990: 198) explains, "An accumulation strategy defines a specific economic 'growth model' complete with its various extra-economic pre-conditions and also outlines a general strategy appropriate to its realisation." This approach allows us to explain the development of capitalism in Mexico not as a process forced onto the masses but rather as the construction of an overarching hegemonic project, the context of which the subaltern classes helped shape. Hegemonic projects involve "the mobilisation of support behind a concrete, national-popular program of action which assert a general interest in the pursuit of objectives that explicitly or implicitly advance the long term interest of the hegemonic class" (Jessop 1990: 208). Hegemony should therefore be thought of not as synonymous with "false consciousnesses" but rather as the outcome of the balance of class forces. As Gramsci (1971: 52, Q 25, §5) explains, subaltern groups can have "active or passive affiliation to the dominant political formations"; furthermore, they can attempt to "influence the programmes of these formations in order to press claims of their own." Article 27 of the 1917 Constitution, which enshrined the responsibility of the state to provide land for those without it, and Article 123, which established one of the most progressive labor laws in the world at the time, are examples of the successful shaping of the new hegemonic project by the subaltern classes.[3] However, as I will now explain, the acceptance of the bourgeois state form as an "autonomous" entity, standing above the class struggle capable of resolving disputes and serving the goals of the revolution, meant that there were form-determined limits to how far the subaltern classes could pursue their demands. Capitalist hegemony needs to be postulated as an elastic concept capable of being stretched in response to particular forces, but unless it is pushed beyond these limits and snapped completely, it is always capable of contraction. This conforms to the point made by Gramsci (1971: 55, Q 25, §2) that "subaltern groups are always subject to the activity of ruling groups, even when they rebel and rise up: only 'permanent' victory breaks their subordination." For this reason, the revolution is best thought of not as an emancipation but "rather [as] a new order of capitalist control" (Womack 1978: 102). However, as will be demonstrated in chapters 4 and 5, within this control, spaces remained for exercising agency and contesting this political project.

Mexico and the Bourgeois State

To examine why the revolution was not an emancipation but a new order of capitalist control, we first have to render a theory of the bourgeois state. Doing so allows us to understand and historicize the key role of the state in the Mexican development process while avoiding "statolatory" (worship of the state's power) (Gramsci 1971: 268, Q 8, §130). The starting point for this investigation entails examining how surplus value in a society is to be appropriated and how this process relates to the political form (Hirsch 1978: 58). The state is required by capitalism by virtue of the fact that there remain vital extraeconomic preconditions that need to be realized in order for production and reproduction to proceed. These preconditions must be secured by an apparently autonomous entity standing outside of the market (Holloway and Picciotto 1977: 79). As we have already seen, the Mexican Revolution helped sweep away the remnants of the precapitalist state built upon extraeconomic coercion, yet it did not do away with all class antagonisms, as was clear from the Constitution of 1917, which enshrined that the system of private property would remain vital to the overarching economic framework. The continued preponderance of foreign capital also remained a vital lever of power, limiting the state's room to maneuver and again highlighting how the struggle for hegemony has to be related to both national and international social forces and the country's wider geopolitical position (Cox 1983: 171).[4] The Mexican state thus remained "directly dependent upon resources generated in the private sector" (Hamilton 1982: 213) while seeking to use these resources in order to pacify subaltern demands. Class antagonism was thus to be *mediated* by the state rather than done away with. However, as John Holloway and Sol Picciotto (1977: 80) make clear, "Seen through the prism of the state, the capital relation is concealed, class struggle is diffused, classes are atomised into a mass of individual citizens — 'the public,' class consciousness is broken down into 'public opinion' to be expressed individually through opinion polls or ballot boxes."

In other words, rather than seeing economic and political conflicts as part of the same process resulting from capitalist exploitation, they are formally separated and channeled into fetishized forms (Wood 1995: 20). The "imagined community" of the nation (Anderson 1991), with its corollary of "national interest," can thus be appealed to in order to move issues away from class struggle and ensure the rule of capital (see chapter 1). In this manner, the Mexican Revolution was to become "the ideological banner legitimising bourgeois rule" (Cockcroft 1998: 108).

The process of state formation did not occur in a vacuum, therefore, but within historically specific structural constraints. Among these were the lack of an economic base, the poor development of the productive forces, the remnants of the old oligarchic state, and the pressure exerted by foreign capital (Hamilton 1982: 63–71).[5] The key issue confronting elites would be how to expand opportunities within a stratified class framework that would serve to alleviate pressure from below. In other words, how could some limited demands of the subaltern classes be successfully incorporated into an overarching hegemonic framework? The answer to this, as it was in the rest of Latin America (documented in the previous chapter), came in the production of a nationally oriented market. The social forces put into motion with the revolutionary struggle, therefore, produced modern Mexico by forcing the creation of a new scale for capital accumulation. There was thus nothing "natural" about this national scale. However, important consequences flowed from the creation of this scale. As Neil Smith (1993: 101) argues, the production of scale is "not simply a spatial solidification or materialization of contested social forces and processes; the corollary also holds. Scale is an active progenitor of specific social processes." In contrast to the previous development strategy, in which foreign investment shaped the urban and rural environment, the government in the 1930s "moved to effect an equivalent domestication of the capital market" (Glade 1963: 72). Although the process of a new conscious national orientation to the development of space can be traced to the administration of Plutarco Elías Calles in the 1920s, the Great Depression and its aftermath in the early 1930s proved throughout Latin America to be the key turning point for the evolution of the new development strategy, as the depression altered the field of force under which emergent bourgeois classes could pursue their objectives. Not only did the depression make export-oriented growth untenable due to the high tariffs that were erected in the core states, but it also reduced somewhat the ability of foreign countries to intervene in the affairs of the peripheral ones (Hamilton 1982: 23). Coupled with this was a generalized idea resulting from the depression that it was a crisis of *global* capitalism rather than a crisis of capital per se, and its solution lay in constructing national markets that were less exposed to these world fluctuations. In the case of Mexico, where previously 50 percent of government revenues derived from foreign trade, new sources of productive capital were thus imperative (Cárdenas 2000: 199). Local manufacture of light consumer durables thus began in earnest (Gereffi and Evans 1981: 35).

What would emerge from this would be a Mexican version of the region-wide capitalist development paradigm of ISI. As Enrique Dussel-Peters (2000: 8) argues, ISI "was not only an accumulation strategy, it was also deeply embedded in the emergence of a new political and social consensus among the respective oligarchies, labour unions, agricultural workers, capitalists and state." In other words, ISI was also a hegemonic project developed through the creation of a historical bloc of contending social forces. A historical bloc should be thought of as more than simply an alliance of various social groups, as its creation reflects the dialectical interplay between structure and superstructure. Thus, as Gramsci (1971: 377, Q 7, §21, emphasis added) explains, "Material forces are the *content* and ideologies are the *form*." ISI can thus be postulated as an "organic ideology" that resulted from the synthesis of the material conditions under which social forces sought to press their claims. These material conditions included the breakdown of the traditional agroexport model, nationalist resentment of foreign ownership of key sectors of the economy, working-class militancy, and peasant unrest in the countryside. According to Joachim Hirsch (1978: 82, emphasis added), when investigating the function of the bourgeois state, it is imperative to "embrace the whole of the social, political and *national conditions* of the production of the social formation." As Robert Cox (1983: 168) points out, however, every historical bloc contains a hegemonic social class (in this case, the bourgeoisie). Crucially, then, the system of ISI would take place through a capitalist framework where "the development and expansion of a particular group are conceived of, and presented, as being the motor force of a universal expansion, of a development of all the national energies" (Gramsci 1971: 182, Q 13, §17). The hegemonic project would thus inscribe its own contradictions when the limits imposed by its model of accumulation were reached and class forces began to stretch the elasticity of hegemony to breaking point. This process, I will argue, resulted in a second process of passive revolution with the transition to neoliberalism.

Producing Space and Scale under Import Substitution Industrialization

The historical bloc alluded to would be formally institutionalized through the creation of the Partido de la Revolución Mexicana (PRM, Party of the Mexican Revolution), later renamed Partido Revolucionario Institucional (PRI, Institutional Revolutionary Party), founded in 1929. As Mónica Serrano (1996: 8) documents, since its creation, the party "has asserted a 'peculiar right to rule' linked to its emergence and rise to power in the aftermath of a 'historical crisis,' the Mexican Revolution." If the Mexican Revolution epitomized the conditions of passive revolution, the PRI came likewise to embody the state. Fearing the "Hobbesian potential of Mexican society, the subaltern classes were tied to the government's tutelage through emergent corporatist structures" (Serrano 1996: 6). This was paradigmatic of the model of "controlled inclusion" discussed in the previous chapter. The state, seeking to overcome the violence that had plagued Mexico since 1910, aimed to provide stability by trying to limit the demands placed upon the system, increasing the capacity of the state to meet what demands were made, stimulating cross-class support for the new growth model, and, vitally, retaining the support of key sectors of society that controlled enough resources to threaten the system (Hansen 1971: 175). Key to the construction of this hegemonic project was the *production of space*.

One integral aspect of this project was land reform. A principal cause of the Mexican Revolution and a key source of continuing peasant unrest was the prevailing system of land tenure. Reform of the agricultural sector thus became a central pillar of the administration of Lázaro Cárdenas (1934–40) and would come to serve a key historical social function in furthering the development of capitalism in Mexico (although, as will be demonstrated in chapters 4 and 5, this is only half the story). Under Cárdenas the *ejidos*, government-created communal lands that were reminiscent of the pre-Hispanic form of land tenure, stabilized the Mexican countryside for almost thirty years (McCaughan 1993: 20). The process of land reform profoundly altered the shape of the Mexican countryside. While *ejidal* land in 1930 only accounted for 13 percent of cropland, by 1940 this figure was 47 percent (Hansen 1971: 32). Through the breakup of large haciendas, not only were peasants pacified and the state's legitimacy enhanced, but the land reform process helped destroy a key barrier to capital accumulation, that of the status-based latifundia, with their associated idle means of production. This again vividly demonstrates the power of class struggle in shaping space and the role that passive revolution played. As John Tutino (1986: 8) summarizes, peasants fought for "tierra y libertad." What they got was "tierra y el estado."

The opening of the countryside to capitalization also facilitated the rise of industrialization, as labor was "freed" from debt bondage. Mass migration from the countryside resulted, a process that was accelerated by the transfer of resources away from the agricultural sector due to the uncertainty of its profitability in the face of land reform (Cárdenas 2000: 204). Linked to these processes of land reform were state-led infrastructural projects intended to create a fully functioning "national" market. This market was to be achieved through irrigation works that were designed to increase the productivity of the land and highway construction that would provide for the integration of formerly isolated areas and link industrial and urban centers (Cárdenas 2000: 205–6; Kemper and Royce 1979). The importance of this spatial integration was vital for capitalist development. As David Harvey (2006a: 375) explains, "Spatial integration—the linking of commodity production in different locations through exchange—is necessary if value is to become the social form of abstract labour." Harvey's

TABLE 7. Kilometers of Roads in Mexico, 1930–1975

Year	Total	Dirt	Surfaced	Paved
1930	1,426	629	256	541
1935	5,237	1,760	1,918	1,559
1940	9,929	1,643	3,505	4,781
1945	17,404	2,399	6,842	8,163
1950	21,422	1,865	5,972	13,585
1955	27,431	3,022	5,881	18,528
1960	44,892	6,710	11,203	26,970
1965	61,252	8,448	18,373	34,331
1970	71,520	8,494	21,079	41,947
1975	187,660	75,245	24,434	57,910

Source: Nacional Financiera 1977: 82–83.

TABLE 8. Railroad Services in Mexico, 1921–1975

Year	Freight (million ton km carried)
1925	3,219
1930	4,041
1935	4,596
1940	5,810
1945	8,024
1950	8,391
1955	10,961
1960	14,004
1965	18,326
1970	23,083
1975	33,673

Source: Nacional Financiera 1977: 75.

point can be empirically highlighted through an examination of the road network and rail services in Mexico (tables 7 and 8), key infrastructural developments that allowed for the circulation of commodities.

Postwar Mexico thus saw the increasing production of what Lefebvre (1991: 49, 53–57) calls "abstract space," that is, a space whose primary purpose is the production of surplus value under conditions of wage labor in which "differential space" (spaces not devoted to commodity production) could be maintained only through class struggles. While the dynamism for this construction of abstract space was propelled by the struggles of the subaltern classes and the necessity to expand opportunities for their participation, it was done in a manner that retained support of the elites, whose strategic control of resources allowed them to profit from this restructuring process. This point is summarized by William Glade (1963: 69), who neatly explains the recomposition of class dominance in Mexico: "As the large public works program and urban expansion raised the returns on investment in construction industries, fortunes deriving from urban land ownership began to be invested in cement, glass, iron and steel and other construction industries. To a significant extent, then, the older land-owning group abandoned its passive *rentier* role to become actively involved in new financial and industrial undertakings, including those induced by domestic market growth."

It should further be noted that commercial haciendas, producing for the export market, were largely protected from this process of land reform, leading to the development of a new agrarian bourgeoisie (Cockcroft 1998: 118). The Cárdenas government, then, although making some key concessions to the subaltern classes, did so in a manner that ultimately was consistent with the furtherance of capitalist development. Roger Bartra (1975: 128) describes the function of *ejidos* as "shock absorbers" designed to prevent further violence in the transition to capitalism. Concurring with such an analysis, Gerardo Otero (1999: 33, emphasis added) has argued that "land redistribution in Mexico was the way *chosen* to entrench capitalism in Mexico."

Due to the relatively poor development of the productive forces and weak endogenous capital base, state involvement was vital to the process of capitalist development in Mexico in order to create the material preconditions for the production process that no individual capital either could or would do. A key social function of the state under ISI was, therefore, as an investor creating conditions for expanded accumulation (Fitzgerald 1978). As has already been argued, however, this should not lead us to conclude that the state was "above the classes." Rather, ISI as a policy should be thought of as resulting from the ensemble of class forces brought into the historical bloc within the limits determined by the value-form (Hirsch 1978). State regulation was also vital to developing the national scale for capital accumulation, which was achieved through the creation of a favorable environment for investors, including protective tariffs, regressive taxation policies, subsidies to industry, and direct state ownership of key industries (King 1970). The purpose was to create a stable environment whereby business would save and invest locally through the creation of profitable opportunities (Hansen 1971: 71). This was another central pillar of PRI hegemony as it sought to gain the support of labor and the domestic bourgeoisie by insulating them from foreign competition. These policies were not without their successes. Indeed, the postwar period has often been referred to as an "economic miracle" due to the fact that social mobility increased to a degree unprecedented in Mexican history (Hansen 1971: 181). The gross national product leaped from 13,524,000 pesos in 1910 to 98,200,000 pesos in 1965 (Nacional Financiera 1977: 23). Agricultural and industrial production also increased exponentially during the years following World War II, as figures 1 and 2 illustrate.

The government's industrialization drive profoundly altered the spatial organization of Mexico. From being a predominantly agrarian society (in 1921 close to 70 percent of the population was rural), the nation was transformed

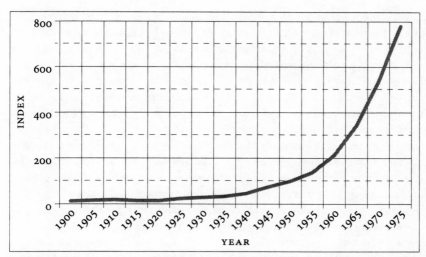

FIGURE 1. Index of the Volume of Industrial Production in Mexico, 1900–1975 (1950 = 100)
Source: Nacional Financiera 1977: 146.

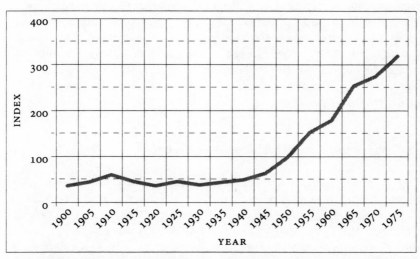

FIGURE 2. Index of the Volume of Agricultural Production in Mexico, 1900–1975 (1950 = 100)
Source: Nacional Financiera 1977: 107–8.

into an overwhelmingly urban one, with these figures reversed by 1976 (Nacional Financiera 1977: 5). This system proved to be relatively stable, as it not only provided increasing opportunities in terms of education, jobs, and social mobility but also demonstrated the possibility for advancement for those who had not yet benefited from new policies (Hansen 1971: 193). Moreover, from a class-theoretical perspective, the system was enormously "successful" in instituting and developing the dominance of the bourgeoisie (Ruccio 1991). Bianca Heredia (1996: 133) documents that from 1940 to 1970 there developed a strong state-business nexus based on tacit coordination and explicit cooperation. In exchange for individuals and companies saving and investing locally, the state gave its active support to private accumulation. However, as Jessop (1990: 210) argues, the long-term success of a hegemonic project "will depend on a flow of *material concessions* to the subordinate social forces." Maintaining a flow of material concessions while seeking to restructure Mexican capital after the "easy stage" of ISI came to an end was something that ultimately Mexico's accumulation strategy could not do without incurring massive debt, which would lead to the breakdown of the historical bloc and the recomposition of the state's social basis with the transition to neoliberalism. Giving more substantial detail to the analysis rendered in the previous chapter, I now argue that the reasons for this breakdown lie in the peculiar nature of the scalar and spatial project of ISI, relying as it did on an extremely narrow market for the consumption of its manufactured goods while being dependent on outside sources to provide the inputs for this production process. This led to an increasing current account deficit, a problem that was temporally displaced—but ultimately therefore compounded— by increased foreign borrowing.

The Contradictions of Import Substitution Industrialization

One of the key contradictions of ISI in Mexico was that it never managed to reduce completely its reliance on an "outside" (as was recognized as a continent-wide problem in the previous chapter). As Marx (1867/1974: 531–36) makes clear, capitalism is not merely a process of production but also one of *reproduction*. That is to say, it must furnish the materials necessary to replace those used up in the course of a year in order for accumulation to continue. It is through this process that the social relations of capitalism are also produced and reproduced. Taking this model of reproduction, we can pick apart the idea that ISI represented a "nation-state phase" of capitalism (Robinson 2003, 2004b). While manufactured goods were indeed produced for the domestic market, key capital goods needed by the Mexican industrialization process were generated in the core countries, which in turn needed foreign markets for their overaccumulation of these Department 1 goods. Thus, while Mexican industrial capital did increase fivefold between 1940 and 1965, imports of capital goods and replacement parts increased more than twelvefold during this period. Import substitution, in other words, was actually "import-intensive" (Cockcroft 1983: 161–62, 179). Furthermore, the capital necessary to invest in the industrialization process was generated through the export of raw materials to the core. Although World War II is often highlighted as a key period for the country's turn inward, in fact, during this period, Mexico's exports actually doubled (Cockcroft 1983: 151). "International" space was thus inscribed in "national" space from the outset (as the previous chapter also illustrated). This point can be further empirically demonstrated if we examine the process of irrigation, a key spatial development that was vital to transforming Mexican agriculture. Loans for this process were provided by the U.S.-based Rockefeller Foundation, and the irrigated land was then to become a key source of (cheap) agricultural exports to the United States (Barkin and Esteva 1986: 124). We can clearly see through an examination of simple reproduction that the core and periphery remained thoroughly interlinked through transnational flows of goods and money (circulating capital, in other words). Expressed another way, there was no period in which a purely national space was instantiated, as the production of capitalist social relations in Mexico always relied upon resources outside its territorial borders. The idea that nation-state-based capitalism came to containerize social relations can thus be shown to be palpably false. It is for this reason that ISI can more usefully be described as a "dependent development" strategy (Gereffi and Evans 1981: 31–32). This description is superior to positing a Eurocentric history of nation-state-era capitalism that elides the very differences in power relations between both states and social classes, as this removes the key conditioning factor of uneven and combined development. Indeed, it was through these links with the global economy that new forms of class struggles began to manifest themselves that would precipitate a second phase of passive revolution in the form of a state-led process of restructuring. Let us now examine this process in more detail.

As mentioned previously, in the aftermath of the revolution, foreign capital was still preponderant in Mexico. Although its dominance was challenged somewhat by Lázaro Cárdenas (most notably with the expropriation of the oil industry in 1938 and, additionally, the nationalization of railways), foreign ownership still constituted a major part of the manufacturing industry. Indeed, by 1972 over half of Mexico's manufacturing firms were foreign owned (Fitzgerald 1978: 266). Dussel-Peters (2000: 44) argues with regard to this point that "a seemingly 'peaceful coexistence' evolved: state owned enterprises and national private firms provided the infrastructure, producing consumer and intermediate goods, whilst TNCs [transnational corporations], with higher total factor productivity and profit rates, concentrated their activities in relatively more advanced manufacturing branches."

The creation of a "national" market actually drew in foreign investors, as high profits could be made inside the protected environment that Mexico offered (Reynolds 1978: 1006). As Cockcroft (1983: 151) documents, U.S. investment "doubled in 1950, tripled in the 1960s and quadrupled in the 1970s." Manufactured goods, despite this *international* composition, were produced largely for *national* consumption, and, as we shall later see, this situation would be a key barrier to further accumulation. Increasingly during this period, Mexico witnessed the concentration and centralization of capital as large enterprises took over small and medium ones. This process can be directly related to the state's particular accumulation strategy, as "the concentration of personal income and the centralization of control over the productive apparatus was financed by the extraordinarily high profits generated in an overtly protective environment carefully shaped by the state" (Barkin 1990: 79). Despite the massive state support it received, domestic industry began to be outperformed by the more efficient transnational corporations. Rather than complementing domestic production with goods that domestic industries could not furnish, transnational corporations in Mexico became increasingly large due to acquisition rather than from Greenfield investment (brand new ventures) (Gereffi and Evans 1981: 45). The new global strategy of these firms, however, needs to be dialectically related to developments within their own national setting. Within Fordist core countries there were fewer opportunities for productive investment during this period, meaning overaccumulated resources sought a productive outlet elsewhere. Concomitantly, the protected environments offered by developmental nations such as Mexico provided incentives to shift production sites there. The uneven development of capitalism and the difference that national spaces contained in social relations can once again be empirically witnessed here in explaining the rise of global capital accumulation.

The spatial significance of Mexico under ISI can be demonstrated by examining the changing composition of postwar foreign investment. Whereas 47 percent of U.S. private investment before World War II had been geared toward export-oriented concerns, by 1959 manufacturing for the domestic market was the key focus (Glade 1963: 8). Indeed, by the early 1970s two-thirds of U.S. investment was in manufacturing (Gereffi and Evans 1981: 40). This would not have happened were it not for the idea of a protected national scale in which capital accumulation could occur, highlighting Saskia Sassen's (2001: 1) argument that the national scale can simultaneously be "one of the key enablers of the global scale." The embryonic formation of a transnational capitalist class therefore took place as "local elites interested in development thus found common ground with many of the TNCs interested in global expansion" (Gereffi and Evans 1981: 40). However, the growth of transnational corporations would ultimately have a corrosive effect on the viability of ISI as a hegemonic project. That growth accelerated Mexico's reliance on capital goods exogenously produced, adding strain to the country's balance of payments (Jenkins 1979: 104). ISI was funded largely through the transfer of resources gained from the exportation of agricultural products, which led to an effort to increase profits in the agricultural sphere through capitalization and mechanization, speeding the dispossession of the peasantry and swelling the urban population. However, owing to the high organic composition of capital that was being imported, not enough employment opportunities were being generated to cope with this urban migration (Fitzgerald 1978: 273; Hamilton 1982: 32).

Meanwhile, due to the reliance on foreign capital to finance industrialization, the government favored large commercial farms producing for export at the expense of *ejidos* (King 1970: 29; Barkin 1990: 22, 34). Market relations rather than productivity governed this decision, as *ejidos* were just as productive as private farms (Hansen 1971: 61). This state support expressed itself geographically, with the government's main investments in irrigation and agricultural equipment being concentrated in the north and northeast of the country, areas that served as platforms for exportation to the United States (for a discussion of the way in which the south of Mexico has historically been neglected, see Dávila, Kessel, and Levy 2002). Uneven development was thus taking place both intranationally and internationally (a point to be discussed in detail in the following chapters). As a means for depressing wages in the industrial sector, price support for basic grains had been frozen since 1962 (Barkin 1990: 26). However, as a response to this freeze, many peasants stopped producing for the market and instead reverted to subsistence farming. The result of the government's agricultural policy, then, was to move the country from a position of virtual self-sufficiency to one where the country had to import basic foods to fulfill the needs of the population. This would further serve to exacerbate Mexico's trade deficit and thus cause additional balance-of-payment problems, an issue that has consistently plagued Mexican development (McCaughan 1993: 12). Moreover, it would also lead to the fracturing of the PRI's hegemony among the peasantry, with new independent unions being formed outside the government's corporatist structures (Harvey 1998: 1; Cockcroft 1983: 249). In order to deal with the growing imbalances in the economy and the increasing demands that were placed upon it from workers, peasants, and the nationally oriented bourgeoisie, the Mexican state turned abroad for loans to oil the creaking wheels of ISI and offset discontent.

As we can see, the conditions for creating an endogenously self-renewing process of production were thus never realized in Mexico. This situation was compounded by the fact that the subaltern classes were largely excluded from entering into consumption of the goods they furnished. As the economic expansion associated with the "easy stage" of ISI came to an end, the PRI thus found its hegemony unraveling due to the fact that it was unable to make the concessions necessary to gain the support of key constituencies. The members of the domestic bourgeoisie saw themselves being displaced by transnationally oriented industrialists, while subaltern classes found their limited inclusion into the hegemonic project increasingly precarious (Davis 1993: 51). ISI thus entered a "structural crisis of accumulation" (McCaughan 1993: 6). However, we can only understand the meaning behind this structural crisis if we pay due attention to the class relations that the accumulation strategy was built upon, which had limited scope for effective demand, leading to overproduction and stagnation (McCaughan 1993: 11). Additionally, the term "structural crisis" only has meaning to the extent that groups of human beings have frustrated needs and make demands that cannot be met. Again (as noted in chapter 1), structure and agency are tightly interlinked (Bieler and Morton 2001). As Gramsci (1971: 113, Q 15, §25) argues in relation to this point, "It seems obvious that the so-called subjective conditions can never be missing when the objective conditions exist, in as much as the distinction involved is one of didactic character."

The starting point, then, for investigating capital restructuring comes from the falling rate of profit and the attempts by the Mexican state to mobilize countertendencies to this fall. As Hirsch (1978: 74) writes in relation to this, "The mobilisation of counter-tendencies means in practice the reorganisation of an historical complex of general social conditions of production and relations of exploitation in a process that can only proceed in a crisis ridden manner." The state-led transition from ISI to neoliberalism perfectly exemplifies this point. The basis for this falling rate of profit was due to the narrow social relations on which capitalism was based and the fact that production in Mexico had always been oriented toward elite consumption. The production of national space—vital to fostering the conditions in which capitalist class processes could be safely incubated—now became a barrier to further accumulation as corporations sought integration into the world market in order to widen their profits. This crisis manifested itself in growing unrest and demands for reform, as well as more radical action with the growth of guerrilla movements in the late 1960s and early 1970s. The state responded to this pressure from the subaltern classes with increasing repression (known as the dirty war). This repression was most dramatically manifested with the massacre of students and workers in the Tlatelolco Plaza in 1968, highlighting Gramsci's (1971: 263, Q 6, §88) point that along the path to hegemony "the armour of coercion" is always latent. This act of repression, however, hugely undermined the legitimacy of the PRI.

The administration of Luis Echeverría (1970–76) sought to deal with the contradictory pressures placed on the state by labor and domestic capital by implementing a new policy of "shared development." A central pillar of this was the so-called Mexicanization laws, which sought to limit the activity of transnational corporations and restore the national basis of accumulation. This involved restricting foreign ownership in strategic sectors and legislating for majority Mexican ownership in others (Weinert 1981: 119). Concomitant with these actions, the state sought to restructure domestic capital in order to reduce its reliance on foreign inputs. The state thus focused on the production of capital goods. Lastly, the PRI sought to revive its legitimacy with the subaltern classes by taking on a greater investment burden in health and education (Fitzgerald 1978: 270; Barkin 1990: 83). However, this attempt to reconstitute the PRI's hegemony highlights dramatically the limits of state autonomy, since the class forces able to influence state policy shifted dramatically in favor of transnationally linked capital. This shift was reflected in the manner in which this faction of capital mobilized successfully to block Echeverría's spending plans and modest tax reform proposals (Davis 1993: 55). Capital export and production cutbacks were the indicators of business opposition (Hamilton 1982: 30). Reforming the basis of Mexico's taxation system, however, was an urgent priority in order to counteract key fiscal imbalances. Although Latin America as a whole had a historically low rate of taxation as a proportion of GNP, with levels at around 20 percent compared with the 30–40 percent taken in the developed world, Mexico stood out as particularly solicitous of business with an average tax rate between 5.7 and 7.7 percent (King 1970: 53). Unable to mobilize sufficient domestic resources from inside its national space, the Mexican government was therefore forced to borrow on international markets. Maintaining ISI as a hegemonic project, which sought, at least nominally, to include all social classes in the development strategy, was thus commanding more resources than the accumulation strategy was able to generate. This pattern of temporally displacing crises, rather than addressing their fundamental cause, became a familiar pattern in Mexico during the 1970s. Neil Brenner (1998: 472) has demonstrated that when spatial and scalar configurations fail to secure the conditions for capital accumulation, they are generally "reconfigured in significant, if always highly contested ways." This indeed was precisely what occurred in Mexico.

Thus, as Morton (2003: 637) notes, "While neoliberalism *had not* taken hold at this time, crucial cleavages within the organisation of the state were developing that would lead to shifts in capitalist accumulation." The context in which the "shared development" strategy of Echeverría was thus articulated was qualitatively different from previous attempts to shore up hegemony. The "stabilizing development" strategy pursued by the administration of Gustavo Díaz Ordaz (1964–70), at least in its early phase, was able to command the support of all factions of labor and capital. However, the logic of capitalist development meant that by the time Echeverría came to power, a "tipping point" had been reached where crucial class divisions had emerged that were becoming harder to reconcile.[6] The struggle of particular factions of the bourgeoisie to accumulate further surplus value through increasing spatial integration with the global market, and attempts by the subaltern classes to resist their deepening exploitation, were the concrete class forces that created this tipping point. As Diane Davis (1993: 52) explains with regard to the outcome of the "stabilizing development" strategy, "By strengthening a few large internationally linked firms to the detriment of national industry and most other subordinate social groups, stabilizing development had fundamentally altered the balance of political power both within the capitalist class and between labour and the state."

It was becoming increasingly clear that the latest attempts to reinvent ISI as a viable accumulation strategy were untenable. Exports were failing to increase, and imports were accelerating too fast, creating current account difficulties and leading to a dialectic of overaccumulation and spiraling inflation in an effort to deal with these difficulties. In order to stabilize the system, further debt was contracted abroad, with this debt itself finally becoming the foundation of economic growth (Rosario Green 1981: 106). In 1976 the cycle of foreign borrowing, capital flight, and a deteriorating current account forced a massive devaluation of the peso. This devaluation was not, however, class neutral. As David Barkin and Gustavo Esteva (1986: 14) note, "The powerful national economic groups took advantage of the situation, centralising their control of strategic resources, reinforcing their links with transnational corporations, and expanding both their operations and their prospects for profits." Under the auspices of the IMF, an austerity program was agreed to by the incoming administration of José López Portillo (1976–82). The program included reducing federal spending, cutting social welfare programs, freeing exchange rates, and limiting wage increases (Cockcroft 1983: 259). The subaltern classes, in other words, were to bear the costs of devaluation in order for the process of private capital accumulation to continue. This would prove to be a recurring motif of Mexican development for the next twenty-five years. Growing class resentment resulted, expressed through increasing labor militancy and peasants organizing outside of traditional corporatist unions. Cockcroft (1998: 256) documents how independent peasant organizations sought a broad alliance with urban squatters, teachers, labor militants, and students, creating the potential for progressive resistance. However, divisions over tactics and ideology would come to split the movement, undermining its capacity for a hegemonic project.

In the face of mounting social pressures, the discovery of vast oil deposits in 1976 was viewed by the government as "black gold" that could again restore accumulation and shore up support through increased social spending. This oil discovery would have profound effects on the structure of the Mexican economy and class structure (as will be discussed further in chapter 5 in relation to Chiapas). By 1982 Mexico had become dangerously reliant upon a single resource, with oil coming to account for almost 75 percent of export earnings (Comisión Económica para América Latina y el Caribe 2007). Resources were diverted from agricultural production to increase productive capacity, once more furthering the growth of proletarianization. Again, however, Mexico found itself reliant on resources outside of its own national space. In order to increase the capacity for oil extraction, the country needed a huge influx of machinery, foreign capital, and technical know-how (Cockcroft 1983: 262–63). This dovetailed neatly with the internationalization of U.S. capital. Indeed, as María del Rosario Green (1981: 112) argues, "Only because of their international lending activities were American banks able to sustain the pace of profit growth." It was the accumulation of vast reserves of "petro-dollars" in Western banks that provided this liquidity, as these dollars would have caused inflationary pressures in core states if they did not find a productive outlet. This merry-go-round of finance capital and debt began to spiral out of control. As discussed in the previous chapter in relation to Latin America as a whole, Mexico in particular became a site for the creation of "fictitious capital." The rapid influx of finance capital was far in excess of Mexican productive capacity, a matter that was compounded when oil prices began to fall in the late 1970s.[7] However, by this time Mexico had the highest per capita debt in the Third World (Cockcroft 1983: 270). There was, then, a growing realization that it would not be possible to repay the debt, a fact confirmed by finance minister Jesús Silva-Herzog in August 1982, as Mexico entered into the so-called debt crisis.

The Silent Revolution as Passive Revolution

This crisis would be perceived as a chance to fundamentally restructure the Mexican economy, as well as other Latin American economies, along neoliberal lines, exemplifying the conditions of passive revolution, in which the state plays a leading role in the process of restructuring and renewing class power. The conditions were, of course, different from those of the Mexican Revolution, but as Gramsci (1971: 114, Q 15, §62) makes clear, the concept of passive revolution should serve as a "category of interpretation" rather than as a specific program (see also Morton 2007b: 15–36). Just as the entry into the crisis came from the breakdown of a particular accumulation strategy and hegemonic project, so the crisis would be used as the basis on which to begin constructing a new historical bloc with an alternative accumulation strategy and hegemonic project. In this sense, the spiraling debt was utilized as a weapon to enforce market discipline. Unable to gain access to capital through private lending, Mexico was forced to adopt IMF-mandated austerity measures, which frequently involved a modification of the debt payments, but only at the cost of increasing its overall amount (see figure 3). This further exposed the country to the pressure of transnational capital, enhancing those factions of capital in Mexico oriented toward global accumulation. Barkin (1990: 7, emphasis added) astutely summarizes the political implications of the debt crisis: "Mexico, like most other third world countries,

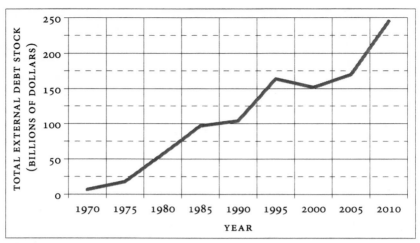

FIGURE 3. Total External Debt Stock of Mexico, 1970–2010 (Current U.S. Dollars)
Source: World Bank.

can never be expected to pay off its debt. Rather, the debt and the crisis that sparked it have already done their service in the international economy. They have *forced a reorganisation of production and of social classes.*"

Bob Jessop (1990: 211) usefully distinguishes between "one-nation" and "two-nation" hegemonic projects. One-nation hegemonic projects offer an expansive form of hegemony in which rights and welfare are extended (albeit unevenly) for the whole population. Compromises or sacrifices are thus required by the leading classes in the form of material concessions to provide stability. ISI can thus be interpreted in this light. Two-nation projects, in contrast, seek only to mobilize strategically significant sectors of the population and offer limited scope for material concessions to the subaltern classes. Neoliberalism in Mexico is thus a paradigmatic example of a two-nation hegemonic project. Duncan Green (1995) has labeled this process of restructuring (which also affected the whole of Latin America) as a "silent revolution" due to the manner in which the voices of the marginalized were sidelined and capitalist processes of exploitation deepened. I argue that a focus on the key role of the state as the facilitator or guiding hand of this process allows us to understand the rise of neoliberalism in Mexico as a second instance of passive revolution.

The discussion hitherto has highlighted how the state has to be located within the historical form of exploitation engendered by capitalist social relations. However, as has been demonstrated through the evolving character of ISI, the precise nature of these relations is far from static, and as ISI progressed, class antagonisms began to be constituted more and more by transnational processes of accumulation, confirming the point made by Gramsci (1971: 117, Q 10ii, §61) that the state is to be understood as "the concrete form of a productive world." The restructuring of the relations between the state and civil society both before the Mexican Revolution and during the transition to neoliberalism must be located in the dialectic between the national and the international and the conditioning factor of uneven and combined development. If the bourgeois state is to survive as an institution, an essential requirement of that survival is to ensure the conditions for continued capital accumulation. However, it was clear that with the declining profitability of ISI, the state's role as a creator of the national scale for the accumulation of capital had reached its limits. This does not mean that the space of the national had become unimportant. Because of the historical relations existing in Mexico and thus the potential for the extensive and intensive enlargement of capital, the space of Mexico was *reconfigured* in order to serve as a site for the accumulation of capital on a global scale.

The role of the state has been fundamental to the reorganization of capitalism in Mexico. As a result of the changing balance of class forces, the country has been transformed from being a key source of investment and the provider of goods for productive consumption (essentially, an ideal collective capitalist) to a country whose function was "to reshape social relations to create an attractive environment that would stimulate industrialists—domestic and foreign—to invest in new competitive ventures which would in turn allow the country to become a responsible participant in the *international* economy" (Barkin 1990: 94, emphasis added).

Making space an attractive destination for foreign capital thus became a vital policy priority. In this regard the state once more became an agent of "primitive accumulation" in Mexico (see chapter 1 for a discussion of this concept). The 1987 Pacto de Solidaridad Económica (Pact of Economic Solidarity) was the first key piece of legislation signaling the state's new policy orientation, eliminating subsidies and dramatically reducing tariff barriers (Dussel-Peters 2000: 65–66; Heredia 1996: 138). The mounting debt burden meant resources were forced to be transferred from social expenditure to debt repayment. This had massive social repercussions, with a 40 percent decline in real wages (Walton and Shefner 1994: 123). Factors such as *ejido* land and parastatals—essential to the stability of ISI—now became the spaces through which the capital relation could be extended. Article 27 of the 1917 Constitution—the cornerstone of the Mexican state's covenant with the peasantry in the aftermath of the revolution— was repealed by Carlos Salinas in 1992, demonstrating the new policy priorities of the state. This reform allowed for the privatization of *ejido* land and also formally ended the petitioning for land reform, signaling the end of the Mexican Revolution while auguring the rise of a new passive revolution. The southern states of Mexico (Chiapas, Oaxaca, and Guerrero, where the largest proportion of communal land is held) have become what Neil Brenner (1997: 280) refers to as "spatial targets" for a new round of capitalist expansion. Just as the uneven and combined development of space within the global political economy was the means by which the crisis built, so too would it be utilized as a means to attempt to resolve that crisis by producing its relation anew in a different articulation.

Taking the declared objective of attracting FDI on its own terms, Mexico has been highly successful, as figure 4 demonstrates. The beginning of the rapid increase of FDI in 1990 coincided with the massive privatization of parastatals and reforms designed to pave the way for entry into NAFTA, such as the reduction of price supports and subsidies to peasants. Mexico has thus gone from being a country that based its accumulation strategy on domestic industrialization and the growth of an internal market to one that seeks further integration into global production networks. This is demonstrably shown in figure 5, which highlights the rise of manufacturing as a percentage of the total value of Mexican exports (from 1992 onward this includes maquiladora goods).

The state has reshaped the space of Mexico so that it now serves a vital new social function in the global division of labor. With Mexico's entry into NAFTA in 1994, its space became essential to the profitability of U.S. capital. By 2000 some 62 percent of FDI in Mexico was U.S.-based, with 86.6 percent being located in the maquiladora sector, where wages are notably lower than in the United States (Dussel-Peters 2000: 124). Maquiladoras, as Gary Gereffi (1995: 134) notes, provide a poor basis for meaningful development, as they offer limited scope for skills upgrades and technology transfers, and they create

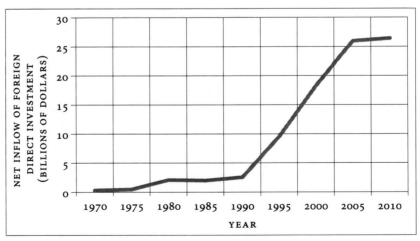

FIGURE 4. Net Inflow of Foreign Direct Investment, 1970–2010 (Balance of Payments, Current U.S. Dollars)
Source: World Bank

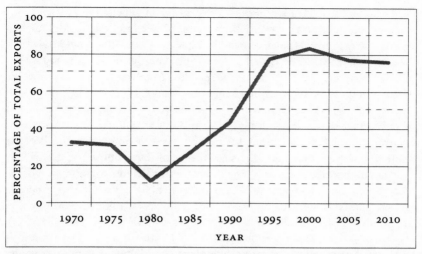

FIGURE 5. Export of Manufactures as a Percentage of Total Exports from Mexico, 1970–2010
Source: United Nations Commodity Trade Statistics Database.

few backward linkages with local society. Mexico may experience economic growth, but it is unlikely to see "development" based on the continuation of this trajectory (see the discussion in the previous chapter).

¡La Lucha Sigue! (The Struggle Continues!)

The move from ISI to neoliberalism in Mexico thus provides concrete meaning for Lefebvre's (1991: 55) claim that "today, more than ever the class struggle is inscribed in space." The debt crisis in Mexico must be understood not only as a *national* crisis of capital accumulation but also as a *global* capitalist crisis. It was through geopolitical competition that the costs of devaluation were exported to Mexico (Harvey 2006a: 438). Devaluation, however, is always a two-sided process that provides opportunity for some and increased exploitation for others (for example, Carlos Slim, one of the world's richest people, made his fortune during this period from the privatization of state-owned industries, as did a number of other tycoons). Marx (1867/1974: 567) captures this essential class dynamic when he declares that the "development of productive power is accompanied by a partial depreciation of functioning capital. So far as this depreciation makes itself acutely felt in competition, the burden falls on the labourer, in the increased exploitation of whom the capitalist looks for his indemnification." This process can be witnessed in the move to create "flexible" labor markets in Mexico as a concomitant to the new export-oriented strategy. In practice this has meant an intensification of the labor process, in which employment status is more precarious and government or union protection limited (McCaughan 1993: 18). Large internationally linked businesses, on the other hand, saw their power augmented and their political centrality increased (Heredia 1996: 142). Other geographical manifestations that resulted from this depreciation include increased migration to the United States in search of jobs, as well as the growth of urban slums (Barkin 1990: 10). A conservative United Nations estimate put the percentage of urban Mexicans living in slums at 19.1 percent, although if a less restrictive definition is used, the number rises to almost two-thirds of the population (Davis 2006: 23). The significance of these slums was briefly discussed in the previous chapter, namely, that they contribute to the growth of the informal economy, helping to mask unemployment figures while also providing a superexploitable workforce, adding further downward pressure on wages in the formal sector. The point was clearly recognized by Marx (1867/1974: 435), who saw that the spatial dispersion of work led to the decreasing power of collective resistance, something capital attempts to build upon with piecework and subcontracting. According to Cockcroft (1998: 236), the growth of slums and the informal economy should not be viewed as precapitalist forms of social relations but rather as a "product and tool of modern capitalist accumulation."

The state has played a key role not only in effecting this transition but also in attempting to deal with the resulting class resentments through a number of social programs such as the Programa Nacional de Solidaridad (PRONASOL, National Solidarity Program) and the Programa de Educación, Salud y Alimentación (PROGRESA, Program for Education, Health and Nutrition, later rebranded Oportunidades and now known as Prospera), as well as widening the sphere of democratic participation. However, these social programs must clearly be interpreted in light of an attempt at the recomposition of PRI hegemony (Morton 2003: 643; Veltmeyer 1997: 234). While not overlooking the importance of widening democratic participation in Mexico and the notable ending of the PRI's seventy-one-year dominance of Mexican politics with the election of Vicente Fox in 2000, widening democratic participation must again be interpreted as a state-led solution to the political crisis provoked by the Zapatista uprising in 1994, as it aimed at pacifying subaltern demands and channeling them onto a more manageable terrain that stays within the limits of acceptable discontent. Rather than genuine democracy, this solution is better theorized as the promotion of polyarchy, understood as the continuation of elite-based rule with carefully managed mass participation (Robinson 1996). As Morton (2005: 190) cogently argues, the democratic reforms were "designed to frame and condition the institutional context of opposition movements. The reform constituted the construction of a specific legal and institutional terrain that was capable of containing popular demands by defining terms and fixing the boundaries of the rules of the game of representation and social struggle."

This attempt at the statization of discontent has not always been successful. The Zapatistas since 1994 have steadfastly continued to resist incorporation into "official" political discourse and have instead created autonomous spaces for horizontal and democratic political practices beyond the purview of the state. Their example has often served as an inspiration to other social movements around the country that have found themselves forcibly disenfranchised from the state's new hegemonic project. In 2006 the Zapatistas began their Otra Campaña (Other Campaign), which ran parallel to the presidential elections. It was intended to begin the process of creating civil society alliances to transform Mexico from the bottom up. The year 2006 also witnessed the explosion of popular anger at the corrupt and repressive governorship of Ulises Ruiz Ortiz in Oaxaca, crystallizing in the formation of the Asamblea Popular de los Pueblos de Oaxaca (APPO, Popular Assembly of the Peoples of Oaxaca). This movement, coming in the wake of the repression of the teachers' union (known as Section 22), must be placed in the context of the increasing inability of the state to attend to wider societal demands, demonstrating the failure of hegemony (Martínez Vásquez 2007: 79).

Conclusion

It has been argued that through an examination of Mexican development in the twentieth century we can identify two particular instances of passive revolution whereby the state has acted as the leading agent of transformation, restructuring social relations and maintaining or furthering class power. These instances of passive revolution must be thought of as protracted processes rather than single, sudden events, the import of which has been to effect "molecular changes which . . . progressively modify the pre-existing composition of forces, and hence the matrix of new changes" (Gramsci 1971: 109, Q 15, §11). Associated with each phase was a particular state spatial project that served a distinct historical social purpose. While the first instance of passive revolution managed to offset the revolutionary impulses of the time and draw the subaltern classes into an expansive hegemonic project through its production of space, it is becoming increasingly clear that the neoliberal passive revolution is failing to do this, as rather than opening new possibilities for the subaltern, the new spatial strategy is threatening long-held revolutionary desires for a different way of life. As the Mexican state has sought to open new spaces for capital, new spaces of resistance have proliferated. It is to these spaces of resistance that we now turn, with detailed case studies of the southern states of Oaxaca and Chiapas.

CHAPTER FOUR

The Changing State of Resistance

Defending Place and Producing Space in Oaxaca

The first aim of capitalism is to isolate the producer, to sever the community ties which protect him.
    —**Rosa Luxemburg,** *The Accumulation of Capital*

While over the centuries, the Valley of Oaxaca's population has retained many indigenous cultural features, these now seem in opposition to capitalist development.
    —**Scott Cook and Martin Diskin,** *Markets in Oaxaca*

In the summer of 2006, Oaxaca de Juárez—the historic capital of Oaxaca State—known for its quaint charm and tranquil ambience, resembled something more akin to a war zone. Thousands of barricades were erected throughout the city around key public offices, and a state of "ungovernability" was declared.[1] For five months no official government functioned as a battle was waged to control public space. Instead, informal neighborhood organizations sprang up, with popular "people's councils" replacing official political parties as the local centers of power. Out of this cacophony of voices and searing anger, directed at one of the most corrupt and repressive governors in recent history, a disparate collective of social movements, trade unions, and civil society organizations came together under the banner of the Asamblea Popular de los Pueblos de Oaxaca (APPO, Popular Assembly of the Peoples of Oaxaca). Some immediately drew the analogy between events taking place in Oaxaca and those of the Paris Commune (Gustavo Esteva, interview with the author, Oaxaca, 2009). Since this time, the sharpened social tensions have barely receded. While the Mexican state and transnational capital continue to attempt to reconfigure Oaxaca into a new site of accumulation, so too has Oaxaca been at the forefront of resistance to neoliberalism in Mexico.

In exploring the spaces of capital and the spaces of resistance, we have so far outlined an abstract theoretical analysis of the production of space and the role of class struggle in this process (chapter 1) before moving on to consider the meso level changes that have taken place within the global economy (chapter 2). The key themes emerging from these chapters, such as the role of the state within capitalist development, passive revolution, the geopolitics of devaluation, and the antinomies surrounding the production of spatial scales, were then discussed in relation to both regional and national developments (chapters 2 and 3, respectively). It is now time to extend the concrete level of analysis further through detailed local case studies of the southern Mexican states of Oaxaca and Chiapas, beginning here with Oaxaca. This exploration of the subnational scale should complete our picture of the production of space and provide us with the tools to understand the dynamics and contradictions inherent in the latest phase of capitalist expansion, as well as offering insights into the alternative geographies that are currently being produced in opposition to this process. A focus on specific regional history is also an essential element in the dialectical method, as it allows us to explore not only how particular places are incorporated and transformed by an overarching structure of articulation but also how these places themselves produce this structure and, furthermore, how they seek to contest, resist, or reshape it (Chassen-López 2004: 17; Wolf 1955: 455).

Through an exploration of spatial production in Oaxaca, this chapter reveals that not only does the process of capitalist expansion unfold in a highly uneven manner, but (as was stressed in chapter 1) it is this unevenness itself that induces the particular manner of (attempted) transformation. Thus, as Patricia Martin (2005) has submitted, we need to be attentive to the differing topographies of social relations at localized spatial scales if we are to understand the particular trajectories of capitalist development in a wider setting. The same is equally true of resistance to this process. Gerardo Otero (1999: 22) argues succinctly with regard to this resistance: "Peasants in different parts of the world or in different regions within a country . . . may have diverse structural capacities depending on their distinctive histories and cultures, or the villages or regions where they develop." With this concept in mind, the chapter also forces us to reconsider the agency of political transformation. Through an exploration of struggles to defend place and produce alternative spaces, the chapter challenges the traditional Marxist notion of class struggle in which developments among the peasantry are subordinated to the struggles of the working class, who necessarily occupy a vanguardist position (Gramsci 1971: 15, Q 12, §1; Trotsky 1930/1962: 61). This exploration of indigenous and peasant agency also stands in stark contrast to the approach of some recent Marxist-inspired analyses of transformation in Latin America that have put forward the view that developments in the world economy are leading to the disappearance of the peasantry as the forces of global capitalism wrench them from the land and force them into proletarianization (Robinson 2008).[2] However, as will be highlighted here, this view takes a rather large leap over historical contingency (Block 2001). This chapter therefore seeks to take a more nuanced approach that recognizes this process as being far from complete or uncontested. Instead, concurring with Eric Wolf (1955: 462, emphasis added), I argue that it is extreme folly to "visualise the development of the world market in terms of continuous and *even expansion*, and to suppose therefore that the line of development of particular peasantries always leads from lesser involvement in the market to more involvement."

Via a historical-geographical sociology of Oaxaca, I explore three interlinked themes. First, I document the historic struggles over the production of space in Oaxaca. I advance an argument that the retention of collective property, as well as wider indigenous communal traditions, provides a crucial basis for resisting capitalism in the present day. Second, I offer a spatial rendering of hegemony in its localized form. In other words, I explore how wider global and national trends articulate themselves within their intimate class culture, defined as "the culture of class in a particular setting" (Lomnitz-Adler 1992: 28). Bringing together the insights of Trotsky, Gramsci, and Lefebvre, I introduce the concept of "uneven and combined hegemony." Consequently, rather than postulating a monolithic "global" or "national" hegemonic project (Jessop 1990: 201–11; Robinson 2004b, 2008; Hardt and Negri 2000), I demonstrate how these projects are struggled over and renegotiated at the local scale. An overarching project with a particular social logic can thus manifest itself differently in particular contexts that are dependent upon the social forces within a given place. Third and finally, I will focus on the dialectic of passive revolution and resistance to it in the localized setting of Oaxaca. In relation to this last point, I will examine key social movements in Oaxaca that acted as important precursors to the APPO and explore how social struggles have now evolved.

The chapter is set out as follows. First, it explores the historical space of Oaxaca in relation to the impact of Spanish colonialism. Second, the text examines the liberal era from independence to the outbreak of revolution. These sections lay the basis for considering the evolution of collective property in Oaxaca, as well as its relationship to the national and the global. Third, the chapter scrutinizes the changing space of Oaxaca in the twentieth century, with a particular focus on how these changes fit into the Mexican state's hegemonic project of nation building along the capitalist lines of ISI (analyzed separately in the previous chapter). The fourth and final section explores the increasing clash of opposing spatial projects in Oaxaca following Mexico's neoliberal turn, as global capitalism increasingly seeks to expand and transform Oaxaca into an area for surplus value creation, on the one hand, while in opposition, subaltern social forces seek to extend the spaces of autonomous, democratic participation, based in the state's indigenous traditions and histories of struggle. These last two sections allow us to explore the dialectic of passive revolution and resistance to this process of incorporation.

Situating the State of Oaxaca

Located in the southwest of Mexico, Oaxaca encompasses a rich variety of contradictions. It is rugged and geographically isolated, and over the last century it has had minimal influence on the national political agenda. It has therefore been described as being both literally and metaphorically peripheral to national life (Clarke 1992: 153). However, historically with Porfirio Díaz and Benito Juárez, Oaxaca has produced two statesmen who have profoundly influenced Mexico's transition to modernity. It furthermore remains a tourist "hot spot," with thousands flocking each year to see the colonial city of Oaxaca de Juárez, enjoy the indigenous markets, and relax on its spectacular beaches. Indeed, the national state has actively sought to *produce* Oaxaca precisely in this image. Oaxaca is often portrayed as a traditional state, as well as being a bastion of PRI support. However, the municipality of Juchitán was the first place in which the PRI experienced a dent in its electoral hegemony with a defeat from a radical, indigenous, and leftist-oriented social movement in 1981 (see Campbell et al. 1993).

According to the Programa de las Naciones Unidad para el Desarrollo (2009: 6), Oaxaca ranks thirty-first out of Mexico's thirty-two federal entities on its Human Development Index. More than 60 percent of the population live in poverty, with more than 23 percent defined as living in a situation of extreme poverty (Instituto Nacional de Estadística y Geografía 2014). However, despite having only 3.4 percent of the national population, Oaxaca contains over one-fifth of all the nation's 2,438 municipalities, numbering 570 in total. Of these, 418 since 1995 have governed themselves according to their own *usos y costumbres* (practices and customs).[3] For these reasons the state has often been portrayed as a backwater, untouched by the hand of modernity (Chassen-López 2004: 4). However, this is to take our very understanding of the term "modernity" from a highly Eurocentric perspective, as it fails to grasp how so-called traditional and modern societies have mutually conditioned one another (Mallon 1995: 8). The high number of municipalities in Oaxaca did not fall from the sky, nor was it created by chance. Rather, it is the result of a long process of struggle for autonomy (Esteva 2001; Corbett and Whiteford 1983: 16). Members of the largely indigenous population have not simply been victims who have had a new way of life imposed on them; instead, they have actively contested and negotiated various hegemonic projects to refine them toward people's specific needs (Hesketh 2016). This historic resistance continues to inform contemporary struggles. As the title of this chapter suggests, although Oaxaca has had a long history of resistance stretching back half a millennium, this should not be taken to imply that the people's resistance has remained unchanged. To do so would romanticize indigenous peasant culture and hold communities static. Such a position serves to deny peasants their role as "potential makers of history" (Chassen-López 2004: 343). As Ernesto Laclau (1977: 157–58) has argued, this means we cannot essentialize traditional paradigms of social groups; instead, we need to examine how such views become utilized and expressed as new forms of antagonism. In this way, ideas and local practices are transformed into resources for self-determination. Forms of struggle and political organization, as we shall see, have been constantly reinvented in Oaxaca (see Sorroza Polo and Danielson 2013). As Kiado Cruz (interview with the author, Oaxaca, 2009), a member of the Zapotec community of Yagavila in the Sierra Norte, elaborated with regard to this reinvention, "If we did not constantly reinvent forms of life and other things, it would not be possible to be a community."

What is most remarkable about Oaxaca is its property regime. To this day, 75 percent of land is communally held in the form of either *ejidos* (34 percent) or *tierras communales* (communal lands, 41 percent) (extrapolated from Instituto Nacional de Estadística y Geografía 2014). Three prominent local nongovernmental organizations (NGOs) have concluded, therefore, that "it is precisely in Oaxacan territory where one can observe and study the survival of ancient agrarian structures" (La Ventana, Investigación y Divulgación A.C., Tequio Jurídico A.C., and Servicios para una Educación Alternativa A.C. [EDUCA] 2013). To demonstrate how such a remarkable arrangement came about, I will now explore the changing historical sociology of space, beginning with the colonial era. The purpose of this exploration is to call attention to the way in which property relations evolved in the state, as this process not only informs the manner in which capital is seeking to expand in Oaxaca but also provides the territorial basis for the counterspaces of resistance.

Caciques, *Cabildos*, and Communities: Producing the Spaces of Colonial Oaxaca

Oaxaca has a long history of exceptionalism in terms of its property relations compared to other regions of Mexico. The Spanish arrived in the Valley of Oaxaca in 1521 and immediately began altering the spatial practices they found. Recalling the point made in chapter 1 with regard to colonial representations of space, it was from this gaze that the space of Mexico was viewed as an unknown territory to be discovered, and the perspective of the indigenous population was ignored (Bonfil Batalla 1996: 8–9). Preexisting communal spaces of power were reconfigured by the Spanish Crown to serve its primary interest, which was, of course, the extraction of tribute (Cook and Diskin 1976: 9; Taylor 1972: 198). The development of land tenure in Oaxaca, however, stood in contrast to that in the northern and central states, which have often been assumed to be paradigmatic of colonial social property relations. Instead of the hacienda developing to displace communal land, as happened widely elsewhere (as discussed in chapter 3), "late colonial Oaxaca did not experience a dramatic expansion of Spanish landholdings" (Taylor 1972: 7–8). This lack of Spanish expansion is partly related to the physical geographical features of the state. As Colin Clarke (1992: 152) explains, the largely mountainous topography of Oaxaca was "inimical to agricultural development of a hacienda or plantation type." The fierceness of native resistance and their determination to hold onto their communal land, however, were also fundamental to the evolution of this property regime (Murphy and Stepick 1991: 18; Taylor 1972: 197). Spanish colonialism thus developed alongside the survival of the native nobility in the form of *cacicazgo* landholdings (noble estates). These local caciques (native chiefs), in fact, were to play a crucial mediating role for the Spanish Crown and would help facilitate the extraction of tribute (Taylor 1972: 35–37; Knight 2002b: 14). Recognizing what existed already in native practice therefore became a method for transforming it (Wainwright 2008: 53). This is not to say that the experience of colonialism did not affect in any manner the preexisting forms of space. Rather, the spatial terrain was shaped by asymmetrical relations of force with a particular social purpose in mind, one that nevertheless was forced to recognize the power of already existing social relations at the community level. Commenting upon this, Guillermo Bonfil Batalla (1996: 9) argues: "Geographical transformations did not take place on an empty landscape. Rather, the changes Europeans introduced affected groups of people with a cultural heritage elaborated over many centuries in the same places, where local adoptions allowed different sorts of responses."

As well as being decimated by disease brought by the Europeans, some indigenous communities found themselves physically transferred to new locations in what were known as "civil congregations" (Cline 1949). The spatial practices of village life were also modified as the Spanish sought to introduce the *cabildo* (town government), which they used in their own domestic municipalities (Chassen-López 2004: 286). This type of government conformed to the Spanish preference for a "nucleated grid community with a concentrated civil-commercial and religious precinct (the plaza)" (Whitecotton 1977: 180). This reorganization of space is a classic example of what James Scott (1998: 2) describes as "seeing like a state," where concentrated power is used to attempt to resettle and render people more legible for a particular social purpose (in this case, easier social control and mobilization of labor and resources). These so-called *pueblos de indios* were intended to serve three functions for the Spanish Crown: (1) the curtailment of power of the new colonial landholding class, (2) the simpler identification of group units to mobilize and extract resources from, and (3) the creation or enhancement of communal obligations to which labor should be dedicated (Wolf 1955: 457). Their creation can thus be thought of as a spatial strategy for the mobilization of social labor under historically specific class conditions. However, owing to the intensity of struggle in Oaxaca, a far greater number of municipalities were created there than in other parts of Mexico in an effort to divide and rule the population more efficiently. By the end of the colonial period the *cabildo* was a spatial reflection of the clash of social forces and the contested nature of the regime of power. The Crown had managed to introduce the civil-religious *cargo* system, which was intended to be a means of control that would aid in preserving social peace and the extraction of tribute. The system was supposed to be secured through the *comprador* classes in the form of indigenous caciques, who were the only ones entitled to hold positions of authority, as well as being the only ones able to participate in the electing of community representatives. However, the power of the caciques was gradually eroded by the resistance from the commoners to the abuses that took place. Far from simply being an instrument of control, the *cabildo* was contested and renegotiated to protect and serve community needs (Whitecotton 1977: 180–91; Frye 1994: 326). We can see here, therefore, the very real dynamics of class strategies for the production of space. As Scott (1998: 49) elucidates with regard to this issue, "We must keep in mind not only the capacity of state simplifications to transform the world but also the capacity of the society to modify, subvert, block and overturn the categories imposed upon it."

From the beginnings of the colonial era, the indigenous population was forced to pay tribute through the *encomienda* system, in which the Crown granted land rights to a particular individual from whom the Crown could then claim an amount of particular goods from specified places. Labor could also be demanded from these places in what was known as the *repartimiento*. Recalling the discussion from chapter 1 with regard to the manner in which social labor is mobilized, we can see that under Spanish colonialism the mode of exploitation did not divorce the primary producers from their means of production but rather sought to requisition both their products and their labor power (often through the use of or the threat of force). As Ronald Waterbury (1975: 420–21) explains in relation to this, "Removal of the Indians from their land would have been contrary to the economic interests of the most powerful class in the province: the Spanish merchants." What this section has highlighted thus far is the retention not only of communal property but also, more fundamentally, of indigenous territory. This is vital, as the politics that accompany this retention (collective decision making and work) are essential bases for resisting modern encroachment. As Ana María García Arreola (interview with the author, Oaxaca, 2015) from the Oaxacan NGO EDUCA outlines, "Here in Oaxaca there was a strong internal structure of government over the land because in the communities the entire system of government is a function of the land and the communities' necessities. . . . They [the communities] have strongly conserved their assemblies and the system of *cargos*." Let us now move to see how this process continued to interact with national and global forces.

From Liberal to Revolutionary Oaxaca

Space in Oaxaca, as it was throughout Mexico, began to be profoundly altered during the liberal era. The advent of independence witnessed a collapse in the export economy of the state. This collapse was intimately linked to the production, or lack of production, of space, as the region's poor transportation infrastructure meant that it was susceptible to competition on a world scale if other places could ensure a faster turnover time for products. Such competition from Guatemala in cochineal production (cochineal is a red dye made from the dried bodies of cochineal insects, and up to this time it had been the dominant export of Oaxaca) during the 1820s and the exploitation by colonial powers of their territories for both cochineal and indigo (India in the British case, Indonesia in the Dutch) would lead to the spatial devaluation of Oaxaca (Tutino 1993: 53; Clarke 1996: 268). Following this devaluation, Oaxaca reverted to becoming a regional peasant economy, with trade being centered in the capital city (Murphy and Stepick 1991: 27).

Throughout the whole of Mexico, the two foremost spatial projects of the liberal era were the creation of infrastructure (regarded at the time by elite classes as synonymous with civilization) and the increasing privatization of property (Chassen-López 2004: 47). It was thought that these developments would make Mexico more attractive to foreign investors, who were needed to transform the country into a modern state. Both the ideology and the necessary capital for the liberal project were thus imported and set to work in local conditions. Benito Juárez and Porfirio Díaz epitomized the maxim that Henri Lefebvre (1991: 190) would later stress: to change life, it is necessary to change space (a recurring theme of state planners).

As we saw in chapter 3, the beginnings of modern state formation in Mexico took place during this period in the shadow of Western capitalist expansion. Liberalism in Mexico was an imported ideology that was wielded by elite classes in the attempt to mimic the European road to modernity and impose change (Chassen-López 2004: 4). Led by Juárez (1858–72), the liberals came to power determined to transform Mexico from its colonial heritage. This strategy involved breaking up landed estates held by the church and communal property held by indigenous communities. Both were viewed as impediments to the spread of individual property holdings. Aided by state power, which acted as a nodal point through which European and American interests were wielded, laws were passed in Oaxaca in favor of privatization. However, in response to the efforts to privatize communal lands, rebellions took place in "most of the seven districts of Porfirian Oaxaca" (Chassen-López 2004: 80).

Foreign capital poured into Mexico during the Porfiriato, in line with the ideology of the Científicos (as documented in the previous chapter). Oaxaca was not immune to these changes. Indeed, it had its very own Científico governor, Emilio Pimentel (1902–11). Thus, Porfirio Díaz, in both a direct and an indirect manner, did much to influence the development of his *patria chica* (native region) (Overmyer-Valázquez 2006: 23, 55). The decline of cochineal prices on the world market, as well as the aforementioned competition from other regions, had led to Oaxaca becoming transformed into a center for light industry and handicrafts (Kemper and Royce 1979: 279). Additionally, since 1863 coffee cultivation had replaced cochineal as the most important cash crop of the state. As links grew with foreign businesses anxious to market coffee beans, the increasing emphasis on coffee cultivation acted as a spur to the privatization of land (Chassen-López 2004: 138, 143). Following national trends, the largest amount of land privatization took place between 1880 and 1910 (Stephen 1998: 12). During this period, some indigenous communities also privatized their landholdings, although this was generally the result of a strategy for survival rather than an ideological shift toward individualism. However, the most salient feature to note is that whereas in other parts of Mexico peasants were rendered landless, in Oaxaca peasants largely retained access to their land. Nevertheless, the process of capital expansion was making inroads, quite literally, into Oaxaca.

Foreign capital was attracted to the state and was utilized both to construct infrastructure and to extract natural resources in the shape of mining industries. In 1876, when Porfirio Díaz assumed power, Oaxaca had no railroads at all. By 1910 it had 1,829 kilometers (1,136 miles) of track (Chassen-López 2004: 48). Railroad construction (as was argued in the previous chapter) cannot be separated from the export orientation of the Porfiriato. This expansion of infrastructure highlights the clashing of distinct spatial projects. In the liberal outlook there was little regard for the distinct places of indigenous communities. They would survive only through their own stubborn defense. The growth of infrastructure induced spatial development and land speculation in sites of close proximity that saw their (exchange) value transformed. The Puebla–Oaxaca railway line, completed in 1892, also heralded the beginning of the mining boom in the state. The railway line was thought to be the physical symbol of Oaxaca's integration into the national state-building project and circuits of global capital. Although mining in Oaxaca is insignificant if taken as a percentage of the country's overall mining exports, this "national gaze" does not tell the whole story, as from a local perspective the mining industry was to rapidly increase the state's linkages with the global economy. Indeed, over one hundred companies set up offices in Oaxaca City (Overmyer-Valásquez 2006: 13). Mining and commerce were to flourish in the state until the outbreak of the Mexican Revolution, heralding the high point of Oaxaca's uneven insertion into the global capitalist system. Importantly, while contributing to elite class formation in the state, the proliferation of mining interests did not threaten village lands during this time but rather was utilized by peasants as a source of wage labor to supplement their subsistence activities (Waterbury 1975: 421–24). What was developing in Oaxaca was, therefore, not a purely capitalist economy but rather a plural or heterogeneous socioeconomic landscape marked by the survival of key noncapitalist elements (Hesketh 2016). While engaging in wage labor helped provide additional forms of class consciousness, it complemented, rather than subsumed, collective consciousness developed in the wider community.

In summary, liberal privatization and infrastructural developmental projects did not leave land tenure in Oaxaca unaffected. Unquestionably, land speculations linked to mining and agrarian capitalism were beginning to make their mark on the state's social relations (Chassen-López 2004: 92; Waterbury 1975). Despite these changes, however, Colin Clarke (2000) concludes that "Oaxaca's peasantries, though undoubtedly dominated socially and politically and exploited economically during the Porfiriato, retained much of their land and maintained their spatial distribution more or less intact." The liberal project was thus not articulated evenly throughout Mexico or in the state of Oaxaca. This is an important point to note, as it means the process of state formation took place on highly differentiated terrain that did not simply become subsumed by the directives of the center (see Joseph and Nugent 1994).

However, despite the fact that the peasantry of Oaxaca managed to retain a large amount of their lands, it should also be noted that the increasing production of capitalist space would change the structural environment in which they operated, creating new class relations from which they were not immune. Massimo Modonesi (2010: 28) reminds us that subaltern actors are not in a relationship of total autonomy from power structures. Rather, their history is dialectically related to such wider relations (as opposed to dualistically running alongside them). The expansion of infrastructure had, in the form of roads, railways, and ports, led to an increase in the capitalization of agriculture and the cultivation of new crops (Smith 2009: 25, 298). As Colin Clarke (1992: 147) summarizes, the peasantry became "increasingly differentiated internally because the economic value of what they control is changed by capitalist investment." This issue of spatial differentiation within Oaxaca serves to highlight that while "everyday forms of resistance" may be important for the protection and retention of place (Scott 1985), it is ultimately a defensive strategy in which subaltern classes remain susceptible to the activities of the hegemonic groups in wider society, groups that may seek to manipulate the spaces they occupy for their own ends (Gramsci 1971: 55, Q 25, §2). Taking our understanding of capital (as was set out in the preceding chapters) as an expansive mode of production that seeks to subordinate and transform space in line with its own logic, this implies that at some point, a purely defensive strategy may no longer be adequate, and political action must be scaled up.

Postrevolutionary Oaxaca: Between Local Practice and National Project

Owing to the fact that the peasants in Oaxaca had not experienced the dramatic dispossession that peasants in other states had, Oaxaca was not at the forefront of the revolutionary struggles (Waterbury 1975). However, the outbreak of the revolution would nonetheless alter the spatial terrain of Oaxaca. It shattered Oaxaca's links with the wider forces of the global economy (Murphy and Stepick 1991: 27). Mining and coffee industries collapsed, and although coffee would recover to again become the main export commodity of the state, mining has (until recently) remained dormant. These developments, however, did not fundamentally alter the class structure of Oaxaca. As Benjamin Smith (2009: 32–33) argues, "The *vallistocracia* may have been trimmed of its exotic imports, its mining and commercial agriculture enterprises left to the malicious militant masses, and its national power delimited, but the Oaxaca City elite maintained extensive commercial, industrial, real estate, and agricultural interests, especially around the state capital."[4]

As has been discussed hitherto, Oaxaca's resources, including its labor power, had been mobilized for various political projects and under various class conditions, of which wage labor was still a relatively minor part. The region had also shifted from being a space that was colonized directly by a foreign power to one that was colonized by an emergent nation-state on behalf of foreign interests. During the Porfiriato, Oaxaca served as a destination that could attract foreign capital due to its natural resources while also serving as an important export center and tourist destination. The state was thus produced as a "moment" of international capital formation. However, it must also not be forgotten that a strong tradition of resistance had remained in the state, resulting in vast tracts of communal land being retained.

Let us now explore how space was transformed with the changing hegemonic project of isi (analyzed in the previous chapter). Under the accumulation regime that emerged in Mexico following the revolution, Oaxaca and the southern Mexican states in general were not considered vital areas for industrial development. Indeed, the lack of industrial development in Oaxaca can be explained usefully in the notion of uneven and combined hegemony (see the introduction). The purpose of this concept is to show how hegemonic projects designed at a particular scale play out differently at other levels where they are contested and rearticulated within local conditions, or what Claudio

Lomnitz-Adler (1992: 28) describes as "regionally differentiated manifestations of class culture."

Following the protracted conflict, the newly formed Mexican state was forced to seek ways to secure its legitimacy. As was discussed in the previous chapter, ISI was a classic example of a one-nation hegemonic project in that it sought to mobilize all sectors of society (Jessop 1990: 211). Land redistribution and industrial development were the key drivers that engendered wider opportunity within the overall framework of capitalist development. However, as has been discussed earlier, Oaxaca possessed a population that was overwhelmingly rural, and the state's indigenous lands had not been usurped to the degree they had elsewhere. There was not, therefore, the same imperative for the national state to create a new spatial terrain in order to win support. Consequently, government spending on industrial development was concentrated largely in the central and northern states, where the majority of the more contumacious population was located. Oaxaca's geographical location and hostile topography also partially explain the government's lack of efforts to expand industry there. Due to the state's mountainous terrain, the cost of installing roads and power lines was twice the national average (Corbett and Whiteford 1983: 16). Instead, land recognition and land redistribution were the mechanisms employed to construct consent. Furthermore, *indigenismo* began to be promoted within the state to increase its attractiveness as part of the tourist trade (Smith 2009: 50). The regime of hegemony constructed in Oaxaca, although definitively part of a wider national project, was therefore founded in particularly localized conditions. According to Francie Chassen-López (2004: 427), "The process of state formation demanded constant negotiations on the local, regional, state and national levels, each in their own particular context but also interconnected."

In the years following the revolution, Oaxaca was slowly drawn into the wider project of passive revolution and *trasformismo* described in the previous chapters. For example, efforts were made to extend the emergent corporatist model of control to Oaxaca. This was done through the creation of the Confederación de Partidos Socialistas de Oaxaca (CPSO, Confederation of Socialist Parties of Oaxaca), an umbrella organization created under Governor Genaro Vásquez in 1926, comprising a union of twenty-six regional parties. No party eventually existed outside of this umbrella, and by 1934 it had been subordinated to the Partido Nacional Revolucionario (PNR, National Revolutionary Party) (Smith 2009: 47). As we saw in the previous chapter, Mexican leaders, following the Great Depression, sought to create a fully fledged national market that would be based on industrial production and include a stable landholding peasantry in the countryside. Essential to this process of modern state formation was the breakup of haciendas, described by Eric Wolf (1959: 245) as "ramparts of power in the countryside." Although attracting little industrial development, between 1917 and 1964 almost all areas of Oaxaca experienced land reform of some kind.

The only places that didn't were those areas that had managed to hold onto their communal land during the colonial period, the so-called *communidades agrarias* (agrarian communities) (although at times the state played an important role in confirming their title). However, the manner in which agrarian reform was carried out reflected the politics of state development combined with struggles for local autonomy. For example, land was predominantly redistributed in areas in which the government sought to increase its tax base, such as Tuxtepec and Pochutla. Areas nearest to the state capital were also given priority (so as to maintain control over them), whereas more peripheral areas were left to cacique control. Lastly, protection was offered to landowners in particularly productive zones (Smith 2009: 58–63, 132). Through these state-led processes of restructuring in Oaxaca, recalcitrant elements were subordinated, subdued, or silenced.

Postrevolution, three distinct patterns of land tenure had evolved throughout Mexico: private property, *ejidal* property, and communal property (in the form of agrarian communities). The latter two have predominated in Oaxaca, accounting for 75 percent of the total area to this day. Between 1900 and 1992, only the states of Durango and Chihuahua experienced more land redistribution. Furthermore, the process of redistribution created more beneficiaries in Oaxaca than in any other state (Instituto Nacional de Estadística y Geografía 1994: 379–80). For reasons such as these, Lynn Stephen (1998: 23) has claimed that subaltern actors in Oaxaca came to have a positive view of the Mexican state, and while not fully acquiescent to it, they viewed it as an ally in the struggle against the elite classes. However, the redistribution of land was far from the only spatial development in Oaxaca during this time. Throughout the period of ISI, resources were increasingly mobilized to serve the new project of building a nationally oriented market. More important than the breakup of the haciendas for the reconfiguration of space in Oaxaca was the investment in large-scale infrastructural projects that have acted as key forces propelling capitalization and urbanization. The state was markedly opened up from 1940 onward by the construction of the Pan-American Highway (Clarke 1992: 148, 157). Arthur Murphy and Alex Stepick (1991: 78) submit that the completion of the highway "literally paved the way for Oaxaca's reintegration with the national economy." Commerce rapidly increased as a result of this highway (Smith 2009: 271). As well as providing for the circulation of goods to and from the state, the highway was also hugely influential in facilitating the rise of tourism in Oaxaca (Kemper and Royce 1979: 280). Other large infrastructural projects included the construction of huge dams to provide hydroelectricity and water for irrigation projects (e.g., the Alemán Dam in Tuxtepec and the Benito Juárez Dam in the Isthmus of Tehuantepec), as well as the creation of a large oil refinery at Salina Cruz. These projects had important consequences for the class composition of particular places. As similar developments had during the Porfiriato, these developments could only proceed through the dispossession of people from the land, with the additional result being an increase in land speculation in the surrounding areas. Furthermore, in an effort to recuperate the costs of the projects, the government sought to reorient agricultural production to more commercial ends (López Monjardin 1993: 69–70; Rubin 1993: 160). Leigh Binford and Howard Campbell (1993: 16) explain how class relations were altered by these spatial developments: "Agrarian capitalism, followed by modern industrial capitalism, penetrated the hitherto merchant dominated economy as the government sought to convert the Isthmus into a full-blown development pole." I would now like to consider how these aforementioned issues combined with new social struggles to form a dialectic of passive revolution, *trasformismo*, and resistance that provides the background to contemporary forms of sociospatial conflict.

Following national trends, Oaxaca has not escaped the process of urbanization. However, this process has not been driven by industrialization, as elsewhere in Mexico. Indeed, the state still lacks a real industrial base, with only textile production, mines, power plants, and sugar refineries providing what industrial production there is (Smith 2009: 52). Instead, state services, commerce, and, importantly, tourism have engendered the state's transformation. Nevertheless, Oaxaca remains an overwhelmingly rural economy. Generally speaking, to possess land in Oaxaca has always meant to be a *minifundista* (small landholder), with the land base too small to provide for all of the subsistence needs of a family or community (Cook 1984: 62). Maize cultivation in Oaxaca, for example, can only provide enough subsistence for around half the year (Cohen 2010: 154). A dramatic population increase has placed even more pressure on peasant communities (as will be seen in the following chapter, the campesinos of highland Chiapas have suffered a similar problem). Lacking the endogenous capacities to satisfy their needs, many rural community members have increasingly had to look outside their communities for employment opportunities (Clarke 2000: 109, 139). This demographic change has led to what Jeffrey Cohen (2004: 5) calls a "culture of migration" in Oaxaca, defined as a pervasive phenomenon in which migration is viewed as a vital strategy for socioeconomic advancement.

Like much of Mexico, Oaxaca went through a politically tumultuous period during the 1970s and 1980s as ISI—as both an accumulation strategy and a hegemonic project—began to stutter. During this time class conflict was manifested in a number of social movements seeking social justice. Land invasions increased markedly, as did student activism. The expansion of police powers, the intervention of the army, and the co-optation of independent organizations were the concomitant responses from the federal government (Martínez Vásquez 1990; Martin 2006: 63). Following the 1968 student massacre at Tlatelolco Square in Mexico City, a radical student organization known as the Federación Estudiantil Oaxaqueña (FEO, Oaxacan Student Federation) emerged in Oaxaca. Members not only got involved in a high-profile campaign to reduce bus fares but

also formed an alliance with the ultimately unsuccessful struggle of the indigenous vendors to resist the relocation of their market from the center of the city
to the periphery—a move insisted upon by merchants for reasons of "hygiene"
(Clarke 1996: 273). Other popular movements such as the Coalición de Obreros, Campesinos y Estudiantes de Oaxaca (COCEO, Coalition of Workers, Peasants, and Students of Oaxaca) also emerged during this period and played a key
role in coordinating disparate social groups. However, without doubt the most
important social movement to emerge in Oaxaca was the Coalición Obrera
Campesina Estudiantil del Istmo (COCEI, Worker-Peasant-Student Coalition of
the Isthmus), which was founded in 1973. The COCEI emerged as a political
response to the changing class relations in the Isthmus. In particular, the movement was a reaction to transformations in space, specifically, the capitalization
of agriculture. Land, as well as access to it and its products, was thus at the heart
of this conflict. As previously explained, the infrastructural development in the
area such as the dam and irrigation projects had developed in tandem with the
needs of the national hegemonic project of seeking to increase the productivity
of the land (Lees 1976: 202–3). It was thought that capital-intensive agriculture
would provide both cheap food for domestic consumption and produce for
export (Binford 1993: 89). This process of commercialization, however, was an
assault on "the most elemental conditions of reproduction" of the largely indigenous peasantry (López Monjardin 1993: 69). Members of the COCEI emerged
in this atmosphere to defend place and local identity. They took part in land
invasions, blocked roads, and involved themselves in union organization while
articulating demands for increased autonomy (Binford and Campbell 1993: 3;
Rubin 1999: 189). The highly localized forms of authoritarianism that had been
developed in Juchitán—reliant as it was upon indigenous cacique rule—had
resulted in corporate institutions affiliated to the PRI being weak or absent. The
COCEI thus developed an important social function as a social movement capable of raising class consciousness in the region (Rubin 1993: 160–62). It was
able to win widespread support from workers and campesinos, culminating in
the electoral defeat of the PRI in the municipality of Juchitán in 1981. The national state's response to this defeat ranged from reform to outright repression,
especially in response to land invasions (Rubin 1999: 182), confirming Gramsci's (1971: 263, Q 6, §88) definition of the state as "hegemony protected by the
armour of coercion."

   It is worth dwelling upon this struggle, as in many ways the COCEI, as a
pioneer for indigenous autonomy, the defense of territory, and cultural recognition, was a direct precursor of the conflicts that are currently taking place in
Oaxaca (Renique 2007; Stephen 2013: 55). That earlier struggle also prefigured
today's struggle because what took place then was a distinct clash of spatial
projects. On the one hand, capital sought to expand into Oaxaca, transforming
it into a space into which the accumulation of surplus value could proceed. On

the other hand, the corollary of this spatial transformation was the transformation of people and their dispossession from their cultural patrimony (Harvey 2003: 137–82; Castro-Soto 2005). The COCEI had some notable successes as a social movement, including leading the first Left-governed municipality under PRI rule, achieving greater cultural recognition for Zapotec people, increasing literacy, and constructing public works projects (Stephen 2013: 59). However, we should also note that the movement eventually became incorporated into the structures of the state, including governing alongside the PRI from 1989 in a classic example of *trasformismo*.

Although the COCEI was repressed between 1981 and 1989, notably via the Mexican army, during Carlos Salinas's regime the state engaged in a much subtler method of passive revolutionary statecraft. Following the contested presidential election of 1988, which many saw as fraudulently stolen from Cuauhtémoc Cárdenas, Salinas launched the *concertación social* (social pact). As Jeffrey Rubin (1997: 190–91) points out, under this program, the COCEI received government funding and recognition. However, the explicit price for this support was a reduction in the group's militancy. As theorized in the previous chapter, this reduction led to the state ultimately leading the processes of renewal in Oaxaca, partially fulfilling but ultimately displacing the more radical agenda of the subaltern classes. This localized articulation of passive revolution can be linked to conditions of uneven and combined hegemony. After all, what Salinas was responding to was the national challenge proposed by the new party of Cárdenas, the Partido de la Revolución Democrática (PDR, Party of the Democratic Revolution). In this atmosphere, radical social movements operating throughout Mexico were also deemed a threat. The COCEI's cooperation with the state quickly led to co-optation, allowing the state to divide and conquer the COCEI and undermine it as a radical force.

However, this history clearly has had an influence on current social movement activism in Juchitán. One of the major forms of contemporary social conflict in Oaxaca revolves around the construction of wind farms by multinational corporations such as Iberdrola, Mareña Renovables, Gas Natural Fenosa, and EDF Energies Nouvelles. These wind farms have largely been constructed in Juchitán, where environmental conditions are most propitious. The construction process has proved to be controversial, however, with some residents claiming that the corporations have failed to inform residents about the projects, blocked residents' access to sacred historical sites, contaminated the fishing sources on which Juchitán is dependent, and failed to deliver on their promises of benefits to communities (Rojas 2005). One of the major groups fighting against wind farm construction is the Asamblea Popular de los Pueblos de Juchitán (APPJ, Popular Assembly of the Peoples of Juchitán). One of the leaders of the APPJ, Carlos Sánchez Martínez (interview with the author, Oaxaca, 2015), explained that the movement arose in 2006 because of the lack of information provided by

Wind farms in Juchitán.

the government in relation to megaprojects in the isthmus such as the 2001 Plan Puebla Panama (PPP), a regional infrastructural project aimed at integrating southern Mexico and Central America.[5] The area was, and still is, being targeted as a key zone of development, yet the people were not consulted and had no idea how these projects would affect their land. Sánchez Martínez stated with regards to this, "We are not against technology. We are against foreigners with money, foreign companies trying to do things with our territory without asking us." In particular, members of the APPJ speak out against the claim that the wind farms represent a green form of energy because of the perceived contamination these wind farms are alleged to have caused, as well as their effect on access to communal land. Sánchez Martínez concluded: "We are being asked to sacrifice ourselves for their pollution. It is a dispossession. We need to hold the wealthy accountable, and we need to defend ourselves." Another APPJ leader, Raymundo Regalado Jiménez, was a former militant in the COCEI (and remains a part of Section 22, the teachers' union). However, he argues that the COCEI has lost credibility; moreover, there has been a general discrediting of political parties. It was in light of this disillusionment, he says, that the APPJ was formed, following the line "no to politicians, no to political parties, and no to elections. . . . We have honored this because of what power has done to other movements"

(Regalado Jiménez, interview with the author, Oaxaca, 2015). This statement clearly reveals the manner in which resistance has evolved over the past few decades and how contemporary struggles are often self-consciously aware of the passive revolutionary tactics employed by the state. In their new strategies, resistance movements are taking steps to avoid these tactics.

The following section seeks to elaborate on these themes and further explore how Oaxaca has been affected by the national turn to neoliberalism. This involves a localized articulation of passive revolution that the previous chapter established Mexico was undergoing at a national level after the debt crisis. Using the arguments presented in chapter 3, I will demonstrate here how Oaxaca has become what Neil Brenner (1997: 280) calls a "spatial target" for a renewed round of accumulation. As Lefebvre (1991: 105) makes clear, ideologies intervene in space in the form of development strategies (see also chapter 3). It is therefore pertinent for us to examine the ideologies of groups that seek to influence the area's development. The World Bank's Southern States Development Strategy (Hall and Humphrey 2003) is perhaps paradigmatic in this regard. Its overarching concern is with the opening of Oaxaca to the vicissitudes of the world market. Gillette Hall and Christopher Humphrey's report makes it clear that infrastructure must be improved in order to encourage investment. Unclear property rights are also said to hinder investment and promote social conflict. The report recommends the reorientation of the economy toward export-based agriculture and production, the latter of which is to be aided by valorizing the low wage base of the area. It is clear from this report that the history of social/ spatial relations in the state is thus of vital importance in dictating the strategy for accumulation there, because that strategy seeks to draw on Oaxaca's lack of developed capitalist social relations in order to insert Oaxaca all the more advantageously into the global system (Massey 1994: 56–57). This strategy is, of course, nothing other than the logic of uneven and combined development, through which new spatial divisions of labor are attempted to be constructed. However, this local history is equally salient to informing the alternative counterspaces of resistance. I will show here that, in contrast to the omnipotent, homogenizing force that neoliberalism is often presented to be, a concrete analysis of Oaxaca reveals both neoliberalism's highly local particularities and its limitations in the face of oppositional subaltern forces. Oaxaca has thus become the site of struggle for survival between two very different spatial projects, both of which seem inimical to each other. Ana María García Arreola from EDUCA, an NGO with twenty years' experience of working with social movements in the region, claims that in Oaxaca there are "two projects of life in conflict: the project of capital and the project of indigenous life." On the one hand, capital must expand into new areas if it is not to perish (owing to capital's inherent dynamics as a mode of production, discussed in chapter 1). On the other hand, the conditions of this expansion would consign an alternative way of life to history. It is through this examination of the refusal of capitalist domination that we can also identify a different theorization of what it means to engage in class struggle.

Indigenous Place versus Neoliberal Space

It is often assumed that the onset of the debt crisis and the fiscal austerity that followed it were felt evenly both spatially and temporally throughout Mexico. However, while public spending was slashed at the national level, the state budget for Oaxaca actually increased in a populist effort to relieve social tensions and stop them from spilling over into the "national agenda." As Richard Snyder (1999: 314) points out, in 1989, during the governorship of Heladio Ramírez López (1986–92), the Oaxaca state government actually received more money than it could spend and was forced to return three billion of the twenty-one billion pesos it had been given. This highlights how national concerns can translate into different strategies for maintaining hegemony in accordance with the struggle of social forces in a particular locale (once again giving meaning to the notion of uneven and combined hegemony stressed in the introduction). We cannot assume that so-called national order changes are experienced evenly throughout the country. A further example of the national changes that were not experienced evenly at the local level is the process of democratization, analyzed by one scholar as the "quintessence of hegemonic practice designed to frame and condition the institutional context of opposition movements" (Morton 2005: 190). While this practice may hold true from a perspective that only examines the national scale, we must also be mindful that the process of democratization at the national level that has accompanied the neoliberal reforms has been a far from even process (Gibson 2005). While we are aware of the importance of wider spatial scales, we must also be wary of adopting a "center-centered approach" that ignores the continuation of "illiberal peripheries" (Snyder 2001: 101). As Oaxacan sociologist Victor Raul Martínez Vásquez (2007: 16) has argued, "It is evident that in some places, like Oaxaca, in recent years not only have the changes seen at the national level not occurred, but the characteristics of the old authoritarian regime have been deepened." This was exemplified in the governorships of José Murat (1988–2004) and Ulises Ruiz Ortiz (2004–10).[6] It is against the background both of localized authoritarianism and of the *attempted* neoliberalization of the nation that we must understand the formation of the APPO.

Demographically, Oaxaca is Mexico's most indigenous state, with over a third of the population identifying as such. It is also diverse, with sixteen separate indigenous groups recognized. This fact meant that the local hegemony of the national PRI could be secured in Oaxaca only in compromise with these groups throughout the ISI period. As Gustavo Esteva (interview with the author, Oaxaca, 2008) explains, it was realized that governing could only take place in Oaxaca "*with* the indigenous people, not *to* them." We can extrapolate from this evaluation that the very process of state formation in Mexico took place under conditions of competing visions of citizenship, nation, and sovereignty (Chassen-López 2004: 314; Eisenstadt 2013; Yashar 2005). A compromise existed whereby certain demands for autonomous decision-making processes were accepted in the communities in exchange for their loyalty to the PRI. As Todd Eisenstadt (2007: 62) explains, under this settlement "votes were harvested by local caciques or chieftains invariably affiliated with the PRI and acting as the communities' interlocutor with the party and the state government (which were fused together as one)." Under this system of semiautonomous governance, other indigenous practices such as community assembly (a forum for discussing all pertinent issues, as well as a group to which all *cargo* holders must submit themselves) and *tequios* (collective work projects for community needs) were maintained.[7] PRI hegemony within the wider society thus could be continued only as long as the indigenous peoples' social conditions could be assured. However, this has been increasingly threatened with the inroads of capitalist development. As one indigenous community member explained, migration and money (in the form of remittances) have affected the horizontality of the community structure and created hierarchies that have often formed into centers of power. Returning migrants are sometimes more reluctant to participate in *tequios* or *cargos* or to pay for the upkeep of the community (Kiado Cruz, interview with the author, Oaxaca, 2009). This dynamic has led some communities to find novel ways of asserting political agency in order to control the timing and rhythm of the migratory process, including sanctions against those not contributing to *tequios* and *cargos* due to their absence (Mutersbaugh 2002: 473, 485). This threat to community reproduction must be placed within a national context in which peasant agriculture has come under attack. This threat was further increased after 1992 with the ending of agrarian reform and moves toward neoliberal policies nationally. This meant the already highly marginalized conditions of existence for Oaxacan campesinos were made even worse.

As has been highlighted hitherto, Oaxaca had experienced heightened social conflict in the 1960s and 1970s. This conflict culminated with the declaration of martial law in response to the power of the COCEO in 1977 (Cook 1984: 73). Alejandro Anaya Muñoz (2005: 594–97) argues that this proliferation of independent popular organizations highlights the PRI's declining legitimacy. At the same time, the First International Forum on the Human Rights of Indigenous Peoples, held in the state in 1989, is cited as evidence of growing political mobilization by indigenous actors. The PRI then began to lose municipal elections in the state. An indication of the declining ability of the PRI to maintain its control over the Oaxacan countryside came in 1995, when the federal government officially recognized the right of the municipalities to choose their authorities based on their own *usos y costumbres*. Although, as we have seen, this practice had often been the reality for many communities before this time, the significance here was that communities could now elect their own representatives without the mediation of political parties. As was mentioned in the introduction, of Oaxaca's 570 municipalities, 418 opted to use this traditional system, which allowed political decisions to be expressed in their own cultural framework. As Luis Hernández Navarro (1999: 159) cogently argues, this process only recognized what existed in practice anyway and, moreover, was the lesser of two evils for the PRI, as it prevented indigenous communities from uniting electorally under an oppositional party banner. Furthermore, Eisenstadt (2007: 55) points out that this legalization followed rapidly on the heels of the Zapatista rebellion (discussed in the next chapter) and thus can be interpreted as a defensive strategy of the Mexican state to avert a wider escalation of indigenous rebellion and prevent the so-called contagion effect of Zapatismo (Muñoz 2005: 596). This legalization must clearly, therefore, be seen as a local articulation of passive revolution. The recognition of *usos y costumbres* was an element of statecraft designed to delimit both wider radical demands and the in-roads of opposition parties (Eisenstadt 2013: 9). As Victor Leonel Juan Martínez (2013: 139) concludes, the "constitutional and institutional design is used both to recognise the exercise of autonomy and to inhibit its true realisation." In tandem with these reforms was a systematic process of repression. In its efforts to counter the rise of Oaxacan guerrilla movements, particularly the Ejército Popular Revolucionario (EPR, Popular Revolutionary Army), which announced their presence in 1996, the Oaxacan state government, rather than seeking to address the material causes of anger, began a campaign of low-intensity warfare against the local population in areas where suspected members were thought to dwell, such as Loxicha.[8] It is vital that we recognize the role of political agency here and the dialectic of struggle involved. First, recognition of *usos y costumbres* was tied to the bottom-up resistance of indigenous communities in Oaxaca.[9] At the same time, limited recognition of indigenous demands made possible their recuperation into state-based projects without wider spatial linkages being formed (Martínez 2013: 140). This policy practice conforms to what Charles Hale (2004) has described as the "indio permitido" (authorized Indian), which signifies the manner in which neoliberalism both enables and limits indigenous subjects. As his wider analysis has demonstrated, the neoliberal state has been content to provide recognition of limited rights, provided they do not contradict the wider economic model of neoliberalism or threaten the wider power structure at large (Hale 2005: 18). This recognition authorizes certain members of a community, but as Hale notes, "When indigenous leaders or intellectuals occupy that authorized space of compromise, they win an important battle in the struggle for recognition. Yet when they exchange protest for proposal, they often lose the inclination to articulate more expansive, utopian political visions with the pragmatic tactics of the here and now" (2005: 20). This process conforms, in other words, to the wider analysis of passive revolution articulated throughout the previous chapter. However, it has been the case in the last decade that the economic model of neoliberalism has in fact been challenged along with the major centers of political power. This means we must explore why this strategy of passive revolution has proven to be unsuccessful or, conversely, why indigenous movements have sought to further their claims for autonomy.

Lynn Stephen (1998: 23) has claimed that historically the national government was viewed in a more positive light in Oaxaca than in neighboring Chiapas owing to issues of land redistribution. However, such support now appears to be seriously waning in some areas as the social conditions of the two states have begun to converge. This needs to be put into the context of the changing national hegemonic project the state is increasingly trying to draw Oaxaca into. One particularly salient feature of the neoliberal turn in Mexico has been that of land reform (or, more accurately, counterrevolution). As described at the end of the previous chapter, the revisions to Article 27 formally ended petitions for land redistribution. However, land reform under Salinas (1988–94) went even further in decimating the social contract that had been built with the peasants, further evidencing the reorientation of the federal government's projects and the recomposition of the national state's social base (Jessop 1990: 207; Stanford 1994: 98; Richard 2008: 401). As well as ending the government's responsibility to redistribute land, reform also made provision for formerly inalienable *ejido* land to be rented or sold. Furthermore, while maintaining limits on the maximum amount of land an individual could hold (100 hectares), corporations could now own up to 2,500 hectares as long as twenty-five individuals were associate members in the new venture (Otero 1999: 47). Despite the rhetoric of support for autonomous *ejidal* organization, these communities lacked the resources to compete successfully in the transition to a fully capitalist market. The new discourse of individual rights was thus insensitive to the highly differentiated capacities to enjoy these rights. The prime motivation for this change in policy was to encourage foreign investment in the agricultural sector and thus increase productivity in a bid to reorient production toward exportation. As Ana de Ita (2006: 158) argues, the agrarian reforms seek to transform the status of land from a social right to a commodity. The *ejidal* sector was also felt to be an unproductive albatross around the neck of a government that was no longer sustainable in the new economic climate. Part of this problem came from the state ownership of the land, meaning *ejidatarios* had only usufruct rights. This legal status prevented them from using the land as collateral to obtain credit (Hansen 1971: 82; Stanford 1994: 100). However, we should not assume that *ejidos* were unproductive; instead, the institutional complex in which they operated was hugely unfavorable to them, as it favored large farms (as was discussed in the previous chapter). Thus, it must be stressed that the decision to attempt to end peasant agriculture does not relate to its "natural" decline as a mode of production "but rather is a clear case of a planned obsolescence" (Richard 2008: 396).

Organizations like the World Bank have argued that the opaque nature of property rights in the southern states is an impediment to investment and increased prosperity (Hall and Humphrey 2003). The Mexican government has sought to rectify this problem through the Programa de Certificación de Derecho Ejidales y Titulación de Solares Urbanos (PROCEDE, Program for the Certification of Agrarian Rights), renamed the Fondo de Apoyo para los Núcleos Agrarios sin Regularizar (FANAR, Support Fund for Nonregularized Agrarian Nuclei). This was a supposedly voluntary program into which communities could enter to officially have their lands demarcated and a title granted.[10] Certification of *ejidal* land is a precondition for the decision to then privatize or rent out the land. Armando de la Cruz Cortés (interview with the author, Oaxaca, 2015) from Tequio Jurídico, an NGO that promotes indigenous autonomy and collective rights to land in Oaxaca, has labeled these programs "the legalization of dispossession." The unclear boundaries of many of the *ejidos* have made them extremely difficult to levy tax upon. Rosaria Pisa (1994: 267, 287) sagely interprets revisions to agrarian property rights as an effort to reclaim territory for taxation purposes. Therefore, this policy needs to be placed in the context of evolving state formation.

In contrast to the school of thought that postulates neoliberalism as leading to a decline of the state, it must be stressed that the introduction of the PROCEDE/FANAR had the opposite effect, increasing the state's regulation and bureaucratization of the countryside, involving as it did the creation of three new institutions, including the agrarian attorney general, the national agrarian registry, and agrarian tribunals (Pisa 1994: 267, 273). Again, the process of "seeing like a state" can be observed, only this time with a distinctly capitalist social purpose in mind. As James Scott (1998: 51) writes with regard to this purpose, "Where the premodern state was content with a level of intelligence sufficient to allow it to keep order, extract taxes, and raise armies, the modern state increasingly aspired to 'take in charge' the physical and human resources of a nation and make them more productive. These more positive ends of statecraft required a much greater knowledge of the society." As a region with a large rural population, Oaxaca has been clearly affected by these developments, although, due to the nature of the different land tenure patterns, the effects have been experienced differently here from how they were in the highlands of Chiapas (as will be discussed in the next chapter). It is also clear from the argument that has been laid out earlier that efforts to transform space unfold in both a spatially and a temporally uneven fashion. However, there has been a consensus among policy planners that the space of Oaxaca must be reshaped in line with those areas in which the state enjoys "comparative advantage" so as to help increase revenues within the reconfigured national accumulation strategy (discussed in the previous chapter). Practically, this plan translates into the exploitation of the state's low wage base, natural resources, and cultural patrimony.

Efforts to reshape the space of Oaxaca are perhaps best encapsulated in the Plan Puebla Panama (PPP, renamed Plan Mesoamerica, discussed more in chapter 5). For international financial institutions, transnational corporations, and state planners, the resource-rich area of the Isthmus of Tehuantepec is central to this project. As one APPO advisor from the region clarified, although there are development projects throughout Oaxaca affiliated to the PPP, the Isthmus is the area in which the majority of projects are concentrated because of its natural resources, including wind energy, hydroelectric dams, and petrochemicals (Valencia Nuñez, interview with the author, Oaxaca, 2009). PPP seeks to transform the space of Oaxaca into part of the southern tourist corridor, necessitating the creation of high-speed *autopistas* (highways) alongside a new *maquiladora* industry.

However, while PPP illustrates the changes the PROCEDE can facilitate, Oaxaca has been far from universally acquiescent to it. In fact, it is the state with the smallest adoption of the program, with only 20.5 percent of the required surface area being certified (Ita 2006: 155). It is becoming clearer that the historical defense of place and the long struggle against exploitation have provided a collective form of social organization through which capitalism can be resisted. Indeed, it is by virtue of the democratic control of their own communities that the indigenous population is able to deny capital the right to expand. As Gustavo Esteva (interview with the author, Oaxaca, 2009) puts it, the spatial structure of the assembly is both an end and a political tool. One example of this is the opposition to Libramiento Sur, a superhighway project costing 548 million pesos, announced officially by the secretary of public works and Caminos y Aeropistas de Oaxaca (CAO, Roads and Airstrips of Oaxaca) in October 2009 (*Noticias* 2010a). This highway was intended to dramatically reduce the time it takes to get to coastal beach resorts such as Puerto Escondido and Huatulco. As should be obvious, a development like this can only take place through the production of space and the transformation of places (indeed, this is its raison d'être). The PROCEDE creates the conditions under which a project like this can be made possible through the alienation or renting of lands. However, Zaachila, one community that is threatened to be directly affected by this highway, began the process of organizing against the development (along with other municipalities). Residents of a large section of this municipality allied themselves with the APPO in a bid to widen their struggle and articulate it within a statewide atmosphere of resistance. Previously a PRI stronghold, a "failure of power" was acknowledged in the community in 2006, and the mayor, José Coronel, was removed from his post as the people decided to revert to using their own *usos y*

Protesting against the proposed superhighway Libramiento Sur.

costumbres, declaring themselves to be an autonomous municipality. In August 2007 the PRI retook power amidst wide allegations of fraud, yet the community has maintained its fierce resistance to the project, with Governor Ulises Ruiz Ortiz being prevented from entering the municipality after barricades were erected and a violent confrontation took place between PRI members and APPO supporters. Meanwhile, the authority of the community assembly has been invoked to challenge any potential threats to the community's lands. The *ejidatarios* of the community claimed that the community assembly had no knowledge of the project, nor did it have the approval of the municipal president (*Noticias* 2009). Representatives from the community were highly visible at the *plantón* (encampment) of 2009 and have managed to put their struggle at the forefront of social movement activism as increasing connections are being made to different localized patterns of exploitation. A mantra often heard around the historic Zócalo, or main plaza, in Oaxaca City during the *plantón* of 2009 was, "Ruiz entiende, la tierra no se vende" (Ruiz understand, the land is not for sale). When the project was finally announced officially, the community assembly voted unanimously to reject it, arguing that it would not only cause irreparable damage to the agriculture, ecology, and water systems of the area but also provoke the community to stop producing things that have cultural value (*Noticias* 2010b). As one *ejidatario* argued, "It is something more than just a field, it is a feeling we carry inside of us. It is a love of our land" (*Noticias* 2010b). This view of land is widely shared among the indigenous population of Oaxaca and indeed throughout Mexico. Speaking of this collective power, Oaxacan intellectual Benjamin Maldonado (interview with the author, Oaxaca, 2008) stated, "The community is fundamental in Oaxaca, not only to construct a social movement that is based in it but moreover because the struggles have been reoriented toward the recuperation of the power of the community . . . and the strengthening of communal life." In other words, communities are able to draw upon traditions of resistance and collective power that have been developed over centuries of struggle, and those traditions are now used to inform present ones. An indigenous community member from the Sierra Norte (Cruz, interview with the author, Oaxaca, 2009) claims that these conflicts are intensifying, as laws are closing down ways to officially gain land, and little land is left to redistribute. He argues that in the context of an expansionary capitalist system, communities defending their land and territory have the potential to form powerful social movements. Indeed, it is this commonality of experience that gives highly place-specific movements that ability to "jump scales" and link to other groups suffering similar experiences. In this case, not only was the community of Zaachila able to link with other groups in the state of Oaxaca facing dispossession, but an alliance was formed with the Frente del Pueblo en Defensa de La Tierra (FPDT, People's Front in Defense of the Land) in Atenco. Atenco, an adherent of the Zapatistas' "Other Campaign" (to be discussed in the following chapter), received national attention when residents successfully blocked President Vicente Fox's plan to construct an airport on their lands and subsequently announced themselves to be an autonomous municipality. The defense of place, therefore, does not preclude wider links being forged; instead, movements can be Janus-faced, simultaneously both introverted and extroverted (Castree 2004: 150).

As mentioned earlier, neoliberal modernizing developments have taken place in Oaxaca under the auspices of highly authoritarian governors. The apogee of this authoritarianism was reached under the governorship of Ulises Ruiz Ortiz (commonly referred to as URO). From the outset of his dubious election (widespread fraud was alleged), his time in office was characterized by the systematic violation of human rights and heavy use of repression against social protest. Epitomizing these actions was the fact that the state came in last place nationally for both transparency and access to information (Martínez Vásquez 2007: 19). Adding to residents' anger was the remodeling of the historical symbols of Oaxaca City, described as the systematic destruction of the state's natural and historical patrimony, actions that benefited URO's cronies (Esteva 2007: 84). Significantly, these projects included moving a key site of authority, the Palacio de Gobierno (Government Palace), from the Zócalo (the historic center of social protest) to a suburb on the outskirts of the town in a bid to "cleanse" public space from undesirable elements (Poole 2009: 147). Deborah Poole (2007b: 10–11) highlights the manner in which cultural diversity came to be promoted in Oaxaca as a commodity and packaged within a framework of individualized rights in a bid to promote the image of the state as a "traditional" indigenous tourist mecca. Furthermore, in 2004 URO introduced the Pact of Oaxaca, in an attempt to prohibit public protests, which were thought to represent a danger to foreign investment.

This clash between Oaxaca's deepening authoritarianism, with its neoliberal features, and increasing societal demands was most visibly manifested with the formation of the APPO in 2006. On May 22, for the twenty-sixth year in a row, the teachers' union began their annual strike, demanding better terms for teachers and improvements in conditions for students and other issues related to teaching, such as better classrooms. Spatial concerns, in fact, were prime motives for the struggle in 2006. As they had done the year before, the teachers demanded the reclassification of various parts of the state. Citing the pressure of tourism as leading to rising prices, the teachers argued that specific places should be rezoned, and higher wages should be paid in those areas.[11] In line with this proposal, a series of megamarches were also coordinated to protest against the repression endured under URO. However, in an atmosphere where social protest had effectively been criminalized, rather than listening to the demands of the teachers, the government, in an extraordinary move, tried to violently dislodge the *plantón* on June 14. The act of public repression has been described by one observer as signifying "a crisis not only of the government but of the political regime" in Oaxaca (Martínez Vásquez 2007: 9).

Following these events (and seeking to galvanize a wider movement), the teachers convened an assembly on June 20 to which they invited various official groups that they hoped to utilize to support their struggle. However, rather than the twenty or so organizations that had been invited to attend, over three hundred civil society organizations arrived, armed with a plethora of social grievances (Gustavo Esteva, interview with the author, Oaxaca, 2008). What had begun as a trade union struggle was thus converted into a wider movement of discontent (Esteva 2007: 80). URO's authoritarian governorship acted as a centripetal force for all of the state's oppositional social forces. Organized political groups that had been repressed under Murat and URO all came together under the APPO banner, including the Frente Amplio de Lucha Popular (FALP), the Consejo Indígena Popular de Oaxaca (CIPO), the Frente Popular Revoluncionario (FPR), the Organización Indígena de Derechos Humanos de Oaxaca (OIDHO), the Comité Democrático Ciudadano (CODECI), the Consejo de Defensa del Pueblo (CODEP), la Organización de Pueblos Indígenas Zapoteca (OPIZ), the Ayuntamiento Popular de San Blas Atempa, and the Nueva Izquierda de Oaxaca, as well as an even longer list of civil society organizations (Martínez Vásquez 2007: 70). As Robert Stout (2010: 37) argues, "The APPO became a symbol of popular cohesion and a trigger for political change." Thousands of barricades were erected throughout the city in a spontaneous rejection of governmental authority. All official government activities were suspended for five months, as a state of "ungovernability" was declared by the APPO. From simply having the *plantón* taking over public space, new encampments were set up around the headquarters of legislative power, the Government Palace, the judicial buildings, and the official house to which the governor had been sent in Santa María Coyotepec (Martínez Vásquez 2007: 80, 89). Human circles were formed around all of the symbols of state power, and public space was forcefully reclaimed in an assertion of what Lefebvre (1996) refers to as the "right to the city." Recalling these events, one participant of the barricades described them as "the moment when the people from below took their lives in their own hands" (Venegas, interview with the author, Oaxaca, 2009). These barricades to defend public space also became the places where for many, political consciousness and the skills for practical collective action began to be developed. Radio and TV stations were also captured to aid in the propaganda war that the government quickly launched. These stations became autonomous space through which a genuine "people's news" was broadcast (Norget 2008; Stout 2010: 32). One of these stations, Radio Universidad, became the most listened to in the city and the central valleys (Martínez Vásquez 2007: 93).

While the mobilization was not only about the demands of the teachers, it would not have come about were it not for the struggle of Section 22, a militant wing of the Coordinadora Nacional de Trabajadores de la Educación (CNTE, National Coordination of Education Workers), itself part of the wider national teachers' union, Sindicato Nacional de Trabajadores de la Educación (SNTE, National Union of Education Workers). It is worth noting that the CNTE itself was formed explicitly in opposition to what some teachers perceived to be a selling out to the state of the official union (Stephen 2013: 40). Historically, teachers have been at the forefront of popular mobilization in Oaxaca. Owing to the lack of industry in Oaxaca, the teachers' union, with roughly seventy thousand members, approximates the nearest thing Oaxaca has to a class-based opposition to the government. Stephen (2013: 37) has argued that Section 22 is the only organization that is capable of mobilizing coordinated action in all of Oaxaca's municipalities. Furthermore, the experience of teachers, living and working in the poorest areas of the state, helps to develop their social consciousness. Thus, as Victor Raul Martínez Vásquez (2007: 59) concludes, over the years the teachers' movement has been converted into "a catalyst for nonconformity and social protest."

Owing to the organization's spontaneous creation, there remained a great deal of confusion as to what the APPO actually was. Esteva (2007: 74) makes it clear, however, that rather than an organization, the APPO must be thought of as a movement, or a movement of movements. Picking up on this theme of plurality, Kristin Norget (2010) argues that despite its amorphous nature, the APPO was often presented as a coherent movement. This was confirmed by those who participated in the movement. They have agreed that "it was not born with a clear objective" (Venegas, interview with the author, Oaxaca, 2009). One clear demand was, of course, the exit of URO. As Esteva (interview with the author, Oaxaca, 2008) said, "This was perhaps the only thing we all had in common." Following a national forum, more general strategic orientations of the movement were formed and demands were broadened. These demands included a minimum standard of well-being, respect for cultural diversity, equality, non-violent resolution to conflicts, a social administration of natural resources, municipal autonomy, multicultural education, the real participation of citizens in political life, and sustainable development (Martínez Vásquez 2007: 98).

Many of the demands that began to be formulated had a long history in Oaxaca, such as teachers' and women's struggles, indigenous rights, and demands for increased autonomy. As Deborah Poole (2007c) notes, "Although the APPO is in many respects a new type of organisation, its novel form is made possible by its grounding in a familiar language of popular democracy, dissent and *rebeldía*." The emergence of the APPO points us toward the failure of social inclusion in Oaxaca and the breakdown of representative democracy. The widespread support the teachers received and the antiauthoritarian response it provoked thus have to be placed in the context of the increasing inability of the local government to attend to the demands of the society. The rise of the APPO can be interpreted as the absence of hegemony and an increasing turn toward repression (Martínez Vásquez 2007: 79).[12] This situation of repression "is just one of the contradictions of the present political and social climate in Mexico, a nation showing the severe contradictions and pains of an unprecedented period of rapid transition" (Norget 2005: 116).

One of the chief accomplishments of the APPO was to politicize everyday control over social space (Gibler 2009: 185). Along with the aforementioned barricades, this politicization was also prominently manifested over the Guala-guetza, a state-sponsored event celebrating Oaxaca's cultural diversity. The APPO held its own rival version of the event.

Analyzing the movement, Norget (2010: 119) makes the argument that while Oaxaca has had a long history of rural radicalism, "what made the APPO unique was its *urban, very heterogeneous profile*" (emphasis added). While this is true in relation to the place-specific location of the protests, to label the movement as merely an urban phenomenon is to ignore a vital component of the historical sociology of Oaxaca in terms of both indigenous migration to urban areas and Oaxaca City's role as a central hub for economic activity (as discussed earlier). Gareth Jones (2000: 201) has argued that for reasons such as these, it does not make sense to analyze urban and rural Mexico as separate from one another. The period of ISI witnessed the ruralization of cities as peasants migrated in search of work during the 1970s, and many Oaxacan peasants continue to seek wage labor for part of the year (Cohen 2010). More than forty of the *colonias populares* (popular neighborhoods) that formed barricades in 2006 came from indigenous communities (Valencia Núñez, interview with the author, Oaxaca, 2009). Furthermore, in relation to Section 22, which was at the forefront of the struggle, Martínez Vásquez (2007: 53, 54) points out that although teachers are often characterized as urban and middle class, "we cannot leave out of recognition that a large number of teachers come from peasant families and indigenous communities." Indigenous community members, he argues, have been important not only to the composition of Section 22 but also, more fundamentally, "in the definition of the organizational strategies, their tactics and their direction." The distinction between rural and urban is, thus, far from clear in the context of Oaxaca and demonstrates the manner in which noncapitalist spaces are able to inform radical possibilities beyond their immediate locale, creating hybrid forms of resistance. However, in many respects, the APPO as a social movement proved to be ephemeral, succumbing to a mixture of state repression and internal division. Over seventeen APPOs were created in the wake of 2006, yet the majority of them have collapsed. This should give us pause for thought. Harvey (2000: 234) has argued that social struggles restricted to one "theater of action" are always liable to being rolled back, without advances in other areas.

Since 2006 struggles have broadened and evolved in Oaxaca. Rather than being defeated, such forms of resistance (as documented earlier in relation to the APPJ) are learning from past mistakes. The current most prominent example of resistance is the struggle against mining interests and wider dispossession. Mexico has in recent years become a prime site for transnational capital investment in extractive industries. This trend has rekindled mining activity in Oaxaca, as it is an area rich in carbon, silver, and gold. During the administration of Felipe Calderón (2006–12), the volume of mining concessions increased by 53 percent nationally. This increase has dramatically impacted Oaxaca, where concessions account for over 20 percent of the territory (González 2012). We can thus note clearly the connections between the arrival of transnational capital and agrarian reform (private companies were previously banned from such associations). However, as Doreen Massey (1995: 7) reminds us, "The world is not simply the product of capital's requirements." Armando de la Cruz Cortés (interview with the author, Oaxaca, 2015) cites the towns of Capulalpam de Méndez and Magdalena Teitipac as the clearest examples of successful resistance in Oaxaca. These communities have united and utilized the internal structure of their community assemblies to force out mining corporations. Another prominent community, San José del Progreso, remains firmly in dispute with the mining corporation Fortuna Silver. These are potential examples of what David Harvey (1996: 32) calls "militant particularism," whereby "ideals forged out of the affirmative experience of solidarities in one place get generalized and universalized as a working model of a new form of society." It is vital, therefore, that struggles such as these, for example, to retain access to land, are linked to a wider analysis of political economy, allowing communities to move beyond their everyday life and connect to other movements (Harvey 2000: 74).

Francisco García López (interview with the author, Oaxaca, 2015), who is on the Comiseriado de Bienes Comunales (Communal Goods Commission) in Capulalpam, highlighted the importance of collective democratic processes when responding to questions about mining in his community: "We have a communal regime, and we are the owners of territory. Whatever decision involves the land, the assembly has to decide." Based on this, the community has refused permission to a Canadian mining corporation, Continuum Resources, to prospect for gold in the community's territory despite the mining company gaining a fifty-year concession from the Mexican state. García López explicitly counterposed the existence of this wider communal regime to the logic of capitalism: "While we keep our way of governing alive . . . we are putting a stop to the voraciousness of capitalism. Every time we have a meeting, every time we have a fiesta, the music we have, the way we live, we are stopping capitalism." This strategy of defending place thus represents an important aspect of class struggle because it is the refusal of the extension of commodification. As Harvey (1996: 401) has submitted, struggles become class projects when they entail "a direct challenge to the circulation and accumulation of capital which currently dictates what environmental transformations occur."

Capulalpam is an interesting case, because it has a long history based on mining and thus seems to have been integrated into the capitalist mode of production. This history provides the community with a clear element of class consciousness. However, in addition to this, communal (noncapitalist) class processes and social practices have remained and been reinvigorated. These practices include collective forms of resource management and decision making that continue to provide vital resources for resistance. This resistance has been strengthened by the community's feeling that it has been abandoned by the nation-state (Aquino-Centeno 2009: 155–57). As García López stated (interview, 2015), "People conserved many traditions and customs. This is a fundamental pillar, because the form with which we govern ourselves does not permit the social fabric to be ripped or broken." There is a combustible situation in Mexico whereby the state claims the right to the subsoil on behalf of the nation and has provided concessions to transnational corporations without the express consent of the affected communities. This has naturally provoked fierce forms of social conflict and potentially provides the impetus for radical action, especially as Mexico is also a signatory to the International Labour Organization's Convention 169 on Indigenous and Tribal Peoples, which recognizes collective rights and the importance of informed consent. Ellen Meiksins Wood (1995) has argued that peripheral forms of capitalist activity tend to be the sources of radical action: "Modern revolutions have tended to occur where the capitalist mode of production has been less developed; where it has coexisted with older forms of production, notably peasant production; where 'extra-economic' compulsion has played a greater role in the organisation of production and the extraction of surplus labour; and where the state has acted not only as a support for appropriating classes but as something like a pre-capitalist appropriator."

At present there are efforts among various NGOs to try to develop more thematic and regional forms of resistance that are linked to issues of natural resources, notably dams and mines (Ana María García Arreola, interview with the author, Oaxaca, 2015). However, the experience of 2006 serves to highlight both the potentiality of such resistance and its limitations. Having a radical history based on different social relations to those of capitalism provides a basis for the possibility of constructing alternative projects. As Kiado Cruz (interview with the author, Oaxaca, 2009) put it, "In Oaxaca we have thousands of hectares of communal land. . . . This implies thousands of hectares of resistance." Communities in Oaxaca are now trying to consolidate and extend these types of social relations to retake control of the production of space. The place of the community is increasingly seen as a method of defense, as the social fabric that has been maintained over the years provides a collective form of power over the community's territory. As Gustavo Esteva (interview with the author, Oaxaca, 2008) put it, "We are resisting by affirming ourselves in place but at the same time opening ourselves to others like us, meaning opening hearts, minds, and arms to create wide coalitions of all those others who share the same predicament."

Understanding the manner in which property relations evolved in Mexico, with the state acting as the arbiter of agrarian conflict and the agent of redistribution, is crucial to understanding the nature of modern resistance movements, as it is now the state that is acting as the intermediary to grant concessions to transnational corporations. While the state may have been an ally of some communities, it is now more and more identified as the principal enemy of indigenous communities in Oaxaca (Cruz, interview with the author, Oaxaca, 2009). As Scott Cook (1984: 76) has argued, centuries of perceived illegitimate rule have built up in Oaxaca an antistatist, "deep home-grown anarchism that cross cuts the rural class structure and pervades rural social consciousness." Oaxaca is clearly an example of a highly global struggle inserted into particularly local conditions. As we saw earlier, autonomy, although a long-articulated demand among the peoples of Oaxaca, is able to resonate with greater force at particular junctures. It would appear that this is one such juncture as the neoliberal project of the state forces communities to defend their land and territory from an expansive capitalist system (Yashar 2005). As Patricia Martin (2005: 217) argues, "The language of autonomy represents a clear stance both against the strengthened role of the local state and against the large scale development projects promised by national and international neo-liberal agendas."

Conclusion

Beginning in 2006, there has been a visible break with government authority in Oaxaca. At the forefront of political struggles has been the teachers' movement, often in alliance with various place-based indigenous communities that fiercely seek to defend land and territory. These movements draw strength from their localized roots, but one issue of vital importance for the future will relate to the wider alliances the Oaxacan movements will be able to form and sustain. Gustavo Esteva (interview with the author, Oaxaca, 2008) stated that one of the biggest problems with the movement in 2006 was the lack of alliances developed at the national level and beyond. Likewise, Lynn Stephen (2013: 64) notes that a major deficit with the APPO was the failure to advance an affirmative program (in spite of some attempts). How the Oaxacan struggles engage with the social maelstrom that is currently emerging in Mexico will therefore be vital to future success. It is clear that movements here must seek to "scale up" their activism, not only fighting place-specific battles but also forging wider spatial links to other centers of resistance.

The issue of wider linkages is especially important in light of the repressive force that was unleashed in 2006. Between June and November, twenty-three people were killed (often in targeted assassinations), hundreds were arrested, and many were tortured (Stephen 2013: 6). The future of Oaxaca thus remains open. It is clear that there is a growing level of political consciousness in the state that is increasingly hostile to Oaxaca becoming an increasing space of capital and instead is pursuing efforts to form alternative counterspaces of resistance. Much effort still has to be made in finding a way to coordinate the disparate interests involved, as well as mediating between urban and rural demands in the efforts to create a viable alternative geographical project. Furthermore, links will have to be built with other movements both nationally and internationally. The Zapatista movement in the neighboring state of Chiapas has perhaps done the most to inspire thinking about how this might be possible. It has managed to transcend interethnic division and instead build an alternative development trajectory based around shared aspirations. It is to that movement that the book now turns.

CHAPTER FIVE

The Clash of Spatializations

Class Power and the Production of Chiapas

> That comes from *afar*. When the river rises, it means a flood has been building in the mountains for a long, long time.
> —E. Zepeda, "It Comes from Afar"

These words, written by a Chiapaneco poet, serve as a metaphor for the Zapatista uprising of 1994. Giving testimony to the protracted process of oppression that the indigenous people of Chiapas have suffered, the Zapatistas described themselves in the "First Declaration of the Lacandon Jungle" as "the product of 500 years of struggle" (Ejército Zapatista de Liberación Nacional 1994: 13). This chapter seeks to explore this historical struggle, extending the concrete level of analysis with a second case study that investigates how the spaces of capital have sought to be extended into Chiapas and, moreover, how spaces of resistance have emerged in response to this extension. Just as the previous chapter sought to excavate where resistance movements came from in Oaxaca, what historical experiences they appealed to, and what was novel about their proposals, so this chapter seeks to do the same with a historical-geographical sociology of Chiapas. Once again, in defense of the long-term perspective that is adopted here, it is worth remembering that the indigenous conception of time in Mexico is circular rather than linear. The past, in other words, is not something dead but rather something that can be returned to and appealed to in order to reimagine the present (Bonfil Batalla 1996: 38).[1]

The importance of the Zapatistas comes not only from their actions and discourse but also from their timing. The uprising and subsequent political project of seeking to build autonomous, democratic, and anticapitalist spaces of decision making confronted and rendered problematic three important theses about transformative politics. The first of these, put forward by Francis Fukuyama (1992), was concerned with politics on a global scale. Fukuyama argued that with the fall of the Berlin Wall and the collapse of Communism, humanity had reached the "end of history." This is not to say that time had literally come to an end; instead, alternatives to liberal-democratic capitalism had been tried and were shown to have failed. Alternative trajectories of development thus no longer existed. The second thesis, put forward by Jorge Castañeda (1994), sought to draw out the implications of Fukuyama's ideas for Latin America. Castañeda claimed that "leftist utopians" in Latin America were now "unarmed" and that change would come about only if these utopians acted in a reformist manner with the state. The armed uprising of 1994, coinciding as it did with the day the North American Free Trade Agreement (NAFTA) took effect, radically challenged both of these theses. As John Holloway and Eloína Peláez (1998: 1) put it, the Zapatistas' revolt "opens a world that appeared to be closed, gives life to a hope that seemed dead."

The final thesis that the Zapatistas have challenged is the centrality of the state as the primary locus of political contestation (Holloway 2002b). As Gustavo Esteva (interview with the author, Oaxaca, 2008) argues, for much of modernity, the nation-state has been "a specific structure that defines political horizons. . . . In the modern mind the state is *the* political horizon." However, over the last two decades, globalization has undermined the foundations of liberal-democratic politics as economic forces have moved increasingly through the global scale (as well as the national and local scales). This movement has rendered problematic the idea of consent and deliberation at a purely national level (see, among others, Held 1993; Tormey 2004: 41; Robinson 2003). In the face of this dilemma, the Zapatistas have provided the clearest example of how it can be possible to construct an alternative political praxis that "reinvents revolution" (Holloway and Peláez 1998). The Zapatistas not only show how alternative spaces of resistance have been formed in the concrete but also demonstrate the importance of constructing an alternative politics on a variety of spatial scales.

The rebellion was, of course, informed by the local conditions that pertained in Chiapas. However, drawing upon the understanding of uneven and combined development through the multiscalar analysis of capitalism that has been expressed throughout the previous chapters, we can also understand Chiapas as a "produced space" that expresses concomitantly the contradictions of both the Mexican national development project and the global capitalist economy (Ceceña and Barreda 1998: 39; Morton 2002: 37). Through their questioning of the legitimacy of the Mexican state and its neoliberal project to "modernize" the nation, the Zapatistas also put into question the social relations upon which capitalism is based. This has allowed the rebellion to have a resonance way beyond the boundaries of Chiapas and Mexico. Drawing upon Neil Smith (1993: 97), the Zapatistas' struggle is not only about the production of *space* but also over the production of *scale* and the level at which this struggle is to operate. As has been pointed out, it has been the Zapatistas' ability "to transform what is in effect a local struggle with a particular set of issues onto a completely different scale of analytics and politics that has made the uprising so visible and so politically interesting" (Harvey 2000: 80). Naomi Klein (2002: 217) thus argues that the Zapatistas have been "both specific and universal."

By demonstrating how space has historically been transformed from the time of colonialism right up to the modern era, we can then provide further empirical evidence for the claim (made in theoretical terms in chapter 1) that spaces are produced and transformed as "moments" of differing modes of production, transformations that themselves create the shifting terrain upon which spaces of resistance are formed. As the title of the chapter suggests, Chiapas is not posited as having a fixed ontological status (Wainwright 2008: 5). As has been highlighted throughout the previous chapters, the capitalist mode of production is *constantly* having to transform the biophysical environment through its search for profit. However, this process is far from uncontested. This chapter is therefore equally concerned to look at how, within the overarching articulation of capitalist hegemony, alternative, emancipatory geographies have been formed that have begun to act as a countertendency to this phenomenon. The chapter addresses a number of key questions: (1) How does capital seek to transform space? (2) What is problematic about this process? (3) How has this process been resisted? (4) What alternative geographies are formed during this process? and (5) How viable are these alternative geographies?

This chapter continues the argument for the relevance of uneven and combined development (as well as uneven and combined hegemony) at a multi-scalar level. We have to look not only at the uneven insertion of Mexico into the global economy but also at the uneven insertion of Chiapas into both the national and the global political economies. Chiapas is both the product of uneven and combined development and the site where this relation is continually reproduced through new spatial divisions of labor. The notion of uneven and combined hegemony (introduced in the previous chapter) will also be extended here. The purpose of this concept is to help explain processes of class and state formation that are differentiated geographically but formed in symbiosis with a broader hegemonic structure (Joseph and Nugent 1994; Wolf 1997). As Gramsci (2011a: 128, Q 1, §43) more poetically stated, "The same ray of light passes through different prisms and yields different refractions of light."

The chapter is structured around four distinct "clashes of spatializations" that, while dialectically related and overflowing into one another, serve as a useful periodization for the production of space in Chiapas. First, I examine the "original" clash between the space of the indigenous communities and that of the Spanish colonizers as a new matrix of power relations was introduced. Second, I detail the clash that occurred during Mexico's liberal period, when labor relations began to be transformed and the national state began to make its presence felt. This process widened into a distinctive clash in the postrevolutionary period of state building, most notably with the process of agrarian reform introduced by Lázaro Cárdenas and the absorption of Chiapas into the national hegemonic project of ISI. This will be detailed in the third section. The fourth section analyzes the final clash, which grew out of the contradictions of this regime of accumulation and the attempted means of resolving it via the opening of new spaces of accumulation (discussed in chapter 3). This clash has taken place principally between the Ejército Zapatista de Liberación Nacional (EZLN, Zapatista Army of National Liberation) and the Mexican state and has involved the reclaiming of territory from the state on which alternative and autonomous governing structures have been constructed (spaces of resistance) alongside the state's attempts to recuperate the recalcitrant population via both coercive and consensual means. Following the method of Gramsci, this analysis allows us to examine "historical moments that articulate the punctual temporality of the event with longer-term forms of historical duration" (Kipfer 2013: 86).

The Clash Begins: Chiapas in the Colonial Era

The Spanish began to definitively colonize Chiapas in 1528, led by Diego de Mazariegos. Prior to this intervention, Chiapas existed in a multiplicity of "ethnic states" with their own territorial boundaries and distinct environments, governed by the local nobility. It was thereafter incorporated into the colonial administration of Guatemala and divided into *encomiendas*, the most desirable of which were located in the more densely populated central highlands (Markman 1984: 47). Although Chiapas did not possess important mineral wealth or gems comparable with other states, it did possess other important primary commodities such as cacao, cotton, wood, and dyestuffs, and it was a region of fertile land. It was from these materials that the colonists sought to enrich themselves through the insertion of the area into the circuits of the global economy, as well as the setting up of unequal relations of exchange within a local mercantile economy (Wasserstrom 1983: 9–11; Viqueria 1994; Ceceña and Barreda 1998: 40). It is clear that a system of domination that entailed the compulsion of labor in order to provide tribute existed before the Spanish arrival. However, this involved neither a wholesale transformation of productive systems nor a process of cultural negation based on alleged racial superiority (Bonfil Batalla 1996: 71–74). As noted in chapter 2, it was colonization that inextricably tied issues of race and class together in Latin America.

Colonization and its aftereffects absolutely devastated the local indigenous population, causing a 50 percent decline in their numbers by 1570 (Harvey 1998: 38). As the region's cheap labor was one of its most important commodities for the colonists, the desire to control labor led to population resettlements into areas where the indigenous population could be the most "productive."

These resettlements necessitated a reorganization of space as sparsely populated villages were drawn into urban centers. Soconusco, for example, was the location of much of the state's plantation, export-oriented agriculture in products such as indigo, cacao, and sugar. However, it was thinly populated and thus required inducements such as the reduction of tribute payments and even brute force to move the labor force there (Collier 1994: 19; Knight 1986: 56; Markman 1984: 47). The early experience of Spanish colonialism in Chiapas, however, was not entirely successful in terms of profit maximization, with settlers experiencing difficulty with credit, high transportation costs, and a precarious labor supply, as well as the continuation of indigenous resistance (Wasserstrom 1983: 38).

Juan Pedro Viqueria (1994: 239) argues that it was between 1670 and 1690 that the original mechanisms were established to ensure tribute payment. As frequently inhered with colonial powers, in order to guarantee a subservient population, it was felt necessary to destroy the indigenous peoples' cultural fabric. This destruction included interfering with local marriage patterns, with noble lineages forced to intermarry with "inferior" lineages, thus discrediting their prestige. *Caciques* (local political bosses) were also installed and removed as colonial interest dictated (Wasserstrom 1983: 19). Issues of cultural negation cannot be understood, therefore, without due consideration of the social purpose of such actions, which in turn cannot be divorced from class projects to control labor and resources.

Unlike Oaxaca, which managed to retain much of its traditional political authority (see chapter 4), Chiapas saw its traditional authority decimated. From 1680 to 1720 there was an increased period of productive development in the region, evidenced by spatial transformations, including a direct opening between Campeche and Guatemala that was intended to break down the isolation of distinct regions and increase commercial activity between them (Viqueria 1994: 240). Between the mid-seventeenth and eighteenth century, Indian townships were set up with a particular division of labor and specialty in mind that the Spanish sought to exploit in order to obtain the maximum amount of tribute. The production of space through the specialization of place helped create identity formation (Collier 1994: 20). This clearly was a class strategy that not only intended to mobilize indigenous labor more efficiently but also sought to create networks of dependency and prevent a more collective consciousness from forming in favor of a fragmented, localized one. This strategy was simultaneously a method of control and a fixing of subaltern class relations (Wainwright 2008: 59).

As well as elite conflict between those overseeing royal offices (*alcaldes mayores*), landowners, and the church, there was continued resistance by the indigenous population, who fought against their subjection by escaping from the towns they had been forced to congregate in. As Sidney Markman (1984: 47–48) explains, a tension existed between the forces of concentration and the forces of dispersion that was not simply based upon a desire to escape the harsh labor conditions but more fundamentally linked to indigenous cosmology about their relation with land. The Spanish believed that the concentration of populations around a fixed, stable center was the only rational and efficient way to organize a productive system. However, this belief was totally at odds with the indigenous spatial practices, which based production on the *milpa* system of shifting agricultural production from place to place (along with the residence of the farmer in a nomadic fashion) in order to maintain harmony with the environment.

Evidence of indigenous resistance can be seen from numerous large-scale rebellions, most notably in 1712 and 1848. On each occasion, the rebellions were precipitated by the increasing levels of exploitation and the inability of indigenous communities to ensure their own social reproduction. Although indigenous people often retained land in Chiapas, extractions in the forms of tribute, forced labor, and other feudal conditions had become increasingly onerous, necessitating the gradual changing of work patterns. Migratory labor on haciendas, plantations, and religious properties became necessary in order to meet the Spanish demands for tribute, which in certain geographical areas had to be paid in cash (Viqueria 1994: 246). With a rapidly declining population owing to disease and famine, the same demands were placed upon a smaller number of people: "A dwindling population thus had to serve a growing parasitic elite" (Knight 2002b: 147). One spatial response to these developments was that many indigenous people abandoned their towns and sought to colonize new areas such as the Selva Lacandona (flight) rather than petition the Crown for their rights (fight) (Wasserstrom 1983: 89). The Selva Lacandona would later become a key base of Zapatismo.

Between Local Autonomy and National Politics: The Formation of *la familia chiapaneca*

By the early nineteenth century, the economic order had evolved. Although the indigenous population had not necessarily been dispossessed of their lands, the wider socioeconomic matrix that they engaged with had led to the transformations of communities, with traditional economic activities being abandoned. While direct coercion did remain (and would remain for some time), it occurred less frequently, with social labor being mobilized through both tenancy agreements and wages (Wasserstrom 1983: 64–66, 104). Payment, however, was frequently made in kind with goods from landowners' stores (*tiendas de raya*), which were oversupplied so as to ensure a continuing debt obligation (Higgins

2004: 83). Chiapas had been the subject of a long struggle between Guatemala (which officially administered it) and Mexico (to which it was formally subject). Following Mexico's independence from Spain, Chiapas became incorporated into Mexico in 1824.

Following independence, the colonial structures of economic exploitation were not fundamentally altered, simply reoriented to serve new masters (Bonfil Batalla 1996: xvi). The native elites of Chiapas favored incorporation into Mexico for a variety of reasons linked to their class position. Not only were commercial links more important with Mexico than with Guatemala, but it was felt that royalist tendencies were stronger in Mexico, and thus the interests of the native elites would be better defended. Lastly, being on the periphery of the Mexican state meant that a large degree of regional autonomy could be preserved, something that was highly prized among the local ruling elite (Benjamin 1996: 7–8; Harvey 1998: 43). Indeed, due to the weakness of the national state, as well as the region's geographical location, Chiapas enjoyed a large degree of autonomy during the nineteenth century (prior to the rule of Porfirio Díaz). However, important changes still did occur. During the liberal period the old *encomienda* was reformed until it morphed into the hacienda of the eighteenth century (Higgins 2004: 42). Owing to the bankruptcy of the national state, after 1826 the government encouraged landowners in Chiapas to denounce communal property and provide alternative claims that would then find legal support, in a bid to increase productive commercial activity and therefore boost state revenues (Wasserstrom 1983: 110). Those Indians in the highlands who remained on their traditional lands were often transformed into tenants and forced to give up labor services (*baldiaje*) for a certain period of time each week if they wanted to remain there (Rus 2003: 262). This tight control of territory by landlords resulted in one-third of highland Indians becoming indentured peons, often prompting indigenous peasants to migrate to lowland ranches to work as either sharecroppers or peons (*mozos*), which were viewed as preferable forms of exploitation. The eventual outcome of these developments was an increase in landlessness and a tightly prescribed social structure with limited capacity for innovation and development (Wasserstrom 1983: 119). The liberal period saw the growth of an entrepreneurial class of landowners in the lowlands of Chiapas. This led to a furtherance of elite class conflict in the state between lowland liberals and highland conservatives. Agricultural production had expanded rapidly in Chiapas after 1832, especially in the areas of cattle ranching and sugar production. However, by far the most important commercial products were cotton and coffee (Wasserstrom 1983: 111–12). It was thus international demand for these commodities that began to transform Chiapas. Summarizing the labor relations that took place during this period, Thomas Benjamin (1996: 5) writes that "the wealth of Chiapas was squeezed from the native population in the form of tribute, tithes, forced labour and forced sales of merchandise for the benefit of a small circle of royal officials, prominent settlers and enterprising friars."

The battle between conservatives and liberals that took place in Mexico during the nineteenth century was mirrored in Chiapas between the oligarchs of the central highlands (who were generally conservative) and the landowners of the central valley (who were generally liberal). This was essentially a divide between old and emerging power (Higgins 2004: 84–85). While new centers of economic power were growing, they had not yet translated into political power, which was still dominated by a handful of caciques who served as intermediaries of the Porfirian state (Harvey 1998: 44). The control of space was a central component of state formation during this time. However, this control was very much formed in tandem with the demands of Western capital, which was attracted to Chiapas for its cheap labor costs but which remained anxious about the supply of this labor. In a bid to reassure investors, a vagrancy law was passed in 1880 that required that the indigenous population remain active during specific parts of the year. In addition, increased head taxes were levied on households (Wasserstrom 1983: 115). These measures were designed to exert compulsion over Indian labor. The spaces of indigenous community thus became a method for controlling the population. The *ayuntamiento* (town council) became responsible for tax collection, and *jefaturas políticas* (district administrative offices) appointed *ladino* (Spanish descendent, nonindigenous person) agents to every village to oversee this process. Furthermore, both workers and their debt obligations were registered with the government in order to tie laborers to a particular locale and prevent them from fleeing. In cases where workers did take up new residence, the *jefatura política* had to be informed by the landowners, and records were kept of these moves (Rus 2003: 265). These controls again highlight the point made in the previous chapter with regard to efforts by the state to simplify and render legible populations it seeks to control (Scott 1998).

As it did on Oaxaca, the experience of Porfirian state building was to have important effects on Chiapas. During this time an informal system of patronage brought the periphery under control of the center (Benjamin 1996: 21). During the Porfiriato, Chiapas experienced profound, uneven development, with the central lowlands and the coastal zones experiencing the most pronounced investment and infrastructural change due to the fact that they were the most productive agricultural zones (Higgins 2004: 116). During the 1870s and 1880s, Chiapas began to be divided into zones of influence (Benjamin 1996: 22). Surveying the situation, Robert Wasserstrom (1983: 116) writes that "expanding national and international markets had divided the state into a series of economic zones in which one or two commercial crops set the pace of life for hacienda workers and Indian villagers alike." One key region of exploitation was the Selva Lacandona. Here European firms set up logging businesses, transforming the nature of Chiapas into "natural resources" that could be commodified and sold on the world market. As Collier (1998: 24–25) notes, this process was controlled by Europeans for the benefit of (some) Europeans. It contributed little to either Chiapas or Mexico as a nation in terms of investment, infrastructure, or skills upgrades.

We can see the difference in the type of economy and varying success of indigenous resistance if we compare the number of municipalities in Oaxaca and Chiapas. Whereas the fierceness of Oaxacan resistance led to the Spanish dividing the state into 570 municipalities in order to better divide and rule the population, in Chiapas the corresponding figure was just 118. This spatial organization demonstrates the far greater power of landowners in Chiapas, as well as highlighting how the regional economies evolved on a different basis, with plantation agriculture and enclave economies being far more prominent in Chiapas (where land was divided into large fincas, or farms), while mining interests dominated in Oaxaca. Both Oaxaca and Chiapas, however, were produced in relation to the demands of the international economy, with the capitalist mode of production acting as the major motor of change, albeit with precapitalist modes of exploitation largely still predominating (Banaji 2011: 74–75). This process of development highlighted above (i.e., the wider capitalist mode of production reinforcing precapitalist modes of exploitation) can be highlighted as a manifestation of uneven and combined development that provided the impetus for localized articulations of class struggles. For example, the lack of roads in Chiapas presented a major impediment to further economic expansion. New road-building projects began to take place under the governorship of Emilio Rabasa (1891–95), including the first highway that connected Chiapas with Oaxaca. These projects increased the links between Chiapas and the rest of the Mexican economy and helped propel a boom in commercial agriculture (Benjamin 1996: 48). Prior to this development of road-building projects, indigenous laborers, known as *cargadores*, had carried products along trails or paths. However, these highway developments were deeply resented by highland elites, who saw spatial integration as a means of undermining their privileged domain of power, which was predicated on their control of indigenous labor, as well as their investment in land and loans that they feared would become worthless if Indian laborers were "freed" (Rus 2003: 274–77).[2] Therefore, there was an emerging clash of spatializations, as one group sought to retain their traditional territorial control, while an emerging group saw the necessity of transforming space to increase their profits. Road building did have the effect of vastly increasing foreign investment in products such as hardwoods, rubber, sugarcane, cacao, and, notably, coffee. It is important to point out that although foreign investment increased and spurred the commercialization of agriculture, this process did not take place through capitalist social relations in which social labor was mobilized without extraeconomic coercion (Benjamin 1996: 33, 85, 25).

Spatial transformations in Chiapas were also induced through geopolitical competition between Mexico and Guatemala. Guatemala had, during this time, constructed a railway from the west coast to the Atlantic Ocean. Fearing secession of the region's plantations, the Mexican state sought to integrate them more firmly into the national economy through their own railway network, which connected western and central Chiapas to the heart of the nation. The construction of the Pan-American Railway facilitated the transportation of coffee to ports in the Gulf of Mexico, reducing turnover time for the product and thereby increasing the commodity's production, as well as the profits derived from it. Aided by these infrastructural developments, from 1890 to 1910 the value of agriculture increased by five times in Chiapas (Benjamin 1996: 85). It is important to note, however, that eastern Chiapas was to remain remote and outside of this modernization process (Collier 1994: 27). The significance of this will become clear later when we consider the fact that eastern Chiapas has been the base of the Zapatista movement. For now, it is sufficient to note that processes of uneven and combined development linked to the national and global economy were taking place within Chiapas, exacerbating class conflict, spatial differentiation, and struggles over spaces more broadly.

In the two decades preceding the Mexican Revolution, foreign investment would also come to fundamentally restructure labor relations in Chiapas and effect profound changes in the scalar organization of the economy, the space of Chiapas, and the spatial practices of everyday life. The 1890s had seen a crisis in the coffee industry. As Jan Rus (2003) documents, both foreign and national investment in the coffee fincas had been encouraged in the lowlands. This investment had been premised on the assumption that highland labor was simply a transferable resource. However, the labor of indigenous communities was already accounted for, as they were used essentially as a "reserve labor force" by the highland elites, in effect continuing colonial policies of *repartimiento*. This arrangement was acquiesced to by the indigenous communities in exchange for a degree of internal autonomy (Rus 2003: 261).

During the Porfiriato, haciendas and ranches vastly expanded in order to produce commodities for export as Chiapas was increasingly integrated into national and global economic imperatives. This integration meant that indigenous people were further dispossessed of their land by foreign business and state officials (Wasserstrom 1983: 108; Bobrow-Strain 2005: 748). Entire villages became tied to expanding fincas, and migratory labor to work on coffee plantations increased (Benjamin 1996: 89). Soconusco was the central target for capital investment spurred by this coffee economy. Foreign-owned farms came to constitute 25 percent of rural property. These investments led to large fortunes, which then acted as a further incentive toward the growth of large estates within Chiapas (Álvarez 1988: 280–81).

Between 1895 and 1910 a transformation of labor relations took place within the state. The number of coffee workers more than quadrupled in this period, from five thousand to twenty-one thousand, with over half of these migrant workers coming from the central highlands as highland landowners now became labor contractors (Rus 2003: 258). Export commodities that would circulate in European and North American capitalist markets were thus being produced in Chiapas, but the labor mobilized to produce these commodities was done in a largely precapitalist manner (e.g., through debt obligations mediated by monetary relations, as well as by direct coercion and dispossession). This symbiosis of modes of production had completely altered the spatial and scalar organization of economic activity in the state. As Rus (2003: 283) explains, "If Chiapas had been a state of largely self-contained regions, each almost sovereign in its isolation as late as the 1980s, by the early 1900s, all had been subordinated to the state and federal government and reorganized to suit the interests of export agriculture." However, a profound new clash of spatializations would occur in the wake of the Revolution between the national state, which sought to transform space in line with its new political project, and local elites, which sought to keep arrangements as they were. Until this point, the Mexican state, although affecting Chiapas in terms of its accumulation strategy, did not really have what could be described as a hegemonic project (in the Gramscian sense of providing intellectual and moral leadership that operated largely through consent). Rather, its policies were carried out through the mediations of the landowning class. It is little exaggeration to say that during the Porfiriato, the landowners were the state. This position was related to their monopolization of territorial control. By 1910 half the labor force of the state was made up of indebted servants (*mozos*). As Neil Harvey (1998: 50) argues, "It was this extensive and intimate control of Indian workers that regional landowners were to defend in their counter-revolution against Carranza and the constitutionalists."

Chiapas and the Revolutionary State: Transformation of Space / *Trasformismo* of Social Relations

Chiapas was not one of the Mexican states that played a prominent role in the Revolution. Here the peasantry was too divided, weak, and spatially isolated to construct an organized challenge to the established order (Benjamin 1996: 92). Instead of a struggle that was given impetus from subaltern classes (as occurred nationally), in Chiapas the Revolution manifested itself as a struggle between elites to control land and (indigenous) labor, the state's most precious commodity (Harvey 1998: 52). This elite conflict was essentially between those who wished to integrate themselves into the wider national agenda and those who preferred to retain local autonomy (Benjamin 1996: 134). During the revolutionary period, the indigenous population was mistreated by both sides, which sought to requisition their food and labor, as well as hand out punishments to suspected collaborators with the other side (Rus 1994: 265). This is not to deny that there were some progressive initiatives resulting from the upheavals. Instead, these initiatives often came from above rather than from local social pressure from below (Reyes Ramos 1992: 41–42). The most significant progressive initiative was the 1914 Ley de Obreros (Workers' Law). Passed by General Castro, this law abolished debt servitude and company stores (*tiendas de raya*) and established a minimum wage and free education (Wasserstrom 1983: 158).[3] However, due to the weakness of subaltern class organization, the revolutionary struggle was initially defeated in Chiapas by the Mapache forces, who, led by Tiburcio Fernández Ruiz[4], sought a restoration of their class power, which had been curtailed with recent developments such as the shift of the state capital from San Cristóbal to Tuxtla Gutiérrez (a move that favored lowland liberals at the expense of highland conservatives). One reason for the Mapache's success lay in their promise to protect regional autonomy against outside interference, something that was prized by both local elites and the indigenous communities (albeit with different rationales). In 1921 Ruiz signed into effect a law that allowed the retention of fincas up to eight thousand hectares for personal use. Furthermore, no limit was placed on the number of family members who could hold properties. In this manner, large estates could be retained through their formal (if not actual) division (Wasserstrom 1983: 159–60). In the subsequent decades, landowners managed to secure power in every government that followed, confirming their continued importance as a social force within the region's political and economic affairs (Bobrow-Strain 2005: 744; Reyes Ramos 1992: 22).

If the initial fire of the Mexican Revolution had failed to spread to Chiapas, the Revolution's institutional phase, led by Lázaro Cárdenas (1934–40), did begin the process of transforming sociospatial relations in the region. Cardenismo, however, was a double-edged sword for the indigenous population, as, while giving them limited land redistribution, it also tied them further to the state's corporatist control and reduced their autonomy (Rus 2004: 214). The key issues on which to elaborate now are (1) why these changes came about, (2) who controlled the process of change, and (3) what the effects of these changes were in the short and longer term.

The activities of political parties, in particular the Partido Socialista del Soconusco (Socialist Party of Soconusco), had begun to help develop political consciousness among the subaltern classes of Chiapas, increasing the militancy of plantation workers. Chiapas really began to be politicized from below around 1920. As Thomas Benjamin (1996: 139) notes, "Indios against ladinos, landless against landed, poor against rich, and workers against capitalists. The politics of class was beginning in Chiapas." Indian activism rather than straightforward benevolence on behalf of the state must therefore be seen as a key component in bringing labor and agrarian reform to Chiapas (Collier 1994: 30). However, equally important were the new political realities the Mexican state faced at the national scale. With the onset of the Great Depression and the collapse of international trade, the government had sought a new political direction and social compact. The Mexican state's new priority of domestic industrialization necessitated the geographical transformation of the hitherto agrarian nation into an urban one and the development of capitalism. This process required the production of cheap foodstuffs in the countryside if it was to be a viable accumulation strategy. In order to achieve this end, land redistribution was necessary to make use of the productive resources of the nation that were often idle or underutilized in prestige-based haciendas. Politically, this entailed mo-bilizing the peasants into the hegemonic project of the state as allies through the granting of *ejidos* in order to defeat the forces of conservatism. As Roger Bartra (1975) has argued, although *ejidos* did not directly facilitate the expan-sion of market relations (they could not be sold or leased, and peasants had only usufruct rights on the land), they did indirectly allow for the expansion of capitalism by preventing wider social discontent via the granting of land titles, thereby acting as "shock absorbers."

However, it was the manner in which this land reform process was carried out within the class conditions of Chiapas that would provide the setting for a new and explosive clash of spatializations that provides the background to the Zapatista rebellion. Following the Zapatista uprising, it became common-place to argue (incorrectly) that the Mexican Revolution never came to Chiapas (Van der Haar 2005). However, this is to completely elide important spatial transformations that profoundly altered the terrain of class relations within the region. The significance of these transformations is aptly described by Aaron Bobrow-Strain (2005: 245, emphasis added), who argues, "During the critical moment of socio-spatial reconfiguration that followed the Mexican Revolution, landowners did not maintain autonomous domains of despotism—'colonial reserves'—amidst quickly thickening post-Revolutionary rule. Rather the con-tours of landed property were made and remade through the *complex interac-tions of landowners, the state, and indigenous peasants struggling over the forms and meaning* of post-Revolutionary rule."

I argue that Chiapas can be seen as a subnational articulation of the process of passive revolution and *trasformismo* that has been outlined in chapter 3 as occurring at the national scale during the revolutionary period. On the one hand, the region became more integrated into the accumulation strategy and hegemonic project of ISI, with processes of land reform helping to stifle conflict between 1940 and 1970. However, the local characteristics and peculiarities that influenced the trajectory of land reform would end in its failure and inform the direction of future struggles, demonstrating how radical discourses can live on even when apparently submerged (Mallon 1995: 317). The deepening insertion into national and global economic activity ultimately served to alter class relations in Chiapas, increasing social stratification and providing the catalyst for the Zapatista antistatist movement.

Ejidos: Spaces of Passive Revolution

Key to processes of passive revolution and *trasformismo* in Chiapas was the production of particular spaces. Crucially, land reform was conducted in a manner that did not adversely affect large landholdings but did provide land for some communities.[5] By 1950 47 percent of land formerly held as fincas had been transformed into *ejidal* property (Van der Haar 2005: 486). However, this was done in a manner in which landowners retained power. In Chiapas agrarian reform led to the coexistence of landowners with new social actors (Reyes Ramos 1992: 22). Far from leading to the straightforward modernization of the region, it confirmed the existence of old forms of authority while also leading to extensive capital investment in activities like cattle ranching, the incipient development of an industrial sector, and the continuation of the export economy, most notably in coffee. In this manner, despite the efforts at agrarian reform, the landowning class still retained their economic dominance, as the finca remained the most important unit of production, although now with a modified form of mobilizing labor. The state-led transformation of Chiapas thus advanced capitalism but without damaging the traditional elite.

The clash of spatial projects between a landlord-dominated region and a newly constructed national state eager to extend its domain of power did not result in either triumphing fully. Instead, what occurred was an extension and reorientation of class power in Chiapas and the development of a new form of "entrepreneurial caciquismo" (boss rule) (Lewis 2005b). Nevertheless, this process of renewal was led by the state, conforming to the conditions of passive revolution outlined in chapter 3. The manner in which land reform took place allowed the landowners to retain the best parcels of land and also all the key economic levers of power such as processing plants, buildings, and storage facilities (Wasserstrom 1983: 164). The *ejidos* created on the peripheries of these estates were often, then, "dependent spaces" that continued to serve the interests of the old masters in their new clothing. In many cases, however, agrarian reform led to an even more profound change in the spatial form of social control and in the means of mobilizing labor. Prior to the Revolution, it was the landlords' territorial control of estates and their tying of peons to the land that ensured the landlords' political dominance. This means of mobilizing social labor was essentially precapitalist, as it was based largely around extraeconomic coercion, or what has been called "political accumulation" (Brenner 1982: 37–38; Wood 2002: 80).

However, an important discourse arose from the revolutionary ideal of land belonging to those who worked it: "La tierra es para quien la trabaja." This discourse had material consequences, as it gave rise to campesinos petitioning for redistribution and state intervention on their behalf. Landowners thus found it less and less desirable to have occupants who had permanent residence on their property, as this carried with it the future threat of petition and expropriation. Instead, they sought to hire sharecroppers, day laborers, and seasonal workers who would be employed through wage work (Rus 2004: 215). Ostensibly, Chiapas was therefore moving toward developing capitalist social relations whereby "material life and social reproduction . . . are universally mediated by the market" (Wood 2002: 7). However, when examining social relations, we have to look at relations not only of production but also of *reproduction* (Otero 1999: 23). This flow of migratory labor was ensured due to the fact that land granted to the indigenous population was generally not sufficient on its own for the communities' reproduction. Wage labor in the lowlands was therefore essential to their cultural survival (Rus 1995: 74–78). Summing up the effects of labor and agrarian reform in the state, Benjamin (1996: 216) concludes that despite the temporary setbacks labor and agrarian reform involved for the landowners, it also "served to provide the state with a large pool of agricultural workers tied to their communities but forced by economic necessity into poorly compensated labour." Landowners could pay low wages because the reproduction of the worker took place within the sphere of the community. In terms of labor relations, a peculiar hybrid was formed in which agricultural producers were "torn between wage-labour and peasant production" (Otero 1999: 9).

While indigenous peoples were excluded from the benefits of capitalist development in terms of social spending and infrastructural development, they were also part of its economic foundation (Ceceña and Barreda 1998: 50). Furthermore, like the capitalist transitions in Europe analyzed by Gramsci (1971: 115, Q 10ii, §61), what occurred in Chiapas was not the liquidation or removal of the landowners as a class but their demotion from their dominant position to one from which they had to share the spoils of political power with new social actors, the most important of which was the national state, which sought to extend its power into Chiapas. In order to achieve this end, new spaces were created outside of the territorial control of landowning estates. In this manner, the government was able to co-opt peasants and ensure "their primary loyalty would be to the state and not their class" (Collier 1994: 32). The hegemony of the PRI was secured through corporatist institutions such as the Confederación Nacional Campesina (CNC, National Peasant Confederation) and the Instituto Nacional Indigenista (INI, National Indigenous Institute), as well as organizations such as Programa de Desarrollo Económico y Social de los Altos de Chiapas (PRODESCH, Program for Social and Economic Development in the Highlands of Chiapas) and the *ejidal* bank.[6] The latter two acted as patronage networks that helped to create chains of dependency and thus extend state discipline (Harvey 1998: 212). The future hope of land reform also served as a means of social control and kept the indigenous population largely quiescent (Rus 2004: 215). This was an unstable equilibrium, however, and could not be maintained in perpetuity. Moreover, this arrangement involved tension in the sense that the spaces granted to the indigenous in which they sought to construct their own political projects were also spaces that represented the power of the national state in Chiapas. A shift in the balance of power for either thus represented a threat to the other.

The institutional phase of the Revolution (from the mid-1930s to the late 1940s) saw the consolidation of *la familia chiapaneca*: "The government of Chiapas completed the political mobilisation of workers and campesinos, fully integrated the regional 'revolutionary' party into the national party of the state, and carried agrarian reform to the indigenous central highlands and the coffee plantations of Soconusco" (Benjamin 1996: 195).[7] In terms of *trasformismo* (solidifying and extending class rule), the process was to be achieved in three main forms. The first involved selective land reform, designed to quell unrest. Up until 1937, the *ejidos* that received definitive titles were located in areas such as Cinalapa, Yajalón, Pinchucalco, and Soconusco, where plantation workers had been the most militant (Wasserstrom 1983: 160). This militant response was aided by the factionalism that developed in the struggles for land, resulting in alliances being formed directly with the state in a vertical manner rather than with other communities in a horizontal fashion.[8] In conjunction with measures such as these, labor and peasant leaders were converted into politicians, resulting in their loyalty being directed toward the national state or particular governments to which their position owed its existence, rather than toward their class constituents (Benjamin 1996: 198). *Trasformismo* of this kind necessitates an important Machiavellian role for political leadership in the process of domination, leading to the absorption of enemies. The result is their "decapitation, and annihilation often for a very long time" (Gramsci 1971: 59, Q 19, §24). The important thing to note is that this reform was mediated by the state, which replaced social classes in leading the processes of struggle and renewal, the classic traits of passive revolution. When these co-optation measures failed, the national state also used repression, including the assassination of prominent Socialist Party members. These events serve as a useful reminder of the role that violence has played and continues to play in Mexican state formation (see Pansters 2012). As Antonio García de León (1994/2003: 15) notes, as a result of the Cárdenas reforms, the majority of agrarian conflicts and syndicalist struggles, as well as forms of social movement activism, were pacified between 1940 and 1970.

However, as was previously mentioned, the manner in which land reform was carried out was partial and insufficient as a resource base for the majority of indigenous communities to fulfill their social reproduction needs. While the discussion so far has focused on tactics from above, we must not forget that we are dealing with the constant process of class struggle over these meanings. Therefore, we must also recognize that, concomitantly, the process of land re- form provided the "physical and social base for development and institutional- isation of indigenous territorial claims" (Bobrow-Strain 2005: 752). Thus, while indigenous peasants and the state were allies at this specific juncture, their spa- tial projects would grow to be irreconcilably hostile as both grew into maturity. A new clash of spatial projects emerged in which the Mexican state has sought to extend the spaces of capital, while the indigenous communities have sought to defend (and expand) their right to collectively held territory. The following section documents the roots of this struggle. It also serves to show how passive revolution is a dialectical process that can serve to create its antithesis (Gramsci 1971: 114, Q 15, §62). It is the struggle of the Zapatistas that concretely represents this antithesis.

Producing State Space in Indigenous Territory

Following land reform in Chiapas, the municipio was the site through which government funding was channeled. In this manner, the state produced depen- dent spaces of political control (Collier 1994: 35). These new spaces have been labeled "institutional revolutionary communities" (linked to the hegemony of the Institutional Revolutionary Party) (Rus 1994). *Caciquismo* had predomi- nated in the period prior to the revolution. During this time, bilingual men had dominated political affairs. In order to prevent future abuses, communities in the postrevolutionary period retreated inward and decided to only appoint monolingual *principales* (elders) who couldn't go behind the back of the com- munity. While corruption was perhaps lessened with this tactic, it also limited the communities' ability to engage with the new national agenda (Rus 2005: 172). Indicative of the new power relations that were being formed in Chiapas was the establishment of agrarian reform committees, as well as organizations such as the Oficina de Contrataciones (Hiring Office) and the Sindicato de Trabajadores Indígenas (STI, Union of Indigenous Workers) following the vic- tory of the Partido Nacional Revolucionario (PNR) candidate in state elections in 1936.[9] Not only were some fincas expropriated and turned over to workers and communities, but the plantation owners had to go to the STI before hiring workers, who were obliged to join the union (Rus 2005: 173). There was a trade-off, therefore, between better working conditions for the indigenous people and increased government control over their lives, highlighting the ambivalent nature of the revolution's outcome (Lewis 2005a). A pivotal point to note is that it was now the state that was mediating social relations and beginning to play a hegemonic role within Chiapas by seeking to instrumentalize space for its own ends to conform to its overall national project. Victory for the PNR in 1936, although key to introducing agrarian reform, also effectively ended independent activity among workers and peasants (Wasserstrom 1983: 162). Radical demands were thus partially fulfilled and thereby displaced, a key hallmark of passive revolution (Callinicos 2010: 498).

The key figure in transforming state-societal relations in Chiapas was Erasto Urbina (Lewis 2005a: 123). He rose to become the head of the Department for Indigenous Protection and through this office was able to consolidate the party's hold over indigenous labor by training a new group of young bilingual men who acted as intermediaries between state institutions and indigenous communities. Communities were forced to accept these bilingual *scribes*, or translators who acted as go-betweens, alongside traditional monolingual elders, as a condition of agrarian reform (Wasserstrom 1983: 173). In this manner, the spaces of indigenous communities were essentially subverted, and new positions of authority were created to mediate relations with the state. Inward-looking, egalitarian structures of native communities, governed by strict civil and religious norms, were in this manner utilized by the state to create institutional revolutionary communities controlled by these young *scribes*, who secured the PRI's vote (Rus 1994).[10] Through the wages they were paid by the state, these *scribes* were also able to become *caciques* themselves, replacing landowners and *ladinos* as power brokers in the community through their monopolization of alcohol sales (essential to many religious fiestas), lending activities, and ownership of key productive assets such as trucks and improved seeds (Rus 2005: 175).

As noted earlier, indigenous communities helped to absorb pressures from the exploitative relations of wage labor that pertained in the region. They were, in other words, a produced space that capital was able to take advantage of by getting egalitarian community structures to provide a social wage (Rus 1995: 74). However, while the creation of institutional revolutionary communities was part of the apparatus of hegemony in Chiapas, this hegemony was far from even in its spatial penetration. In areas such as Venustiano Carranza in northeastern Chiapas, land disputes were far more prominent and *scribes principales* could only retain their legitimacy by regaining land for their communities. The further one moved from the highland communities, the less state presence was felt (N. Harvey 1998: 59, 66). This is important, as it was in this atmosphere of weak state presence that the Zapatista movement grew. Some scholars who have analyzed the Zapatistas' origins have usefully cited the breakdown of PRI hegemony within Chiapas during the period of economic restructuring that took place from the mid-1970s onward (Morton 2013: 206–8). While not seeking to deny the utility of such an analysis, we must take it further and also recognize that this hegemony was never evenly exercised across the territory. Within Chiapas there were some areas in which this hegemony was weak or absent. It was, therefore, possible to construct a new form of sociospatial relations in which social movements, rather than the state, led the process of renewal.

However, despite recognizing that the PRI's hegemony was unevenly exercised, we must acknowledge that the new political formations that were constructed in areas of weak state presence were often intrinsically linked to the breakdown and recomposition of hegemonic practice in other parts of the state. This can best be observed through an examination of eastern Chiapas, specifically, the Selva Lacandona and its surrounding areas, which have been the base of the Zapatista movement. The Selva Lacandona essentially served as the state's form of "spatial fix" to the contradictions of land tenure in Chiapas.[11] Colonization of the Selva was thus encouraged to ease political tensions and diminish class struggles over existing land distribution. Over one hundred thousand colonists settled in the Selva between the 1930s and 1970s (Harvey 1998: 62). These colonists, whose numbers would be increased via religious expulsions and peasant dispossessions in other parts of Chiapas after the 1970s, would vitally reinterpret elements of their culture to place a new emphasis on democratic structures, including consensus, direct democracy, and constant vigilance of leaders by the community assembly, practices that would become integral to the Zapatista movement (García de León 1994/2003: 20).

Let us now explore in more detail how circumstances in Chiapas—linked to wider changes taking place within Mexico and the global economy—altered to precipitate the Zapatista rebellion. These are, naturally, material questions. After a period of improvement from the 1950s that continued for the next two decades, conditions deteriorated after the 1970s, and most rapidly during the 1980s (Rus 1995: 72–73). This deterioration should not be taken to mean simple economic reductionism. We must also examine the changing cultural norms in which key actors are embedded. Nationally, the transition toward neoliberalism not only reshaped the economy but also involved a transformation in citizenship from one based upon tight corporatist control to one based on market mechanisms (N. Harvey 2001; Yashar 2005). How, then, did these developments affect Chiapas?

Chiapas under ISI: Everyday Forms of the State Mode of Production

ISI can usefully be linked to what Lefebvre (1975/2009: 105, 111) calls the "state mode of production," defined as an "ideology of growth controlled by the state."

This involves a change from states concerning themselves essentially with creating the *conditions* for growth to seeking to manage the *space* of that growth (Lefebvre 1991: 23). The state thus comes to promote itself as a stable center and instrumentalize space for particular ends, again exemplifying the conditions of passive revolution touched upon above.

In Chiapas, following the revolution, links with the national and global economy had been increased (Harvey 1998: 48). Most of the productive activities of Chiapas are based at the primary level (agriculture, fisheries, forestry). Therefore, after the Great Depression, the export economy of Chiapas severely contracted, with certain products such as cotton never fully recovering on international markets. Instead, under ISI, the production of grains for the local food market was encouraged. During World War II, when northern states began producing food for export, Chiapas became further integrated into national circuits of production (Ceceña and Barreda 1998: 40). Starting in the 1940s and continuing for the next two decades, the region saw a boom in commercial agriculture due to the rapid rising of commodity prices. During this period, Chiapas became Mexico's principal producer of coffee, corn, and beans, in addition to other commodities such as sugar, rice, cacao, and cotton (Rus 1994: 285). This situation was only made possible, however, due to the production of space by the state, most notably, in road building that was to connect isolated fincas to centers of commercial activity. From having just fourteen hundred kilometers of road in 1940, Chiapas had over six million kilometers by 1970 (Benjamin 1996: 224). Of particular importance was the Pan-American Highway, completed in 1950, which provided links with the national economy (Cancian 1992: 101). Furthermore, in a bid to ensure the security of production, the state made many fincas exempt from expropriation and gave them price support (Rus 1994: 285). This "state mode of production" continued with the further construction of roads that connected the lowland commercial fincas with highland municipios, which was necessary in order to facilitate the vital labor supplies that were needed there. Migratory labor was thus redirected from its previous destination at coffee plantations in Soconusco. This redirection was aided by allowing undocumented Guatemalan workers (who would work for lower wages) to enter Chiapas, highlighting again a particular spatial strategy of the state and the role of classification based on scalar boundaries (Rus 1995: 286). It must be stressed that this process of modernization brought benefits not to the masses but rather to the dominant elites. This helped sharpen class antagonisms within the region, as ethnic differences became "submerged beneath more fundamental differences of wealth, property and power" after 1936 (Wasserstrom 1983: 215). Chiapas under ISI has been aptly described as an "internal colony," with most of the developmental money poured into the state being used to extract resources. With just 3 percent of the national population, Chiapas produced 13 percent of the nation's corn, 54 percent of its hydroelectric power, 13 percent of its gas, 4 percent of its oil, 5 percent of its timber, and 4 percent of its beans. Meanwhile, at the time of the Zapatista rebellion almost half of the region's population did not have electricity, running water, or other basic resources (Collier 1994: 16–17). Subcomandante Marcos, spokesperson of the EZLN, would later declare, "The tribute that capitalism demands from Chiapas has no historical parallel" (2001: 23).

Capital accumulation served to increase social stratification in the region, leading to a period of hegemonic crisis in Chiapas in the 1970s, with an explosion of popular mobilizations against the governing party (as was also occurring nationally). Chiapas also underwent a crisis in agriculture as guaranteed prices for coffee and corn began to fall and machinery replaced human labor. Responding to market prices, cropland began to be replaced by cattle ranching (which doubled in this period). These cattle ranches often expanded at the expense of *ejidos*, further aggravating land conflicts in the state (Benjamin 1996: 231). The effect of this agricultural crisis on jobs can be witnessed by the fact that in the early 1970s 80 percent of the indigenous population could derive their living from this sector, but just a decade later this had dropped to less than 50 percent (Rus 1995: 78–79). However, although a large proportion of jobs were lost in this manner, the situation was ameliorated by public works programs in both Chiapas and neighboring Tabasco. The national oil boom provided the liquidity for infrastructural improvements in dams, roads, oil refineries, and urban improvement. Energy development in Mexico was to have important social and political consequences for the nation. Nowhere was this impact more keenly felt than in Chiapas. Public spending under the Echeverría (1970–76) and Portillo (1976–82) administrations profoundly altered the pattern of economic life in the highlands.

By the end of the 1970s Chiapas had been transformed "from a technological backwater into the producer of about half the country's hydroelectric energy (one fifth of all electric energy) generated in Mexico, and a major producer of petroleum" (Cancian 1992: 48). These developments, as well as school, road, and housing construction, reoriented labor away from traditional maize farming. However, with the onset of the debt crisis after 1982 these work programs were withdrawn, forcing a growing population onto an insufficient resource base. The misery was compounded by the fact that the move away from maize cultivation led to a massive increase in the costs of basic staple foods (Alvarez 1988: 287). This deeper immersion into wage labor led to a move away from rank-based forms of hierarchy to class-based ones (Collier 1994: 120). As has been previously discussed, the PRI's hegemony prior to this move had been secured through the corporatist structures of the CNC and the INI. However, as the economic situation worsened, radical independent groups sprang up, such as the Central Independiente de Obreros Agrícolas y Campesinos (CIOAC, Confederation of Agricultural Workers and Indians), Organización Campesina

Emiliano Zapata (ocez, Emiliano Zapata Peasant Organization), and Política Popular (pp, Popular Politics), as well as the formation of the Unión de Uniones (uu, Union of Unions), the biggest of all the independent unions (Collier 1994: 77). These independent movements "highlight the erosion of corporatist and clientelistic forms of political control" in Chiapas (N. Harvey 1998: 1). It must be stressed that the effects of capital restructuring helped engender these independent peasant organizations as further encroachments were made upon communal property. It was also during this time that a number of guerrillas, radicalized by the events of 1968 (when students were massacred at the Tlatelolco Plaza in Mexico City) and seeing fertile ground for mobilizing discontent in Chiapas, began to organize clandestinely in the mountains of eastern Chiapas. They would integrate into the indigenous communities to form what we now know as the ezln.

The construction of hegemony in Mexico was always an unstable process that, far from being complete, was partial and contested (Roseberry 1994). Subaltern class struggles could only be recuperated into state structures to the extent that a material flow of concessions could be maintained (these material concessions were related not just to money but also to land). However, since the 1970s there has been an increasing turn to repression in Chiapas, with a new wave of torture, displacement, and political assassinations taking place and with some communities coerced into signing documents that required them to give up their struggles for land (García de León 1994/2003: 22–24). The turn to repression, reflecting the declining ability of the state to maintain patronage networks, saw political identity formation take place in which "the state came to be seen as part of the problem, rather than part of the solution" (Van der Haar 2005: 501).

During the presidency of Miguel de la Madrid (1982–88) agricultural subsidies fell by 13 percent annually (N. Harvey 1998: 179). The decline of Mexican agriculture was further accelerated by the signing of the 1987 Pacto de Solidaridad Económica, which sought to reduce wages and price supports. These measures, which hit the peasantry hardest, were compounded by the devaluation of the peso, which led to rising food prices. Although neoliberal reforms had been introduced by de la Madrid, they became rapidly accelerated under Carlos Salinas de Gortari (1988–94). Neoliberalism, in Gramscian terms, had become a new "common sense" among policy makers. These austerity measures hit indigenous communities particularly hard, especially in areas such as public health, as even token salaries were deemed unaffordable (Collier and Collier 2005: 452–53). Furthermore, the two most important cash crops, coffee and maize, were devastated by fluctuating commodity prices. The provision of government credit in this period overwhelmingly went to beef producers, which favored large landholders. By 1990 87 percent of small farmers could not get access to credit (Howard and Homer-Dixon 1996: 12).

The most radical departure was, of course, the reform of Article 27 of the Constitution, which ended the state's historic covenant with the peasantry by abolishing the petitioning for land reform and allowing the privatization and commodification of the *ejido*. In explaining the origins of Zapatismo, it is worth highlighting that Chiapas had the most unresolved land disputes in the country (Van der Haar 2005: 504), again reflecting the importance of class culture in its localized setting. We can appreciate the historical continuities of neoliberalism in Mexico with its earlier liberal version. Both were suspicious of communal property, believing that it was an obstacle to investment and, therefore, progress. However, a whole section of the society was left out of this narrative, their hopes and aspirations not deemed worthy of importance. The indigenous population and the peasantry in this discourse were felt to be an anachronism preventing the nation from modernizing and becoming competitive in the global market.

For state planners, the future of Mexico lay in tying the economy ever more closely to their northern neighbors. These ties were to be institutionalized through the North American Free Trade Agreement (NAFTA). Representing Mexico's full insertion into global circuits of capital, the conditions of NAFTA required Mexico to phase out price support and import restrictions over a fifteen-year period. As Neil Harvey explains, "The rationale for NAFTA was that each country and region should produce goods and services in which they have comparative advantages. The argument implied that over 2 million small producers could not continue to survive as maize producers" (1998: 181). The Zapatistas called NAFTA a "death sentence for the indigenous people," and Marcos declared that the Mexican peasantry were to be "the sacrificial lambs of NAFTA" (Benjamin 1995: 67). Their uprising, timed to coincide with the day that this agreement was due to take effect, thus directly refuted fanciful ideas about the "end of history" (Fukuyama 1992). The Zapatista rebellion puts into question the extension of commodification pushed by the national state. Importantly, their rebellion demonstrated a clear rejection of the peaceful, legalistic negotiations with the state that other peasant movements in Chiapas had previously pursued. These groups either had found themselves co-opted through the process of *trasformismo* (discussed earlier) or were repressed. In contrast to economic modernization theory, which suggests that the development of infrastructure will lead to declining levels of poverty, Chiapas has witnessed the opposite since 1952. Differences between rich and poor have accelerated, leading to class stratification and a decline in living standards (Wasserstrom 1983: 212). Social disintegration and the rise of peasant activism must be linked to "the enormous, sudden and unbalanced development of capitalist investment in the Chiapas agricultural sector" (Alvarez 1988: 288). The reform to Article 27 was the final straw, as it foreclosed the possibility of legal paths to land reform. Within the context of Chiapas, the national state had thus created a situation akin to a pressure cooker, but with safety valves no longer able to function. This buildup of pressure resulted in an explosion on January 1, 1994, as the EZLN emerged to declare "¡Ya basta!" (Enough!) to neoliberal reforms.

Beyond State Space: The Zapatista Challenge

Beginning on this day, the Zapatistas began a territorial response to the Mexican state's policy of dispossession. In an audacious military maneuver, they took over key towns and cities within Chiapas, including Las Margaritas, Altamarino, Rancho Nuevo, Ocosingo, San Cristóbal de las Casas, and Comitán. The Zapatistas have put into practice the maxim of Henri Lefebvre (1991: 190), who stressed that to change life "we must first change space." Following the uprising, they have managed to recuperate 250,000 hectares of land from private hands (Villafuerte Solís 2005: 467). In the wake of the Zapatista rebellion, land invasions multiplied as peasants from a whole spectrum of political positions took over private property. As Bobrow-Strain (2007: 3) illuminates, "Contrary to both the plans of the neoliberal policy makers and the fears of critics on the left, land tenure in Chiapas underwent a rapid repeasantisation and reindiginisation rather than privatisation and concentration."

The space of the community had long been a refuge or defensive bulwark of resistance for indigenous communities. However, as has been highlighted hitherto, it was also a space that was manipulated and used as a means of control by the national state in order to benefit capital accumulation. The significance of the Zapatista uprising has been to move from using the space of the community as a purely defensive means to using it for transformative purposes. As Neil Harvey (2006: 215) succinctly puts it, "Against the effect of economic, ecological and political crisis, the community has been converted into a strategic resource for the reconstruction of the bonds of solidarity and the defence of natural resources." This reclaiming of space has also been developed into a new territorial form of politics. In December 1995 the Zapatistas declared thirty-eight autonomous municipalities, which were to be governed by the people's own political will, beyond the purview of the state. These autonomous municipalities thus represent a rejection of the statization of discontent and instead impose a new territorial framework on the old geographical patterns recognized by the state. The subsequent creation of the Juntas de Buen Gobierno in 2003 was an attempt to further consolidate this process by providing five regional centers of coordination. By 2000 the EZLN had a presence in over a third of all the municipalities of Chiapas (Barmeyer 2009: 23, 62).

The Zapatistas draw on specific indigenous traditions built up in Chiapas and other areas of Mexico. The community assembly, for example, is utilized as a tool to work through problems until consensus is reached. Furthermore, various principles that began to be developed by the Unión de Uniones during the 1970s in dialogue with liberation theology, such as *mandar obedeciendo* (to command, obeying), have been carried on and converted into part of the guiding philosophy underpinning the Zapatista movement (Leyva-Solano 2001: 23–26). The movement also draws upon and expands the pluriethnic conceptions of autonomy that were developed in the eastern part of the state owing to its history of migratory communities (Hernández Castillo 2003: 74–77). This development is in contrast to the practices of communal autonomy practiced in Oaxaca, which are far more ethnically homogeneous.

The Zapatista uprising has also illuminated important dynamics of contemporary class struggles. The rebellion can be interpreted as a refusal of the model of accumulation by dispossession upon which capitalism is increasingly reliant (Harvey 2003: 137–69). It does this by reclaiming social space in which the logic of capital does not operate. Thus, in concurrence with the model of class struggle set out in the previous chapter, the uprising entails a direct challenge to the ability of the state and capital to produce spaces through which new rounds of accumulation can then occur. As William Robinson (2008: 302–3) argues in relation to this point, "The fundamental indigenous notion of 'mother earth,' as something that cannot be 'owned' much less privatized, and which must be respected and sustained, is diametrically opposed to global capitalism's drive to commodify and plunder nature." In this manner, struggles for full cultural recognition are transformed into class struggles. The Zapatista project is also based on collective action for collective need (expressed in the guiding maxim "Para todos todo, nada para nosotros" [For everyone everything, nothing for ourselves]). As Luis Lorenzano (1998: 133) argues, "Zapatismo cannot be understood except as an experience of communal/popular power."

ZAPATISMO AS POLITICAL PRAXIS

Instead of trying to capture state power and use it instrumentally to achieve their objectives, the Zapatistas use a model of organization that is prefigurative, organically constructing new types of social relations as a lived experience of experimentation rather than waiting for some future moment of decisive action.[12] Rather than a "politics of demand," in which state power is reinforced as the supreme arbiter of decision making, the Zapatistas have moved to a "politics of the act," whereby they themselves assume the responsibility for the social (Day 2005: 88–89). The impetus for this decision came when the government refused to ratify the original San Andrés Accords, agreed at peace talks in 1996, and instead finally passed a watered-down version of the bill in 2001 that failed to recognize the Zapatistas' fundamental demands for cultural rights to autonomy and the use and benefit of their territory (Mora 2007: 71; for further details, see People's Global Action 2007).

The lack of progress in negotiating with the national state led the Zapatistas to a process of internal reflection and the eventual creation of the Juntas de Buen Gobierno (JBG) in 2003, which put the San Andrés Accords into effect unilaterally. Rather than the state leading the process of renewal and absorbing discontent in the form of passive revolution, the Zapatistas as a subaltern force managed to keep the initiative. As one member of the JBG of La Realidad (interview with the author, 2009) stated with regard to this result, "With or without laws, we will construct our own autonomy." The Zapatistas have thus learned from the failures of previous social movements in Chiapas that were co-opted and rendered powerless through their involvement with the state. In contrast, they are extremely aware of the dangers of *trasformismo* and passive revolution. They are therefore insistent that their struggle will take place without the mediation of political parties "who find new ways to win, new clothes to wear, new words to say, and new gifts to offer" (interview with the author, La Realidad, 2009). Instead, the Zapatistas have built a form of collective class power that is grounded in their own needs and aspirations.

One major achievement of the Zapatistas has been the general reappraisal of gender relations following the rebellion (Harvey 1998: 224). As Mercedes Olivera (2005: 617) argues, "One of the most important achievements of the EZLN has been the legitimization of female participation in politics, hitherto a reserve of males." Although receiving far less attention in the media, on the same day that the Zapatistas announced themselves to the world with the "First Declaration of the Lacandon Jungle," they also proclaimed the "Revolutionary Women's Law." This law asserted that women were to have full control over their own fertility, the right not to be forced into marriage, and the right to be free from domestic violence (Millán 1998: 74–75).[13]

Women in Chiapas have had to bear the burden of the recent wave of immigration. Many men left communities in search of work as local opportunities have declined (Villafuerte Solís 2005: 469; Davis and Eakin 2013). As well as having responsibility for the household, women have taken over the process of peasant production (Mercedes Olivera, interview with the author, San Cristóbal, 2009). PROCEDE, the government program to regularize land titles (discussed in the previous chapter), has furthermore systematically excluded women from the process of land reform by determining certification status only in relation to (male) heads of households (Olivera 2005: 615). Women's participation in the EZLN can thus be related to resistance against this attempted gender silencing. Gender struggles cannot be divorced from wider class issues related to the manner in which capitalism operates in Chiapas. It is estimated that women constitute a third of the EZLN's membership and make up a significant part of the Comité Clandestino Revolucionario Indígena—Comandancia General (CCRI—CG, Clandestine Indigenous Revolution Committee—General Command), the EZLN's military command. Women have also been at the heart of key symbolic acts of the Zapatistas, including Major Ana María leading the military occupation of San Cristóbal and Comandanta Ramona leading the Zapatista delegation in peace talks with the government. Women's mobilization was also decisive in the fight to evict federal forces from the autonomous municipalities. The Junta de Buen Gobierno (JBG) of La Realidad (interview with the author, 2009) identified the participation of women as being one of the key aspects of change they had witnessed in the community since 1994, especially since the inception of the Juntas in 2003. The revival of traditional Mayan medicine in daily life within the autonomous communities has also proved to be empowering, as women's knowledge has become increasingly valued (N. Harvey 2006: 229). Indigenous feminism, therefore, has been spearheaded by the Zapatista movement (Hernández Castillo 2002). This is not to claim that a situation of perfect equality now exists within Zapatista communities. Indeed, a 2004 communiqué from Marcos entitled "Two Flaws of the Zapatista Movement" recognized that the participation of women was not increasing as much as it should have done, and although the "Sixth Declaration of the Lacandon Jungle" (Comité Clandestino Revolucionario Indígena—Comandancia General 2005) recognized that the position of women had improved, further progress was still demanded. The Zapatistas are not simply trying to restore past conditions but rather to create an alternative future. This involves conscious work, as many aspects of Zapatismo are not found within traditional communities (Lorenzano 1998: 129, 134).

As should be clear, the rejection of alien determination implies the rejection of the state as an organization that places itself above society (Lefebvre 1966/2009: 147–50). After all, the state is not just a form of social relations but a process of forming social relations (Holloway 2002a: 94). This has been a conscious decision by the Zapatistas that relates to the experience of betrayal by the state, which culminated with the revisions to Article 27 of the Constitution. As Gemma Van der Haar (2005: 489) argues, the EZLN "sought to displace the state and deny the Mexican government legitimacy because the latter had betrayed the revolutionary project. The EZLN revived Zapata, whereas the Mexican state had declared him dead." Indeed, the invoking of Zapata was an important discursive move due to his symbolic referent in Mexico as the emblematic defender of the peasantry. His image provided a means of claiming historical legitimacy for EZLN's struggle, which reached out to wider sectors of Mexican society (Rajchenberg and Héau-Lambert 1998: 23–34). This highlights the point raised in the introduction with regard to the fact that the Zapatistas' struggle is thus not merely confined to the local production of space but is also a struggle to insert itself onto wider scalar dynamics.

THE SPACE AND SCALE OF THE ZAPATISTAS

Politically, we can identify the production of three spatial scales at which the Zapatistas' politics now functions within their territorial zone of influence.[14] These are the community level, the municipal level, and the level of the Caracoles, which operate on a regional scale. These spatial scales are linked together as networks of resistance (Gonzalez-Cassanova 2005). The Caracoles are an example of urban experimentation on behalf of the Zapatistas. They contain the economic foundations of Zapatismo, as well as schools, health clinics, and meeting centers.[15] The premise of creating this level of government was to coordinate better the efforts of the autonomous municipalities, to counter the uneven development that had taken place between areas under Zapatista influence,[16] and to provide a focal point for people wishing to engage with the movement.

Drawing on the indigenous tradition of the *cargo* (discussed in the previous chapter), members of the community assembly are elected to the municipal government, where they generally serve a term of two to three years. The municipal government includes the general command, the agrarian council, and the honor and justice commissions. Members work for one or two days a week and then return to their communities. Members of the municipal government are further divided into three teams of seven or eight people who occupy positions on the JBG. These teams rotate every ten days or so and sometimes longer, depending on the region in question (JBG La Garrucha, interview with the author, 2009).[17] The principle of rotation is important for a number of reasons, both economic and political. Economically, it is vital to allow members to return to their communities to be able to plant and tend crops (as work on the Junta is an unpaid responsibility rather than a position of prestige). However, rotating in this manner also ensures that representatives are constantly in contact with their social base. As Marcos (2004) explained, it is a new way of doing politics "so that the task of governing is not exclusive to one group, so that there are no 'professional' leaders, so that learning is for the greatest number of people, and so that the idea that government can only be carried out by 'special people' is rejected." Gramsci (2011b: 229, Q 4, §55) viewed this form of governing as an essential hallmark of democratization. A member of the JBG at La Realidad (interview, 2009) described the Juntas as a space in which they learned to construct autonomy. Therefore, "the Junta is like a school where we learn to govern." This model of governance conforms to the theory of autogestion described in chapter 1. It also overcomes one of the potential problems inherent to this concept, namely, the formation of a bureaucracy (Lefebvre 1966/2009: 147). Some have argued that autogestion dovetails with neoliberal ideologies of self-help (Higgins 2004: 140). However, this ignores the key differences of

Zapatista primary school, Oventik.

social purpose. As Lefebvre (1979/2009: 128–29) makes clear, the latter consists in "transferring the problems, but not the privileges of the central power to grassroots organization."

Education itself is perhaps the most advanced aspect of Zapatismo, not only in the sense that it is the most active and pervasive, with each community now having a school, but also in the sense that it is seeking to ground itself within the people's own reality in terms of history and social environment.[18] Education promoters are now sent to each village, where math, history, and language are taught in whatever language the children speak (education promoter, interview with the author, La Realidad, 2009). A system has been created whereby those who gain literacy can then serve the community either through working on the Juntas or themselves becoming education promoters and thus collectively raising the community.

Another important aspect of the Zapatistas' autonomous project is their provision of justice and law based on the indigenous tradition. This aspect is grounded on the principle of reparations rather than the Western system of punishment. Someone found committing a crime is sentenced to work in the community, and the appropriate sentences are decided by village assemblies (JGB, La Realidad, JGB, La Garrucha, interviews with the author, 2009). Indeed, non-Zapatista communities have been known to ask the Juntas to adjudicate in particular disputes, helping to soften traditional intracommunity tensions (Tom Hansen, interview with the author, Apizaco, 2008; Stahler-Sholk 2014: 198).

Overcoming alienation has also been important in the realms of production and social reproduction of the community. The Junta de Buen Gobierno at La Garrucha (interview with the author, 2009) stressed that their elders had lived through suffering and had bosses to answer to, but the Junta members had never known bosses. In a misinformed analysis of the movement, Tom Brass (2005: 665) labels the Zapatistas "petty smallholders" primarily interested in protecting their private property. However, this ignores the fact that from their inception the Zapatistas have promoted collective ownership rights, an example of which was the Revolutionary Agrarian Law declared in 1994 (Lorrenzano 1998: 139). Alongside subsistence production on the milpa (conducted largely on family plots), production is frequently organized in cooperatives and is taking place more and more in a collective manner, as one Zapatista confirmed (interview with the author, La Realidad, 2009; see also Stahler-Sholk 2014: 195). In La Realidad there is a bank that provides loans with an interest rate of just 2 percent. Interest is charged only so that extra funds can be generated for the community. Jorge Santiago (interview with the author, San Cristóbal, 2008), the former director of Desarrollo Económico y Social de los Mexicanos Indigenas (DESMI, Economic and Social Development of Indigenous Mexicans), a San Cristóbal–based NGO that has worked for over thirty years in Chiapas with indigenous groups, argues that the Zapatista communities have been involved in a profound process of change. Although collective work has a long history in Chiapas, the idea of collective ownership of property, in terms of the means of production, has been something new that the Zapatistas have contributed to. One example of this is the women's collective from Oventik, Mujeres por la Dignidad (Women for Dignity). They formed in 1997 and now have over seven hundred members from over four municipalities. Products from Zapatista communities, including clothing, artwork, coffee, and other items, are sold within TierrAdentro, a Zapatista solidarity café in San Cristóbal.

Lastly, the Zapatistas have developed their own autonomous health service. At the level of the Caracoles, the overall health needs of the various communities are coordinated via the Commission for Health. At the level of the municipal council, there is the Coordinación de Salud (Health Organization), representing health promoters and local municipalities. Finally, there are the local health councils, made up of health workers and community members (Cuevas 2007). Each autonomous municipality now has its own health clinic, with prominent hospitals such as the clinic Commandata Ramona located in La Garrucha and the clinic Guadalupana in Oventik. These clinics conduct health consultations and minor surgeries within Zapatista territory and are free for Zapatista members, while people from non-Zapatista communities are only asked to pay

Zapatista autonomous health clinic, La Garrucha.

a small fee. These developments highlight the revolutionary transformation in conditions of everyday life that the Zapatista struggle has brought about.

THE SCALE OF THE ZAPATISTAS

However, it is not just within Chiapas that the Zapatistas have had an influence. As was mentioned in the introduction, the Zapatistas' politics has operated on a variety of spatial scales, including local, regional, national, and transnational components. At the national scale, the Zapatistas have undoubtedly been the most influential social movement that the country has seen since the Revolution. The Zapatista rebellion has also been hailed as "the most powerful force for democratization in Mexico" (Collier and Collier 2005: 450). Not only did the emergence of the Zapatistas coincide with the ending of the PRI's seventy-one-year rule in 2000, but additionally, the Zapatistas have opened the political terrain for a plethora of civil society groups to flourish (Gilbreth and Otero 2001: 8–9). This includes the creation of the Congreso Nacional Indígena (CNI, National Indigenous Congress), which has helped give voice to indigenous peoples as political subjects in Mexico. The greater visibility of civil society groups was further enhanced with the Otra Campaña (Other Campaign), which took place in 2006 alongside the national presidential elections. This campaign was designed to build networks with other social movements across Mexico that were "below and to the left." The Otra Campaña has sought to put into practice ideas about autonomy on a wider scale and seeks to construct a national political force that is not a traditional party that aspires to office (Mora 2007: 65–67).[19] This strategy, which struggles against the dangers of passive revolution, contests the process of democratization that tried to absorb opposition movements into an acceptable sphere of discontent (Morton 2005: 190). Although their efforts have not been covered by the mainstream news, the Zapatistas have formed and fortified alliances with various social movements across Mexico, for example, the Frente de Pueblos en Defensa de la Tierra (FPDT, People's Front in Defense of the Land) in Atenco, the Consejo Nacional Urbano Campesino (CNUC, National Urban Peasant Council) in Tlaxcala, and the Frente Popular Francisco Villa Independiente (FPFV, Independent Francisco Villa Popular Front) in Mexico City. Tom Hansen (interview with the author, San Cristóbal, 2009), whose organization, Mexico Solidarity Network, works in close association with many of these movements, refutes claims that the Other Campaign has not been a success and instead argues that it cannot be evaluated after only two or three years but rather is a thirty- to forty-year project: "The ideological foundations of autonomy are not something that can take root overnight. It takes a lot of education and practical experience to internalize something that isn't corporatist organizing." The Zapatistas have helped inspire a new conception of thinking about political organization that explicitly rejects the Leninist model of vanguardism, whereby social struggles are subordinated to the interests of the party.[20]

The Zapatistas have also been involved in the politics of resistance at the transnational scale. Their example has proved to be hugely inspirational in the alter-globalization movement (Collier and Collier 2005: 451; Morton 2002: 28), as well as having a particular resonance in Latin America (Zibechi 2004).[21] Through their skillful use of the internet to disseminate communiqués, the Zapatistas have generated what Harry Cleaver (1998: 81) refers to as the "electronic fabric of struggle." The numerous *encuentros* (encounters) organized in Zapatista territory have attracted participation from a wide transnational network of support. This has not only proved key in providing material support for the struggle but also protected the communities from military attacks that had been encouraged by private capital.[22] The internet was key to scaling up the Zapatistas' political project. However, the Zapatista resistance project has developed a relationship with transnational solidarity activists based upon mutuality; that is, it does not depend on a one-way flow of resources. Instead, activists come to Zapatista territory to learn and share experiences (Olesen 2004: 225; Andrews 2010). The Zapatistas have also helped to redefine strategies of resistance in an age of global capital. This stems from their consolidation of local power, but with a supranational projection that critiques neoliberal capitalism.

This process has proved hugely influential in their resistance to megaprojects such as Plan Puebla Panama (discussed below), where over one hundred social movements have created a network of resistance that is based in their everyday social reality while still looking for alternative means of integration (Corando and Mora 2006: 36; N. Harvey 2006: 214–15).

STATE RESPONSES TO THE STRUGGLE TO SHAPE SPACE

The Zapatista project has, of course, been taking place concomitantly with increased activities of the state to reabsorb this social struggle into its hegemonic structure. The Zapatistas, after all, offer a clear challenge to the logic of the state, usurping its monopoly on territorial control, as well as taking over key functions usually associated with the state, such as the provision of education and health and the administration of justice. The fact that the Juntas function every day is a powerful inspiration for others to follow. While not necessarily offering a model to copy, the Juntas allow people to expand their horizons of the possible. The response by the Mexican state has gone through various phases. The first of these was a direct military response aimed at coercing the recalcitrant population. According to Ernesto Ledesma (interview with the author, San Cristóbal, 2009), former director of CAPISE (an NGO that monitored militarization and human rights violations in Chiapas), there still remain fifty-nine military bases within indigenous territory, many of which encircle the political nerve centers of Zapatismo. However, generally speaking, the direct military response has been replaced by more subtle means of economic coercion and political pressure in conjunction with the use of state-backed paramilitary violence against the Zapatista communities.[23] Tom Hansen (interview with the author, San Cristóbal, 2009) of Mexico Solidarity Network defines the situation in Chiapas as one of low-intensity warfare, and it has aimed to reconstitute state hegemony while undercutting support for the Zapatistas. As an example of this, 13 percent of agricultural property in Chiapas was redistributed between 1996 and 2000 (Bobrow-Strain 2007: 4). This redistribution was clearly not what Carlos Salinas had in mind when he declared land reform over. Government aid programs have been targeted to communities that were formerly aligned with the Zapatistas, such as CIOAC and ARIC. Various inducements have also been offered to those communities that took over land in the wake of the rebellion in order to normalize their titles under PROCEDE (shifting the ultimate legal form of control over land). Miguel-Angel García Aguirre (interview with the author, San Cristóbal, 2008), director of Maderas del Pueblo, states that these inducements have escalated tensions within and between communities, as the Zapatistas do not allow their members to accept government aid programs. The effect has been to make some former Zapatistas leave the movement owing to the harshness of material conditions associated with *resistencia* (Barmeyer 2003).

Many government programs such as Plan Cañadas, Programa Integral para el Desarrollo Sustentable de la Selva (PIDDS, Integral Program for the Sustainable Development of the Jungle), and Proyecto de Desarrollo Social Integrado y Sostenible (PRODESIS, Socially Integrated Social and Development Project for Sustainable Development) have targeted the Selva Lacandona area, the base of the Zapatista movement. They are interpreted by some as counterinsurgency tactics that dovetail with the new accumulation strategy of the Mexican state in Chiapas (Mercedes Olivera, interview with the author, San Cristóbal, 2009).[24] The Mexican state has also offered numerous spatial responses to the Zapatista challenge. One response has been to remunicipalize the region in an effort to undermine the autonomous communities and reassert the state's power to name and shape space (Leyva-Solano 2001: 35; Leyva-Solano and Burguete 2007). More recently, there has been a development project under the governorship of Juan Sabines (2006–12) of creating sustainable rural cities (SRCs). The state government has identified the dispersion of the population as one of the greatest problems for the economic modernization of Chiapas and a prime factor explaining rural poverty. Therefore, in a five-year developmental project, the state government proposed constructing twenty-seven "rural cities" that would congregate populations into large communities. This is a clear effort by the state to reterritorialize communities through offering material incentives such as housing, jobs, and social services. Drawing from the work of Alan Gilbert and Peter Ward (1984, 1985), who investigated similar issues of government intervention, housing policy, and community action programs in the 1980s within Mexico City, we can see these actions as attempts by the state to relegitimate itself. This should be interpreted both as part of the lineage of rural social control over indigenous communities by the state and as an aggressive response to the Zapatista challenge (Soto and Banister 2016; Wilson 2011). In other words, it is another attempt to articulate a passive revolution in light of the challenge to state power. As a developmental project, however, the SRCs have largely resulted in abject failure (Bellinghausen 2013a, 2013b).

Some scholars have questioned whether autonomous politics can be viable without the conquest of state power, arguing that these projects do little to affect the resources in state hands (see, among others, Brass 2005: 667; Stahler-Sholk, Vanden, and Kuecker 2007: 9; Callincos 2003: 94). However, this argument is misguided in a number of respects. For example, it conceives of state power as something that can be taken and, moreover, assumes that state power exists only as a center of power linked to institutional and juridical forms. However, as this chapter earlier indicated, the state in Chiapas functioned through the control of political communities. Therefore, the struggle against state power is something that takes place "first and foremost on a daily basis, in communities, *ejidos*, unions, schools, churches, and many other sites" (N. Harvey 1999: 260). The Zapatistas, in other words, have not left the state intact; instead, they have taken power from it through their appropriation of land and production of alternative space. Lefebvre (1991: 383), in identifying the intimate connection between capital accumulation and the role of the state, argues powerfully that "pressure from below must confront the state in its role as organizer of space, as the power that controls urbanization. . . . The state defends class interests while setting itself above society as a whole, and its ability to intervene in space must be turned back against it, by grass-roots opposition, in the form of counter-projects designed to thwart strategies, plans and programmes imposed from above."

This is exactly what the Zapatistas have done. As Neil Harvey (2005: 629) states, even though the Zapatista support base is in northern and northeastern Chiapas, "the ripple effects of Zapatismo are felt throughout the state." This can most clearly be seen in the struggles between two very different visions of the future. As is the case with Oaxaca, so too is Chiapas a "spatial target" for the expansion of capital in Mexico. In the wake of the rebellion, Chiapas has been disproportionately targeted with government programs such as PRONASOL and PROCAMPO in an effort to buy calm and win back support (Bobrow-Strain 2007: 178). However, these locally specific responses need to be placed within the context of a new accumulation strategy based on increasing global investment in Mexico. Key to this is Plan Puebla Panama (renamed Plan Mesoamerica), which seeks to integrate southern Mexico and Central America into a free trade zone in the same manner as other economic blocs that have created economies of scale. Key to this plan are agricultural plantations controlled by multinational corporations, transnational road networks, interoceanic canals, and the development of new port capacities linked with commercial corridors (Corando and Mora 2006: 26). Since the passage of NAFTA, state planners have recognized that while the northern parts of the country have been able to take advantage of free trade with the United States, the south has had neither help from the state nor access to markets, leaving it unable to increase its competitiveness in the global economy (see Dávila, Kessel, and Levy 2002; N. Harvey 2006: 212). Furthermore, there has been a realization among some elites that the old economic models of development, based on extensive cattle rearing, petroleum, extraction, and agricultural colonization, have created ecological problems and contributed to political agitation. These realizations have led to the development of a new "ecological" model of capitalism for the southern Mexican states (N. Harvey 2006: 205). As has been noted by Dianne Rocheleau (2015: 705), "This strategy relies on massive state investments in transportation infrastructure and social re-engineering of territorial identity and extent, as well as the location, lives and livelihoods of indigenous and campesino communities. The federal and local state plans for these takings and remakings of territory have been maintained as de facto state secrets, protected from scrutiny by indigenous, political, social and human rights organizations."

A tension has also emerged between various fractions of capital that seek to utilize the resources of Chiapas in different ways (extracting resources versus preserving them). Nevertheless, the state's developmental projects continue to pursue this contradictory matrix of road building, resource extraction, monoculture, and ecotourism (Rocheleau 2015: 702). On the one hand, over five hundred thousand hectares of concessions have been granted to mining corporations, and the increased planting of monocultures such as African balm and eucalyptus threaten the area's biodiversity and water resources, according to Gustavo Castro-Soto of the NGO Otros Mundos (interview with the author, San Cristóbal, 2009). On the other hand, these projects have taken place alongside the promotion of ecotourism by the government, with plans to construct new tourist corridors to places such as Palenque and the Montes Azules Biosphere that will dramatically reduce the time it takes to reach these areas. This ecological model is thus a myopic one that does not include the indigenous people in its model, or at least claims to know their interests and assumes what sort of people they wish to become. As Neil Harvey (2006: 211) argues, state planners view Chiapas as "a region without people, without a history, but supposedly a future." Conflicts over these projects have escalated in recent years.[25] Indeed, it is clear that the discourse of environmental protection is being invoked to harass and marginalize the Zapatistas as the main oppositional force (Paulson 2000; Rocheleau 2015: 709). In explaining this situation, Mercedes Olivera (interview with the author, San Cristóbal, 2009) argues, "The government is defending its social and political project. Whatever group is against that is an enemy of the state."

The Zapatistas have remained resolute in the face of these processes. According to Dolores Camacho Velázquez (cited in Bellinghausen 2013b), whereas other peasant organizations have been successfully absorbed into state projects, the Zapatistas are the only significant group still fighting for fundamental land rights. Despite the military encirclement, the autonomous communities have been maintained, and remarkable achievements have been made in the face of overwhelming hostility. According to Tom Hansen (interview with the author, San Cristóbal, 2009), the new generation of Zapatistas has "internalized a strong sense of pride in Zapatismo," giving them both a greater sense of confidence and a better understanding of where they want to go. They thus retain a moral authority and continue to occupy a hugely symbolic reference for wider anticapitalist struggles in Mexico and beyond.

Conclusion

Chiapas has long been a site of political contestation through which important spatial developments have taken place. Under colonial administration these developments involved the reorganization of economic activity and the division of space into territorial units of control. Although this feudal mode of production did indeed construct its own distinctive space, it was one in which things remained produced *in space*, rather than space itself becoming the object for constant transformations for the production of surplus value. In examining how capital sought to transform space, we explored the development of foreign capital investments around the 1890s and its effects on sociospatial relations within the state. The chapter demonstrated how labor relations began to be fundamentally transformed and space began to be used instrumentally to facilitate greater returns. The chapter then considered the changing dynamics of spatial production with the move toward the state mode of production during isi following the Revolution. All of these projects required a "clash of spatializations" that negated indigenous knowledge and practices. The development of capitalism within Chiapas was analyzed as taking place both rapidly and unevenly, creating social divisions within communities and threatening socioecological problems. Although contested by various groups, most notably since the 1970s, the most radical challenge to the logic of capital has come from the Zapatistas, who since 1994 have offered an alternative geographical development project that has transformed the everyday reality of Chiapas, as well as that of Mexico and other parts of the world. This project has demonstrated the importance of collective power over resources and also has had far-ranging implications for theorizations of strategies of resistance, operating as it does on a variety of spatial scales but without taking state power.

The pressing task for the future will be not only to maintain these autonomous spaces in the face of attempts by the state to take back control but furthermore to extend such a politics of autonomy onto wider spatial scales. It is here that the greatest challenge and paradox to the Zapatista project of political transformation has been found. While proving relatively successful in transforming their own conditions of everyday life within Chiapas, the Zapatistas have been less successful in their attempts to bring together a concerted counterhegemonic movement at the national level that has the power to challenge the dominant orientation of the Mexican state, hence the possibility for the reemergence of passive revolutionary tactics to absorb these fragmented manifestations of discontent.

December 21, 2012, saw the reemergence of the Zapatistas into the public spotlight. Mobilizing around forty thousand members of their support base in a silent march, they peacefully occupied five key municipal towns across Chiapas and announced a new series of communiqués calling for the formation of a noninstitutional alternative (i.e., a non-state-based Left) within Mexico. They also detailed specific initiatives to take place within their own Caracoles (such as the Escuelita Zapatistas, discussed further in the conclusion). With the PRI having been returned to power at the national level earlier in 2012 following the election of Enrique Peña Nieto, and with the nation still in the grip of escalating violence linked to the drug trade, the Zapatistas' task will not be easy. However, as this chapter has demonstrated, this is a struggle with long historical roots and is likely to endure. When questioned what the future held for the movement in the face of mounting state repression, one Zapatista (interview with the author, La Realidad, 2009) replied, "They want to bury us, but they have forgotten that we are seeds."

CONCLUSION

It is our conviction and practice that to rebel and to fight it is not necessary to have leaders nor caudillos nor messiahs. To fight, all that you need is a bit of humility, some dignity, and a lot of organization.
—Subcomandante Marcos, "Entre la luz y la sombra"

Reflecting upon the rise of Fascism in Europe following the Great Depression, Henri Lefebvre (1947/2008: 153) wrote, "One day individualism begins to collapse (and not as a result of a crisis of ideas or 'world views,' but because of a *material* crisis, both economic and political), and these erstwhile individualists rush headlong to form a crowd, a horde, urged on by the most insane, most loathsome, most ferocious 'ideas' leaving the last vestige of human reason behind."

It would not be engaging in hyperbole to claim that today we are once again living in a period of worldwide material crisis, with some even warning of the dangers of an emergent twenty-first-century Fascism as a potential response to this crisis (Robinson 2013). Alongside the economic crisis that has engulfed the global economy since 2007–8, we are also facing an unprecedented ecological crisis in the form of climate change (Castree 2010). Adding to this general instability is the ongoing "war on terror" which, fifteen years after it was first declared, shows no signs of ending anytime soon and has been interpreted by some as a clear example of a new imperialism (Callinicos 2009; Harvey 2003). What connects these issues is, of course, the way they are related to the dynamics of capitalism as a mode of production. As Lefebvre (1976: 107) astutely notes, "Wars and cyclical crises have the same result: they liquidate excess (things and men)." Rather than viewing crises as anomalies, we should instead interpret them as essential moments in the cycle of accumulation, devaluation, and a restarting of accumulation (Bieler and Morton 2015). However, the specter of climate change and ecological crisis that is haunting the world is a scenario from which we may not be able to rebuild. It is against this background, therefore, that the "big questions" are once again being asked, even if the answers are not yet known. For instance, we are forced to question what "growth" means, what its effects are, and whether it can continue ad infinitum (Harvey 2010: 27).[1] Can global capitalism be reformed to become a more benign type of social democracy or new global Keynesianism, as some are calling for (e.g., Held 2004; Piketty 2014)? If not, what alternatives might there be, and how viable are they? While not offering definitive answers, this book has sought to contribute modestly to the debate not only by highlighting some inherent problems with the spaces of capital but also through an exploration of counterspaces formed in resistance. In highlighting some of these counterspaces that are being actively built, the book has also tried to demonstrate the continuing possibility for alternatives, seeking to shift these in the popular mind from being nowhere to "now here" (Gibson-Graham 2006b: xxvi).

In the aftermath of the global financial crisis, it would appear that Jamie Peck and Adam Tickell's (2002: 381) assertion that neoliberalism is "the common sense of our time" may be beginning to unravel. If, as Gramsci (1971: 184, Q 13, §17) claimed, crises do indeed provide a terrain more favorable to the dissemination of certain modes of thinking, then it is vital at this juncture that we engage in critical reflection, utilizing "good sense" to move toward the production of space that is a collective work. At the same time, as the quote at the beginning of the chapter highlights, this possibility (in relation to the above discussed issue of moving toward good sense) must be tempered with the undeniable fact that during periods of material crisis the potential also exists for the most reactionary form of ideas to take hold. Indeed, this makes the task of those opposed to the logic of capital all the more urgent. For as Gramsci (1971: 276, Q 3, §34) also recognized, when the old is dying but the new is not ready to be born, "in this interregnum a great variety of morbid symptoms appear."

This conclusion will add some further reflections to the issues touched upon above while relating them to the key themes that have been covered in the course of the book so far, namely, the production of space, class struggle, hegemony, and passive revolution. The conclusion is organized in the following manner. First, the main contributions made throughout the book will be summarized. Second, the central arguments of the previous chapters will be revisited. Third, a discussion will be offered regarding the current conjuncture in Oaxaca and Chiapas. Finally, a number of crucial questions for future developments are reflected on.

Results and Prospects: A Space Odyssey

The book has highlighted how struggles over space (and what spaces contain) are an integral feature of the global political economy. Through the analysis conducted at a variety of spatial scales (abstract, meso, and concrete), the notion of uneven and combined development has been deployed to understand the historical-geographical sociology of state formation (extending this sociology into processes of everyday state formation). Unlike the extant literature on uneven and combined development within the historical sociology of international relations, the book sought to deploy the term in a way that was more attentive to issues of the spatial and, furthermore, in a manner that was germane to contemporary struggles (and thus it actively researched and evaluated alternative praxes).

The multiscalar analysis that the book adopted has also been vital to providing a corrective to perspectives that have hitherto focused solely on macrohistorical structures, or the nation-state level, or, conversely, the local area studies approaches that have failed to adequately theorize the interconnections between the local, the national, and the global. The concept of uneven and combined hegemony was developed in an effort to overcome and transcend these separate follies, informed with both an abstract theory and empirical evidence that space and scale are always socially produced and subject to change. It was through the medium of class struggles that changes were shown to come about both through the efforts to expand spaces of capital accumulation and through subaltern struggles to resist this expansion and to create counterspaces, or spaces of resistance. The notion of passive revolution—defined as a class stratagem that aims to defuse radical subaltern pressure through the "statization" of their demands and consequent (re)absorption—was utilized as a key explanation of how this reabsorption and domestication of subaltern demands occurred through processes of restructuring that have served to further the development of capitalist social relations. This concept thus can aid our conclusion, not so much in providing an answer to Lenin's (1902/1987) famous question of "what is to be done?" but rather as a strategic orientation as to what is to be avoided. As the idiom goes, forewarned is forearmed. In concurrence with Anne Showstack Sassoon (1980: 205), the concept of passive revolution can be seen to function at two different levels: first, as an interpretation of history, and second, as a theoretical problem for thinking about change.

An overarching concern of this book has been with space and with class struggles to control the production of space. Within Mexico, the existence of a clash between two distinct spatial projects has been empirically demonstrated. This clash is only likely to intensify in the coming years, not just in Mexico but throughout Latin America. Recent controversial projects such as the proposed superhighway to be built through the Territorio Indígena y Parque Nacional Isiboro Secure (TIPNIS, Isiboro Secure National Park and Indigenous Territory) in Bolivia and the currently planned Nicaragua canal are indicative of this clash. At the global level, China's "One Belt, One Road" infrastructural project (along what was the former "Silk Road") promises to add a new dimension to geopolitical conflict and uneven development (*Economist* 2015). Following the analysis set out in chapter 1, the reason for this uneven development is to be located in the expansionary logic of capital, which remains tied to an ideology of growth (Harvey 2001; Lefebvre 1975/2009: 105). Capital, as was highlighted, seeks to create its own distinct geography via a permanent process of primitive accumulation. That is, it seeks to transform preexisting spaces into abstract spaces that are amenable to further surplus value extraction. However, as was made clear, two caveats remain that impede this process. First, the precapitalist landscape on which capital unfolds influences its trajectory (e.g., in the form of the existing interstate system, which prevents a global "law of value" being established). Second (and the greater subject of our analysis throughout the book), resistance in the form of counterspaces also thwarts capital's attempts to transform the world in the realization of its own concept. Capitalism was therefore postulated not as a complete totality but rather as a system that aims toward totalization (Lacher 2006: 103–4). Indeed, as Rosa Luxemburg (1913/2003: 397–98, 447) noted, a major contradiction of this system is that while it is predicated on expansion, this very logic of expansion undermines the basis on which it is able to grow (by undermining the continued existence of non-capitalist space).

Chapter 2 explored the changes in spatiality associated with the process of neoliberal restructuring, specifically within the Latin American context. In particular, this chapter explored the contradictions of ISI as a spatial and social project for development and inclusion, leading to the rise of neoliberalism as the region's new developmental paradigm. This chapter thereby gave an empirically informed theoretical analysis of the logic of uneven and combined development and the power geometries involved in it. However, at the same time as it explored the creation of new spatial divisions of labor, the chapter concomitantly highlighted resistance(s) that this process has provoked. Key issues that emerged through this discussion were those of passive revolution and *trasformismo* as elite class stratagems, on the one hand, and the overt politicization of space as a strategy for resistance movements, on the other.

Chapter 3 then shifted scales to examine these general trends in more empirical detail. This is a vital step for capturing both the *specific* and the *general* conditions of state formation, as Marx (1875/1996: 610) makes clear. In this chapter, passive revolution and hegemony were deployed in relation to understanding the production of space and scale in modern Mexico. Following the general analysis set out in chapter 2, the contradictory dynamics of capital accumulation tied to the spatial projects of ISI were revealed in greater detail, and the tensions that have resulted from the neoliberalization of space were discussed. This analysis allowed such tensions to be more fully explored in chapters 4 and 5.

These latter two chapters sought to synthesize all the key theoretical points established in the preceding chapters, as well as construct new insights from empirical investigation into movements of resistance. Chapters 4 and 5 therefore served multiple functions, including exploring how the shift from one mode of production to another alters the production of space, while at the same time examining how precapitalist spaces and social relations alter the topography of capitalism as they unfold in symbiosis (the "combined" part of uneven and combined development). These chapters also sought to provide a corrective to studies that have focused solely on the national scale or, conversely, have sought to explore local dynamics without attention to shifting national and global scales. This corrective was accomplished through the development of the concept of uneven and combined hegemony. Exploring state formation in Oaxaca and Chiapas also allowed the book to be the first text of its kind to consider the dynamics of passive revolution at a subnational scale in terms of everyday forms of state formation. Finally, these chapters responded to the lack of engagement in the historical-geographical materialist literature with concrete movements of resistance. This response was done by conducting a detailed discussion of emergent alternative geographical projects that have been formed with the loose coalition of movements associated with the APPO in Oaxaca and the aftermath of these struggles, as well as autonomous communities constructed by the Zapatistas in Chiapas. What, then, is the current conjuncture of these movements at the time of writing?

Struggles Unconquered

OAXACA

In 2016 the Comisión de la Verdad de Oaxaca (Oaxacan Truth Commission), tasked with investigating human rights abuses during the 2006 uprising, reported that violations by the state were "massive and systematic" and included arbitrary detention, torture, and extrajudicial killing. However, the shadow of this repression has not been banished to the past but rather returned during 2015 to preemptively stop teachers from once again launching new social struggles against the sites of power.

Alongside continuing efforts to organize against mining exploitation, wind parks, and other forms of transnational development projects, a crucial current battleground in Oaxaca is the struggle of the teachers against the national Education Reform Law, which includes plans for privatization of schooling, standardized curricula, and punitive teacher evaluations based on a culture of surveillance. Critics have noted that these reforms do not sufficiently take into account geographical sensitivities that are linked to various forms of inequality, most notably, between rural and urban schools (Hernández Navarro 2016).

These reforms threaten some of the last social rights of the Mexican Revolution such as the right to free education and job security. They are also a blatant attempt to undermine the power of unions as an oppositional force (Larson 2015). These threats have been seen most visibly in Oaxaca with the disbanding of the Instituto Estatal de Educación Pública de Oaxaca (IEPPO, State Institute of Public Education of Oaxaca), which was effectively controlled by Section 22 and indeed originally had been designed as a method of incorporating the radical teachers into state structures in order to provide a bridge to wider social movements. Along with the closing of IEPPO, members of Section 22 have been targeted with bank closures and arrest warrants following the attempt by some members to sabotage election materials as a response to the government's policy. In addition, ten thousand extra federal police were deployed to Oaxaca in 2015 to contain protests and ensure that the events of 2006 were not repeated and that space could not be reappropriated. Renata Bessi and Santiago Navarro (2015) point out that the federal police trained in this operation and the equipment they used (such as helicopters) are linked to the U.S.-sponsored Merida Initiative. This program of funding and training is ostensibly to fight the war on drugs, but, in effect, it is about containing threats to capital accumulation, or "armoring NAFTA" as Thomas Shannon, then U.S. assistant secretary of state for Western Hemisphere Affairs, admitted (Carlson 2008: 17). This is a demonstration of the new offensive of capital and is the latest in a round of attempts by the Mexican state to break powerful working-class unions following the evisceration of the Sindicato Mexicano de Electricistas (SME, Mexican Union of Electricians) and the Sindicato Nacional de Trabajadores Mineros, Metalúrgicos y Similares de la República Mexicana (National Union of Miners and Metal Workers) (La Botz 2015).

Oaxaca is not alone in this struggle, however, as this education reform is also opposed by teachers' unions in Guerrero, Michoacán, Chiapas, Veracruz, Quintana Roo, Baja California, and Jalisco (Arriga Lemus 2014). An ongoing difficulty has been maintaining long-term public sympathy for the teachers' cause. Not only do their strikes impact children's education, but also the wider tactics employed (such as roadblocks, installations, etc.) can cause disruption to daily life. Much depends not only on how the state responds to their demands but also on whether the teachers are able to articulate their current demands into a wider social struggle, converting themselves into a form of social movement unionism with key strategic allies. Indeed, this remains a global challenge for unionized workers and reflects the very real process of class struggle in action (Bieler 2012: 374; Bieler, Lindberg, and Sauerborn 2010: 258).

CHIAPAS

With regard to Chiapas, although Subcomandante Marcos had largely disappeared from public view following the 2006 Otra Campaña, it was in 2014 that his "death" was officially announced. At the same time, however, he was "reborn" as Subcomandante Galeano (following the assassination of education promoter José Luis Solís López, also known as Compañero Galeano, in May of that year). His future role within the Zapatista movement remains unclear, but Subcomandante Moises had by this time already replaced Marcos as the official spokesperson for the EZLN, reflecting part of the evolution within Zapatismo to which we now turn.

During his farewell speech, Marcos documented the changes within the Zapatista movement since its inception. As well as the obvious generational change (discussed in the previous chapter), he also noted the changing racial and class composition of the movement away from its origins in middle-class (and mestizo) intellectuals to a fully fledged indigenous peasant organization. Ideologically, there has also been a shift from vanguardism (of the founding guerrilla insurgents) to ruling by obeying linked to the civilian communities. Nevertheless, the key role of the armed movement was stressed as a legitimate form of violence: "The violence of below in the face of the violence of above" (Marcos 2014). A riposte was also given to those on the Left who have criticized the Zapatistas for not engaging in electoral politics and who thus considered the movement to be a failure. As Marcos (2014) outlined with regard to this position, "If being consistent is a failure, then inconsistency is the path to success— the route to power. But we don't want to go there. It doesn't interest us. Within these parameters, we prefer to fail rather than to win."

A key danger for the Zapatistas is the lack of attention to their plight. As one Zapatista in La Realidad (interview with the author, 2009) put it, "It is important that people do not forget that we are still here, struggling." It is for this reason that the Zapatistas have consistently sought to innovate and engage with the wider world rather than simply turning inward. While they had largely been ignored by the mainstream media since 2006, this isolation was shattered with their public reemergence on December 21, 2012 (symbolically, the predicted date of doomsday in the Mayan calendar). In their biggest mobilization since the uprising of 1994, more than forty thousand members of the civilian movement silently and peacefully occupied five municipal seats of Palenque, Altamirano, Las Margaritas, Ocosingo, and San Cristóbal de las Casas in Chiapas. Their message was clear and defiant, describing themselves as "we who never went away, despite what media across the spectrum have been determined to make you believe" (Ejército Zapatista de Liberación Nacional 2012). The same communiqué documented the improved living conditions of Zapatista communities, as well as their pride in their achievements since 1994, including ecologically harmonious production, culturally appropriate education, and self-governance. The communiqué also announced the next stages of the movement, which include the reaffirmation of their participation in the National Indigenous Congress, their reinitiation of contact with adherents of the "Sixth Declaration of the Lacandon Jungle," the building of bridges to wider social movements (without trying to lead or supplant them), the continued rejection of all political parties, and a call to respect the original San Andrés Accords and end the militarization of Chiapas (Ejército Zapatista de Liberación Nacional 2012).

Their latest major initiative has been the Escuelita Zapatista, designed to teach "freedom according to the Zapatistas." The first course, which ran in August and December 2013 and January 2014, attracted thousands of activists from across the world to Zapatista territory. These participants then accompanied families in their day-to-day tasks and were encouraged to ask questions about the praxis of Zapatismo, learning as they did so and deciding themselves what to do with their experiences. It is hard to predict how successful such initiatives will be in the long term and how stable and lasting these alliances will be. However, as Luis Hernández Navarro (2012) argues, these initiatives demonstrate the continued capacity of the Zapatistas to influence debates around politics in Mexico and beyond. The summation of the basis of Zapatismo offered by Marcos (2014)—"Don't sell out, don't surrender, don't give up"—is a testament to their enduring relevance and perseverance.

Final Reflections: The Struggle for Utopian Space

Many radical intellectuals have borrowed from Gramsci (1971: 175, Q 6, §86), citing with regard to social transformation that they retain pessimism of the intellect but optimism of the will. However, this is surely no longer sufficient (if it ever was) for transformative activity. What is required is engaged and purposeful (optimistic) intellectual activity combined with an optimism of the will to put ideas into material practice. John Holloway (2002a: 53) has argued that an essential aspect of transforming the world is to direct both critical thought and action toward fetishism (a form of reification that endows commodities with a life of their own). However, the issue of fetishism can be approached in two different ways. The first of these is what he calls "hard fetishism." According to this view, capitalist social relations are treated as an established fact that was constituted at some historical juncture and now stands as a "thing" to be destroyed at some point in time (presumably when the "balance of forces" allows). Given what has been argued in earlier chapters with regard to the persistence of spaces of resistance, coupled with the warning not to ascribe rigidity or coherence to a category such as "mode of production," this is a view that we should clearly reject. A more fruitful approach can be found in what Holloway calls "fetishisation as a process," which postulates that capitalism does not have an objective and durable existence but instead is a contested set of social relations that must constantly seek to (re)produce themselves in new (and profitable) ways (Holloway 2002a: 78–89). This view is helpful for two main reasons. First, as was highlighted in chapter 1, we must defetishize space in order to change it. Whereas capital remains tied to blind "ideologies of growth," social criticism must stress how such growth is often predicated on the exploitation of labor and the destruction of natural resources. This can aid debates about what growth we want (if any), how we can link production to socially useful endeavors, and how we then define what in fact is socially useful. Second, viewing fetishism this way serves as a more empowering tool for social movements, as whatever "power-over" capital contains, it is based on our own expropriated "power-to" (Holloway 2002a: 28). This tool clears the way for enacting collective power to achieve political transformation, as it recognizes that nonalienated forms of labor, fulfillment, and so on are not things that are to be constructed following some final messianic battle but rather exist in the here and now, albeit often as thwarted tendencies (Lefebvre 1976: 16). Fetishization as a process conforms to the understanding of class struggle that has been stressed throughout this work, namely, as a relational category rather than a fixed identity. The import of the concept of passive revolution is that it points us toward the very dangers of how these class struggles can be absorbed and their emancipatory tendencies blocked (see also Morton 2013). It is precisely when action is informed by this alternative view of fetishisation and cognizant of the dangers of passive revolution that real changes can begin to occur. As Lefebvre (1964/2009: 60) put it, "Once social forces begin moving, everything happens, as if under this house, under this edifice that seemed solid and balanced, the earth begins to move. And there promptly appear fissures where once we saw a vertical rock face."

How can we best reflect on the future of these developments? Gazing through a crystal ball to make concrete predictions is neither possible nor desirable. Nevertheless, certain empirical trends can still be observed and challenges theorized. In this sense, two related issues stand out as perhaps the most significant. The first is the challenge that social movements seeking to construct counter-spaces face in attempts by the state to reabsorb them through passive revolutionary tactics. The second issue relates to understanding this mode of struggle within the broader dynamics of what is occurring in Latin America.

Within Mexico (as well as worldwide), neoliberalism has been characterized not only by a "rollback" of welfare measures associated with the "developmental state" but also a "rollout" of new measures involving the active construction and normalization of neoliberal space (Peck and Tickell 2002: 384). However, this effective removal of the subaltern classes from "controlled inclusion" is not without its problems, as the last two chapters have shown. Indeed, as William Robinson (2008: 280) has aptly noted, the crucial class function that the state plays within capitalist social relation has become impeded by its perceived lack of legitimacy. However, he is surely wrong when he claims that all forms of responsibility, however minimal, have been abandoned (Robinson 2008: 320). Rather, as Peck and Tickell (2002: 396) have argued, it has been (and continues to be) necessary to construct "new modes of institution building designed to extend the neoliberal project, to manage its contradictions, and to secure its legitimacy." Mindful of the explication in chapter 3, which detailed that passive revolution should serve as a category of interpretation rather than a particular program, we must remain attentive to the manner in which new forms of state formation seek to reabsorb subaltern struggles such as those associated with the APPO and the EZLN.

The words of Henri Lefebvre are prescient here. Although he never used the term "passive revolution," he nevertheless usefully points to the dangers of it, warning social movements of "the triple trap of *substitution* (of authority for grassroots action), *transfer* (of responsibility from activists to the 'leaders'), and *displacement* (of the objectives and the stakes of social protest to the goals set by the 'bosses' who are attached to the established order)" (Lefebvre 2003: 99, emphasis added). In branching out to wider spatial scales, how then can we square the tactics of these Mexican social movements with the wider changes that are taking place in Latin America? In a series of polemical responses to John Holloway's (2002a) thesis of changing the world without taking power, many have sought to point to examples in countries such as Venezuela, Ecuador, and Bolivia to highlight conversely the necessity of taking state power in order to achieve social justice (see, among others, Robinson 2008: 341–48; Wilpert 2006). However, arguably more important is the *strategic direction* in which a movement is heading. This requires us to go back to the fundamental Marxist critique of the state as a special type of organization that is superimposed upon society rather than subordinate to it (Marx 1875/1996: 610; Lenin 1917/1987b: 301). Neither Marx nor Lenin thought structures of authority would disappear overnight. Rather, what their critique illustrated was the necessity of extending the participation of the subaltern classes over their everyday lives. What we have to examine, therefore, is whether social struggles are reconstituting society as society or in fact reconstituting the power relations of the state (Lefebvre 1976: 125). Genuine freedom, after all, requires "the exercise of *effective* power" (Lefebvre 1947/2008: 172). This again is where the concept of passive revolution can aid us, as we need to be attentive not only to where the initiative for social change comes from but also to whether this participation becomes a permanent feature of social life or remains restricted to privileged moments.

Through a witty amalgamation of two Greek words, Thomas More (1997) in his classic novel *Utopia* defined the word as the "good place" that was in fact "no place." With this in mind, we can make sense of Lefebvre's (1996: 151) argument that everyone who has plans to change the world must be thought of as a utopian. Consider the logic of capital as it has been outlined in the preceding chapters. What is it trying to do if not to create what it deems to be a good place (where the conditions for capital accumulation can flourish) from not yet existing places (in the indigenous regions of Oaxaca and Chiapas, where, historically, little in the way of capitalist social relations has existed)? Here we see the continuation of a colonial mode of thought that sees actually existing communities as essentially blank on their map of the world.[2]

On the other hand, resistance movements are not seeking to hold place and space static, nor, as chapters 4 and 5 indicated, do they simply aim to return to traditional forms of community.[3] Rather, they are seeking a transformation from something that as yet is not a fully formed reality. Autonomy remains, therefore, a dialectical concept, "simultaneously a documentation of where we are, and a projection of where we could be" (Pickerill and Chatterton 2006: 731). As Massimo Modonesi (2010: 145) further explains, "In this case autonomy does not designate only the form of the emancipated society of the future—the end—or the meaning of the struggles of the present—the process—rather it characterises their sense and orientation as anticipation of emancipation, as a representation in the present of the future liberation."

This anticipation of emancipation is especially significant for Latin America, where "the 'not yet' occupies a significant place" for politics (Dinerstein 2015: 60). With regard to this mode of argument, David Harvey (1996: 436) postulates that resistance can be thought of as a "living utopianism of process" rather than a fixed and nondialectical utopia that itself does not recognize the transitory nature of its own form. It was this aspect of transformation that Lenin (1917/1987b: 330–32) failed to grasp, believing instead that with revolution came a withering of democracy. However, democracy (understood in its true meaning as the rule of the people) is not a stable condition but rather a constant process in action (Lefebvre 1964/2009: 61). What we can therefore observe in Mexico, Latin America, and perhaps the world as a whole is a battle over the meaning of the future utopia and how that utopia is best constructed. This battle does not have a definitive end point. As Oscar Wilde (1891/2009: 27) famously stated, "A map of the world that does not include Utopia is not worth even glancing at, for it leaves out the one country at which Humanity is always landing. And when Humanity lands there, it looks out, and, seeing a better country, sets sail."

The invoking of utopia should not, however, be mistaken for idealistic wish thinking. Terry Eagleton (2005) exposes the fallacy with this position, pointing out that "it is the hard-nosed pragmatists who behave as though the World Bank and caffe latte will be with us for the next two millennia who are the real dreamers, and those who are open to the as yet unfigurable future who are the true realists." Likewise, Marx and Engels (1848/2000: 258–59) contemptuously wrote of those who were not prepared to understand the ephemeral nature of their current circumstances: "The selfish misconception that induces you to transform into eternal laws of nature and of reason, the social forms springing from your present mode of production and form of property—historical relations that rise and disappear in the progress of production—this misconception you share with every ruling class that has preceded you."

It is clear that these spaces of resistance face many challenges. Foremost among them is the need to "scale up" their activism while avoiding becoming reinscribed into the state apparatus and neutralized via means of passive revolutionary activity. This will be far from an easy task, and the future of these struggles can by no means be assured.

For now, however, we can simply say a crack or, rather, multiple cracks have been opened in history (see Holloway 2010). These cracks can serve as a window through which we may glimpse, if only fleetingly, another world: another world that is possible and ever more necessary.

NOTES

INTRODUCTION

1. For a wider critique based on this lack of geographical appreciation with reference to uneven and combined development, see Rioux (2015).

2. I have followed the international standard for referring to Gramsci's work using the notebook (Q) and the note number (§). The concordance table for this system can be found on the International Gramsci Society website, http://www.internationalgramsci society.org.

3. Although the term "mestization" refers literally to the miscegenation of indigenous ethnicities with white Europeans to produce the figure of the mestizo, this term by itself is quite misleading, as it is equally about the negation of indigenous cultural practices through assimilation into wider Western norms.

4. For a collection of essays inspired by this point, see Castree et al. (2010).

5. This argument was in fact originally made by Ernest Mandel (1968: 91).

6. The important recent contribution by Anievas and Nişancıoğlu (2015) and the edited volume by Anievas and Matin (2016) have further reinforced this intellectual trend.

7. The relevance of this method to current debates in historical sociology was introduced by Morton (2010).

CHAPTER 1. Geographical Politics and the Politics of Geography

1. Claudio Lomnitz-Adler (1992: 248) has questioned whether this spatial dichotomy between "México profundo" and "México imaginario" offered by Bonfil Batalla can be sustained, implying as it does a fixed ontological status to each paradigm. The argument, in other words, ignores how space is produced and transformed. It also elides how all traditions are to one degree or another "invented" (Hobsbawm and Ranger 1992). In this manner, Bonfil Batalla's thesis becomes reactionary rather than revolutionary.

2. As Thomas Piketty (2014: 186) notes, the breakup of the Soviet Union concomitantly witnessed the largest wave of privatizations in the history of capitalism.

3. This rejection of the singular narrative has been at the heart of much of postcolonial theory (see Ashcroft, Griffiths, and Tiffin 2002).

4. Marx and Engels wrote in *The Communist Manifesto* about capitalism producing

its own gravedigger in the form of the proletariat. Holloway claims Gramsci's concept of hegemony erases this.

5. For an argument that uses similar statistics to cover the same period but grounds the analysis in issues of class politics, see Duménil and Lévy (2004).

6. Lest this be thought of as something of an abstract discussion, numerous authors have shown that the way in which we conceive of space has direct political effects. For example, European colonial expansion could be justified on the basis that particular territories appeared blank on European maps (Ó Tuathail 1996: 25). As Doreen Massey (2005: 4) powerfully argues with regard to this mindset, it ignores the essential multiplicity of the spatial and is a systematic means of denying other cultures and peoples their own history (cf. Wolf 1997). It is this very type of discourse, however, that dominates modern developmentalism. Thus, spaces that have not subjected themselves to capitalist social relations are derided as "backward" and in need of transformation or opening (as will be explored in detail in chapters 4 and 5).

7. Perhaps the paradigmatic example of this would be Baron Haussmann's redesigning of Paris under Napoleon III to deal with concerns about potential insurrectionary activity (Scott 1998: 61). However, a stroll through any major Mexican city (as just one example) reveals the manner in which street names foster a sense of collective national identity, bearing as they do the names of the larger-than-life characters of the country's history, as well as symbolic dates.

8. Michel Foucault in his work on the prison (1979) and the clinic (1989), although tracing the genealogy of these spatial developments, fails to explore the possibilities for their transgression.

9. Kees van der Pijl (2007) has recently made the case for looking at historical forms of spatial integration through the concept of "modes of foreign relations." However, this ignores the fundamental question of why it is that a society spreads beyond its immediate locale. Modes of foreign relations can thus be better understood as arising from the imperatives generated from the mode of production, as this chapter will seek to demonstrate.

10. Engels (1935: 333) offers a useful periodization to show how particular periods of class rule display corresponding changes in state formation, from the ancient societies of the Greeks, through the Middle Ages, to the present. This nexus between the state and class power will be thoroughly discussed when the notion of passive revolution is introduced in chapter 2 and continued in the following chapters.

11. This point is, surprisingly, not considered by Harvey (2001: 326), who rejects claims that "a prior theorization of the rise of the capitalist state is necessary to reconstruct the historical geography of capitalism."

12. In Marx's classic example, it did not matter whether capital was invested in an education factory or in a sausage factory, as in both cases, the laborer was stamped with the same effect of producing profit for the proprietor.

13. Trotsky (1919/1962: 175) discusses this problem with regard to the role of state formation in Russia, demonstrating how the absolutist state evolved by relying on advanced forms of technology and social control developed in the West to sustain backward forms of social relations, leading to rising contradictions and eventually revolutionary outbreak. Adolfo Gilly (1983), drawing upon Trotsky, applies the same argument to Mexico.

14. For a detailed discussion of the themes of social relations in relation to Latin America, see the collection of essays in Lander (2000).

15. "Value-form" means that for all commodities to be exchangeable, they need to be comparable (e.g., be an increment of labor power).

CHAPTER 2. Latin America and the Production of the Global Economy

1. FDI refers to a strategic controlling investment in another country by a company or individual.

2. These responses by the elite classes are particularly evidenced in the turn to military/authoritarian regimes in Brazil (1964), Argentina (1966), Chile (1973), and Uruguay (1973).

3. Eurodollars are US dollars held outside of the United States and so not under the jurisdiction of the Federal Reserve.

4. The first oil price rise came in 1973 and was a response by the Organization of Arab Petroleum Exporting Countries (OAPEC) to the U.S. support for Israel during the Yom Kippur War. The second shock in 1979 followed in the wake of the Iranian Revolution.

CHAPTER 3. From Passive Revolution to Silent Revolution

1. Indeed, it is notable that Semo's thesis contains no actual reference to the work of Gramsci.

2. This is, of course, again a simplified picture that necessarily elides specific regional variations where divergent trends can be observed (see, e.g., Chassen-López 2004). Such disparities will be considered in chapters 4 and 5.

3. This law legislated for a maximum eight-hour day, the right to form unions, the right to strike, and the protection of foreign workers.

4. In relation to Mexico's geopolitical position, Nicolas Higgins (2004: 128) notes that in comparison with other revolutionary regimes such as the Soviet Union and Cuba, Mexico enjoyed an overwhelming degree of international legitimacy.

5. An example of the pressure brought to bear by foreign capital was the cessation of production in the oil industry, supported by the U.S. State Department in response to the doubling of taxes on oil exports introduced by the administration of Álvaro Obregón (1920–24) (Hamilton 1982: 71).

6. This notion of "tipping points" is taken from Sassen (2006).

7. As Jessop (1990: 199) makes clear, the rates of return on money capital are always ultimately dependent upon the performance of productive or industrial capital.

CHAPTER 4. The Changing State of Resistance

1. It is important to note that this claim regarding "ungovernability" was advanced by the APPO as a political strategy. However, it was not officially recognized by the Senate, which would have given the APPO the power to remove the governor from office. The fact that the national government chose not to take such action speaks to important issues around the politics of scale and the contradictory process of democratization in Mexico with the emergent PAN reliant on support from the PRI as interlocutors (see Gibson 2005).

2. For a rebuttal of this point about declining peasant agency, see Morton (2007a).

3. *Usos y costumbres* involves a grounding of politics in the community assembly, from which members are elected to serve civil and religious *cargos* (positions of responsibility, literally meaning "burdens") of a period usually up to three years. These positions are seen less as positions of prestige and more as a community service that people have an obligation to take part in.

4. The term "Vallistocracia" has been coined to describe the ruling elite of Oaxaca. It refers to an elite of owners, political classes and intellectuals that come largely, although not exclusively from the central valleys (Martínez Vásquez 2007: 27).

5. Indigenous resistance to state-based megaprojects that have elided democratic consultation has been a growing phenomenon throughout Latin America in recent decades (Veltmeyer 2012: 75–77).

6. As an example of these authoritarian practices, during his five years in office Murat suspended 140 (25 percent) of Oaxaca's municipalities. This intervention took place largely in urban areas of opposition control (Gibson 2005: 116). Ulises Ruiz Ortiz gained even wider infamy for the widespread use of repression and practices of crony capitalism. One high-profile target of repression was the Left-leaning Oaxacan daily newspaper *Noticias*, which was openly critical of him.

7. A recent survey revealed that *tequios* are conducted in 79 percent of Oaxacan municipalities, religious *cargos* in 81 percent, civil *cargos* in 86 percent, and government cargos in 96 percent (Sorroza Polo and Danielson 2013: 170).

8. Following state repression, when state and federal soldiers were sent into the community, five hundred local residents were arrested after being accused of links with the EPR. Twelve men remained imprisoned until 2009, despite widespread irregularities and abuses, including well-documented allegations of torture. Four of the twelve were released on July 18, 2009, but eight remain political prisoners to this day.

9. It is important at the same time that we do not idealize *usos y costumbres* as a panacea for development. Important exclusions do remain in terms of representation, notably of women, those outside of the *cabecera* (head town), and other minorities (Eisenstadt 2013: 5).

10. We may question, however, just how "voluntary" this project was. Ana de Ita (2006: 152) highlights how certificates of entry into PROCEDE were often illegally demanded by local and regional authorities for receiving subsidies and credit. On government program, PROCAMPO, was in fact made dependent on entry into the PROCEDE (Pisa 1994: 290). Community representatives from San José del Progreso whom I interviewed also spoke about being tricked into agreement and their ignorance of PROCEDE's ramifications (interviews with community members by the author, Oaxaca, 2009).

11. An identical claim had been successfully raised in previous months in neighboring Chiapas.

12. As evidence of this point, 2006 represented the first time in which the PRI suffered an overwhelming historical defeat in Oaxaca, losing nine of eleven electoral districts.

CHAPTER 5. The Clash of Spatializations

1. This perspective on time was confirmed by a member of La Realidad's Junta de Buen Gobierno (interview with the author, 2009), who stated, "We look to our past to create our future."

2. As Aaron Bobrow-Strain (2007: 65) notes, the state governor in 1898 was offered a thirty-thousand-peso bribe to cancel the planned road that would connect *fincas* with remote markets and ports.

3. Of course, debt servitude was only abolished in law. In reality, it would persist for many decades in Chiapas.

4. *Mapache*, which literally translates as "raccoon," was the name of a coalition of ranchers and planters alongside their subservient labor populations.

5. The actual amount of land redistributed and the number of beneficiaries created, however, were extremely small compared with other states. Only the Federal District and Southern Baja California had less land redistributed (Instituto Nacional de Estadística y Geografía 1994: 379).

6. Noting this change in class relations, Thomas Benjamin (1981: 132) states, "The [*ejidal*] bank became a bureaucratic hacendado, the ejidatario a peon of the bank."

7. *La familia chiapaneca* is the name given to the local elite class, made of up landowners and commercial interests.

8. These tactics of divide and rule, inherited from colonial times, persist into the present.

9. This was the former name of the PRI.

10. Following the analysis set out in Rus (1994), these so-called Institutional Revolutionary Communities can equally be labeled "passive revolutionary communities."

11. The term "spatial fix" was coined by David Harvey (2006a), who used it to demonstrate the manner in which the contradictions of capital accumulation are displaced in one place by expanding into another.

12. One Zapatista (interview with the author, La Realidad, 2009) explained that the importance of the movement was that they were making plans for a new life: "When it rains one prepares by getting an umbrella and wearing adequate clothing. . . . The world economic system is going down the toilet. We are preparing for what comes after. . . . When you want to change the world you need to prepare for it."

13. Women's control over their own fertility is of considerable importance given reports about the high percentage of indigenous women who have been sterilized without their permission (*Proceso* 2013).

14. Owing to the varied and geographically dispersed nature of Zapatista communities, practice between them can vary. For an excellent set of commentaries on different aspects of Zapatismo in everyday life, see Baronnet, Bayo, and Stahler-Sholk (2011).

15. Literally meaning "snails," the Caracoles are a novel regional form of governance whose purpose is to coordinate the autonomous municipalities.

16. For example, a 10 percent tax is made on all solidarity contributions from NGOs working in Zapatista territory. A 10 percent tax is also levied on any government project that wants to pass through the Zapatista zone of influence (JBG member, interview with the author, La Realidad, 2009; Stahler-Sholk 2007: 57).

17. In La Garrucha the JBG is staffed by an eight-member team, with two members from each of the four municipalities, who in turn represent around 211 communities. In La Realidad it is a seven-member team, also representing four municipalities and around 150 communities.

18. For a detailed analysis of Zapatista education, see Baronnet (2012).

19. It should be noted that the Otra Campaña was hindered by the weight of state repression, most notably manifested in Texcoco and neighboring San Salvador Atenco, where the FPDT had allied itself with the Zapatistas' "Sixth Declaration of the Lacandon Jungle." In the wake of this repression, Subcomandante Insurgente Marcos announced the campaign's cessation and issued a red alert throughout rebel territory.

20. Marcos (2003) made his position on this matter abundantly clear with a communiqué entitled "I Shit on the Revolutionary Vanguards of This Planet."

21. The alter-globalization movement rose to prominence during the protests against the WTO in Seattle in 1999 and seeks to recast corporate globalization to ends more compatible with social justice.

22. An infamous memo from the Chase-Manhattan Bank in 1995 called for the Mexican government to "eliminate" the Zapatistas "to demonstrate their effective control of the national territory and security policy" in order to reassure stock markets.

23. For updated information on such violations, see the website of Fray Bartolomé de Las Casas Centro de Derechos Humanos, www.frayba.org.mx.

24. The Selva Lacandona is an area of increasing strategic importance to the Mexican state. It contains a huge amount of Mexico's biodiversity and thus has become essential to projects of ecotourism and bioprospecting.

25. A long-running case involves the *ejidatarios* of San Sebastián Bachajón. This conflict has taken place in relation to a dispute over who had the right to control cultural sites such as the famous Agua Azul and Misol-Ha waterfall (Bellinghausen 2009).

CONCLUSION

1. The limits to growth in relation to ecological concerns were keenly discussed previously in the 1970s (Meadows et al. 1972). However, it appears that these issues are being debated again with renewed vigor.

2. For an actual illustration of this with regard to state projects planned in Chiapas, see Rocheleau (2015: 710).

3. Although as Marx (1871/2000: 588) noted, "It is generally the fate of completely new historical creations to be mistaken for the counterparts of older and even defunct forms of social life, to which they may bear a certain likeness."

BIBLIOGRAPHY

Agnew, J. (1994) "The territorial trap: The geographical assumptions of international relations theory." *Review of International Political Economy*, 1 (1), 53–80.

Agnew, J., and Ó Tuathail, G. (1992) "Geopolitics and discourse: Practical geopolitical reasoning in American foreign policy." *Political Geography*, 11 (2), 190–204.

Alvarez, F. (1988) "Peasant movements in Chiapas." *Bulletin of Latin American Research*, 7 (2), 277–98.

Amin, S. (1974) *Accumulation on a world scale: A critique of the theory of underdevelopment*. New York: Monthly Review Press.

Anderson, B. (1991) *Imagined communities: Reflections on the origin and spread of nationalism*. Rev. ed. London: Verso.

Anderson, K. B. (2010) *Marx at the margins: On nationalism, ethnicity, and non-Western societies*. Chicago: University of Chicago Press.

Andrews, A. (2010) "Constructing mutuality: The Zapatistas' transformation of transnational activist power dynamics." *Latin American Politics and Society*, 52 (1), 89–120.

Anievas, A. (2010) *Marxism and world politics: Contesting global capitalism*. London: Routledge.

Anievas, A., and Matin, K. (2016) *Historical sociology and world history: Uneven and combined development over the longue durée*. Lanham, Md.: Rowman and Littlefield International.

Anievas, A., and Nişancıoğlu, K. (2015) *How the West came to rule*. London: Pluto Press.

Aquino-Centeno, S. (2009) "Contesting social memories and identities in the Zapotec Sierra of Oaxaca, Mexico." PhD diss., University of Arizona.

Arriga Lemus, M. (2014) "The struggle to democratise education in Mexico." *NACLA*, 47 (2), 30–34.

Ashcroft, B., Griffiths, G., and Tiffin, H. (2002) *The empire writes back: Theory and practice in post-colonial literatures*. London: Routledge.

Baer, W. (1972) "Import substitution and industrialization in Latin America: Experiences and interpretations." *Latin American Research Review*, 7 (1), 95–122.

Banaji, J. (2011) *Theory as history: Essays on modes of production and exploitation.* Chicago: Haymarket Books.

Barkin, D. (1990) *Distorted development: Mexico in the world economy.* Boulder, Colo.: Westview Press.

Barkin, D., and Esteva, G. (1986) "Social conflict and inflation in Mexico," in N. Hamilton and T. Harding (eds.), *Modern Mexico: State, economy and social conflict.* Thousand Oaks, Calif.: Sage Publications.

Barmeyer, N. (2003) "The guerrilla movement as a project: An assessment of community involvement in the EZLN." *Latin American Perspectives*, 30 (1), 122–38.

Barmeyer, N. (2009) *Developing Zapatista autonomy: Conflict and NGO involvement in rebel Chiapas.* Albuquerque: University of New Mexico Press.

Baronnet, B. (2012) *Autonomía y educación indígena: Las escuelas zapatistas de la Selva Lacandona de Chiapas, México.* Quito: Abya-Yala.

Baronnet, B., Bayo, M. M., and Stahler-Sholk, R. (2011) *Luchas "muy otras": Zapatismo y autonomía en las comunidades indígenas de Chiapas.* Mexico City: CIESAS.

Bartra, R. (1975) "Peasants and political power in Mexico: A theoretical approach." *Latin American Perspectives*, 2 (2), 25–45.

Bellinghausen, H. (2009) "Inquietante 'normalidad' viven Zapatistas en torno a zona de balnearios fluviales." *La Jornada*, http://www.jornada.unam.mx/2009/05/02 /index.php?section=politica&article=024n1pol (accessed May 6, 2016).

Bellinghausen, H. (2013a) "Otro fracaso: Ciudades rurales sustentables." *La Jornada*, http://www.jornada.unam.mx/2013/05/04/sociedad/040n1soc (accessed March 3, 2016).

Bellinghausen, H. (2013b) "Villas rurales y ciudades sustentables en Chiapas: Ejemplos de despilfarro y corrupción." *La Jornada*, http://www.jornada.unam.mx/2013/05/05 /politica/019n1pol (accessed March 3, 2016).

Benjamin, M. (1995) "Interview: Subcomandante Marcos," in E. Katzenberger (ed.), *First World ha ha ha! The Zapatista challenge.* San Francisco: City Lights.

Benjamin, T. (1981) "Passages to Leviathan: Chiapas and the Mexican state, 1891–1947." PhD dissertation, Michigan State University.

Benjamin, T. (1996) *A rich land, a poor people: Politics and society in modern Chiapas.* Rev. ed. Albuquerque: University of New Mexico Press.

Bernstein, H. (2010) *Class dynamics of agrarian change.* Halifax: Fernwood Publishing.

Bessi, R., and Navarro, S. (2015) "Oaxaca, Mexico, faces police militarization as governor acts to pre-empt education protests." *Truth Out*, August 1, http://www .truth-out.org/news/item/32114-oaxaca-mexico-faces-police-militarization-as -governor-acts-to-preempt-education-protests (accessed May 3, 2016).

Bieler, A. (2012) "'Workers of the world, unite'? Globalisation and the quest for transnational solidarity." *Globalizations*, 9 (3), 365–78.

Bieler, A. (2013) "The EU, global Europe and processes of uneven and combined development: The problem of transnational labour solidarity." *Review of International Studies*, 39 (1), 161–83.

Bieler, A., Lindberg, I., and Sauerborn, W. (2010) "After 30 years of deadlock: Labour's possible strategies in the new global order." *Globalizations*, 7 (1–2), 247–60.

Bieler, A., and Morton, A. D. (2001) "The Gordian knot of agency-structure in international relations: A neo-Gramscian perspective." *European Journal of International Relations*, 1, 5–35.

Bieler, A., and Morton, A. D. (2008) "The deficits of discourse in IPE: Turning base metal into gold." *International Studies Quarterly*, 52 (1), 103–28.

Bieler, A., and Morton, A. D. (2015) "Axis of evil or access to diesel?" *Historical Materialism*, 23 (2), 94–130.

Biersteker, T. (1995) "The 'triumph' of liberal economic ideas in the developing world," in B. Stallings (ed.), *Global change, regional response: The new international context of development*. Cambridge: Cambridge University Press.

Binford, L. (1993) "Irrigation, land tenure and class struggle in Juchitán, Oaxaca," in H. Campbell, L. Binford, M. Bartolomé, and A. Barabas (eds.), *Zapotec struggles: History, politics, and representations from Juchitán, Oaxaca*. Washington, D.C.: Smithsonian Institution Press.

Binford, L., and Campbell, H. (1993) Introduction, in H. Campbell, L. Binford, M. Bartolomé, and A. Barabas (eds.), *Zapotec struggles: History, politics, and representations from Juchitán, Oaxaca*. Washington, D.C.: Smithsonian Institution Press.

Block, F. (2001) "Using social theory to leap over historical contingencies: A comment on Robinson." *Theory and Society*, 30 (2), 215–21.

Bobrow-Strain, A. (2005) "Articulations of rule: Landowners, revolution and territory in Chiapas, Mexico, 1920–1962." *Historical Geography*, 31, 744–62.

Bobrow-Strain, A. (2007) *Intimate enemies: Landowners, power and violence in Chiapas*. Durham, N.C.: Duke University Press.

Bonefeld, W. (2001) "The permanence of primitive accumulation: Commodity fetishism and social constitution." *Commoner*, September, http://www.commoner .org.uk/02bonefeld.pdf (accessed October 4, 2015).

Bonfil Batalla, G. (1996) *México profundo: Reclaiming a civilization*. Translated by P. A. Dennis. Austin: University of Texas Press.

Brass, T. (2005) "Neoliberalism and the rise of (peasant) nations within the nation: Chiapas in comparative and theoretical perspectives." *Journal of Peasant Studies*, 3–4, 651–91.

Brenner, N. (1997) "State territorial restructuring and the production of spatial scale." *Political Geography*, 16 (4), 273–306.

Brenner, N. (1998) "Between fixity and motion: Accumulation, territorial organization and the historical geography of spatial scales." *Environment and Planning D: Space and Society*, 16 (4), 459–81.

Brenner, N. (1999) "Beyond state-centrism? Space, territoriality, and geographical scale in globalization studies." *Theory and Society*, 28 (1), 39–78.

Brenner, N. (2004) *New state spaces: Urban governance and the rescaling of statehood*. Oxford: Oxford University Press.

Brenner, R. (1982) "The agrarian roots of European capitalism." *Past & Present*, 97, 16–113.

Bruff, I. (2010) "European varieties of capitalism and the international." *European Journal of International Relations*, 16 (4), 615–38.

Bulmer-Thomas, V. (1994) *The economic history of Latin America since independence*. Cambridge: Cambridge University Press.

Burawoy, M. (1998) "The extended case method." *Sociological Theory*, 16 (1), 4–33.

Burchardt, H. J., and Dietz, K. (2014) "(Neo-)extractivism—a new challenge for development theory from Latin America." *Third World Quarterly*, 35 (3), 468–86.

Callinicos, A. (2003) *An anti-capitalist manifesto*. Cambridge: Polity.

Callinicos, A. (2007) "Does capitalism need the state-system?" *Cambridge Review of International Affairs*, 20 (4), 533–54.

Callinicos, A. (2009) *Imperialism and the global political economy*. Cambridge: Polity.

Callinicos, A. (2010) "The limits of passive revolution." *Capital and Class*, 34 (3), 491–507.

Callinicos, A., and Rosenberg, J. (2008) "Uneven and combined development: The social-relational substratum of 'the international'? An exchange of letters." *Cambridge Review of International Affairs*, 21 (1), 77–112.

Cameron, M. (2009) "Latin America's left turn: Beyond good and bad." *Third World Quarterly*, 30 (2), 331–48.

Campbell, H., Binford, L., Bartolomé, M., and Barabas, A. (eds.) (1993) *Zapotec struggles: History, politics, and representations from Juchitán, Oaxaca*. Washington, D.C.: Smithsonian Institution Press.

Cancian, F. (1992) *The decline of community in Zinacantan: Economy, public life, and social stratification, 1960–1987*. Stanford, Calif.: Stanford University Press.

Cárdenas, E. (2000) "The Great Depression and industrialization: The case of Mexico," in R. Thorp (ed.), *An economic history of twentieth century Latin America*, vol. 2. Oxford: Palgrave Macmillan.

Cardoso, F. H., and Faletto, E. (1979) *Dependency and development in Latin America*. Translated by M. Uruidi. Berkeley: University of California Press.

Carlson, L. (2008) "Armouring NAFTA: The battleground for Mexico's future." *NACLA*, 41 (5), 17–22.

Castañeda, J. (1994) *Utopia unarmed: The Latin American Left after the Cold War*. New York: Vintage.

Castañeda, J. (2006) "Latin America's left turn." *Foreign Affairs*, 85 (3), 28–43.

Castree, N. (2000) "Marxism and the production of nature." *Capital and Class*, 24 (5), 5–36.

Castree, N. (2004) "Differential geographies: Place, indigenous rights and 'local' resources." *Political Geography*, 23 (2), 133–67.

Castree, N. (2010) "Crisis, continuity and change: Neoliberalism, the Left and the future of capitalism." *Antipode*, 41 (s1), 185–213.

Castree, N., Chatterton, P. A., Heynen, N., Larner, W., and Wright, M. W. (eds.) (2010) *The point is to change it: Geographies of hope and survival in an age of crisis*. Oxford: Wiley-Blackwell.

Castro-Soto, G. (2005) "Impacto y consecuencias de las represas." http://www.ciepac .org/boletines/chiapasaldia.php?id=456 (accessed September 14, 2009).

Ceceña, A. E., and Barreda, A. (1998) "Chiapas and the global restructuring of capital," in J. Holloway and E. Peláez (eds.), *Zapatista! Reinventing revolution in Mexico*. London: Pluto Press.

Chang, H. (2010) "*Hamlet* without the prince of Denmark: How development has disappeared from today's 'development' discourse," in S. Khan and J. Christiansen (eds.), *Towards new developmentalism: Market as means rather than master.* Abingdon: Routledge.

Chase-Dunn, C. (1999) "Globalization: A world-systems perspective." *Journal of World-Systems Research*, 5 (2), 187–215.

Chassen-López, F. (2004) *From liberal to revolutionary Oaxaca: The view from the South, Mexico 1867–1911.* University Park: Pennsylvania State University Press.

Ciccariello-Maher, G. (2013) *We created Chavez.* Durham, N.C.: Duke University Press.

Clarke, C. (1992) "Components of socio-economic change in post-revolutionary Oaxaca, Mexico," in M. P. Moya, F. C. Abellan, and C. G. Martínez (eds.), *America latina: La cuestion regional.* La Mancha: Universidad de Casalle.

Clarke, C. (1996) "Opposition to PRI 'hegemony' in Oaxaca," in R. Aitken, N. Craske, G. A. Jones, and D. E. Stansfield (eds.), *Dismantling the Mexican state?* London: Macmillan.

Clarke, C. (2000) *Class, ethnicity and community in southern Mexico: Oaxaca's peasantries.* Oxford: Oxford University Press.

Cleaver, H. (1998) "The electronic fabric of struggle," in J. Holloway and E. Peláez (eds.), *Zapatista! Reinventing revolution in Mexico.* London: Pluto Press.

Cline, H. (1949) "Civil congregations of the Indians in New Spain 1598–1640." *Hispanic American Historical Review*, 29, 349–69.

CMWP. *Mexico.* Baltimore, Md.: Johns Hopkins University Press.

Coatsworth, J. (1998) "Economic and institutional trajectories in nineteenth century Latin America," in J. Coatsworth and A. M. Taylor (eds.), *Latin America and the world economy since 1800.* Cambridge, Mass.: Harvard University, David Rockefeller Center for Latin American Studies.

Cockcroft, J. (1983) *Mexico: Class formation, capital accumulation and the state.* New York: Monthly Review Press.

Cockcroft, J. (1998) *Mexico's hope: An encounter with politics and history.* New York: Monthly Review Press.

Cohen, J. (2004) *The culture of migration in southern Mexico.* Austin: University of Texas Press.

Cohen, J. (2010) "Oaxacan migration and remittances as they relate to Mexican migration patterns." *Journal of Ethnic and Migration Studies*, 36 (1), 149–61.

Colás, A. (2005) "Neoliberalism, globalisation and international relations," in A. Saad-Filho (ed.), *Neoliberalism: A critical reader.* London: Pluto Press.

Collier, G. (1994) *Basta! Land and the Zapatista rebellion in Chiapas.* Oakland, Calif.: Food First Books.

Collier, G., and Collier, J. (2005) "The Zapatista rebellion in the context of globalization." *Journal of Peasant Studies*, 32 (3–4), 450–60.

Collier, G., with Quaratiello, E. (2005) *Basta! Land and the Zapatista rebellion in Chiapas.* Rev. ed. Oakland, Calif.: Food First Books.

Comisión Económica para América Latina y el Caribe. (2007) *Statistical yearbook for Latin America and the Caribbean 2006.* Santiago, Chile: United Nations.

Comité Clandestino Revolucionario Indígena—Comandancia General. (2005) Sixth declaration of the Lacandon jungle. *EZLN Communiqués*, July, http://flag.blackened .net/revolt/mexico/ezlnco.html (accessed July 7, 2010).

Cook, S. (1984) "Social differentiation, and the construction of provisional Mexican capitalism." *Latin American Perspectives*, 11 (4), 60–85.

Cook, S., and Diskin, M. (1976) "The peasant market economy in the valley of Oaxaca in analysis and history," in S. Cook and M. Diskin (eds.), *Markets in Oaxaca*. Austin: University of Texas Press.

Corando, J. P., and Mora, A. V. (2006) "México y Centroamérica: Hegemonía, resistencias y visibilidad social," in D. V. Solís and X. Leyva-Solano (eds.), *Geoeconómica y geopolítica en el área del Plan Puebla-Panamá*. Mexico City: CIESAS.

Corbett, J., and Whiteford, S. (1983) "State penetration and development in Mesoamerica, 1950–1980," in C. Kendall, J. Hawkins, and L. Bossen (eds.), *Social change in heritage of conquest: Thirty years later*. Albuquerque: University of New Mexico Press.

Cornelius, W., Eisenstadt, T., and Hindley, J. (1999) *Subnational politics and democratization in Mexico*. San Diego: Centre for U.S.-Mexican Studies.

Coutinho, C. N. (2012) "A época neoliberal: Revolução passiva ou contra-reforma?" *Revista Novos Rumos*, 49 (1), 117–25.

Cox, R. W. (1981) "Social forces, states and world orders: Beyond international relations theory." *Millennium: Journal of International Studies*, 10 (2), 126–55.

Cox, R. W. (1983) "Gramsci, hegemony and international relations: An essay in method." *Millennium: Journal of International Studies*, 12 (2), 162–75.

Cox, R. W. (1987) *Production, power and world order: Social forces in the making of history*. New York: Columbia University Press.

Cox, R. W. (1989) "Production, the state and change in world order," in E. Czempiel and J. Rosenau (eds.), *Global changes and theoretical challenges: Approaches to world politics for the 1990s*. Toronto: Lexington Books.

Cox, R. W. (1999) "Civil society at the turn of the millennium: Prospects for an alternative world order." *Review of International Studies*, 25 (1), 3–28.

Cox, L., and Nilsen, A. G. (2014) *We make our own history: Marxism and social movements in the twilight of neoliberalism*. London: Pluto Press.

Cuevas, J. H. (2007) "Salud y autonomía: El caso Chiapas." *Report for the Health Systems Knowledge Network, World Health Organization*, March, http://cdrwww.who.int/social_determinants/resources/csdh_media/autonomy_mexico_2007_es.pdf (accessed May 6, 2016).

Dávila, E., Kessel, G., and Levy, S. (2002) "El sur también existe: Un ensayo sobre el desarrollo regional de Mexico." *Economiá Mexicana*, 11 (2), 205–60.

Davis, D. (1993) "The dialectic of autonomy: State, class and economic crisis in Mexico, 1958–1982." *Latin American Perspectives*, 20 (3), 46–75.

Davis, J., and Eakin, H. (2013) "Chiapas' delayed entry into the international labour market: A story of peasant isolation, exploitation, and coercion." *Migration and Development*, 2 (1), 132–49.

Davis, M. (2006) *Planet of slums*. London: Verso.

Day, R. (2005) *Gramsci is dead: Anarchist undercurrents in the newest social movements*. London: Pluto Press.

Del Roio, M. (2012) "Translating passive revolution in Brazil." *Capital and Class*, 36 (2), 215–34.

Dietz, J. (1989) "The debt cycle and restructuring in Latin America." *Latin American Perspectives*, 16 (1), 13–30.

Dinerstein, A. C. (2015) *The politics of autonomy in Latin America: The art of organising hope*. Basingstoke: Palgrave Macmillan.

Dirlik, A. (1997) *The postcolonial aura: Third World criticism in the age of global capitalism*. Boulder, Colo.: Westview.

Dirlik, A. (1999) "Globalism and the politics of place," in K. Olds, P. Dicken, P. F. Kelly, L. Kong, and H. Wai-chung Yeung (eds.), *Globalization and the Asia-Pacific: Contested territories*. London: Routledge.

Duménil, G., and Lévy, D. (2004) *Capital resurgent: The roots of the neoliberal revolution*. Translated by D. Jeffers. Cambridge, Mass.: Harvard University Press.

Dussel-Peters, E. (2000) *Polarising Mexico: The impact of liberalization strategy*. Boulder, Colo.: Lynne Rienner.

Eagelton, T. (2005) "Just my imagination." *Nation*, May 26, http://www.thenation.com /article/just-my-imagination/176 (accessed May 11, 2016).

Economist. (2015) "Where all silk roads lead." May 11, http://www.economist.com/news /china/21648039-through-fog-hazy-slogans-contours-chinas-vision-asia-emerge -where-all-silk-roads (accessed May 4, 2016).

Eisenstadt, T. (2007) "Usos y costumbres and post-electoral conflicts in Oaxaca, Mexico, 1995–2004: An empirical and normative assessment." *Latin American Research Review*, 42 (1), 53–77.

Eisenstadt, T. (2013) "Reconciling liberal pluralism and group rights: A comparative perspective on Oaxaca, Mexico's experiment in multiculturalism," in T. A. Eisenstadt, M. S. Danielson, M. J. B. Corres, and C. Sorroza Polo (eds.), *Latin America's multicultural movements: The struggle between communitarianism, autonomy, and human rights*. Oxford: Oxford University Press.

Engels, F. (1935) *Herr Eugen Dühring's revolution in science: (Anti-Dühring)*. Translated by E. Burns. Edited by C. P. Dutt. London: Lawrence.

Escobar, A. (2001) "Culture sits in places: Reflections on globalism and subaltern strategies of localization." *Political Geography*, 20 (2), 139–74.

Esteva, G. (2001) "The meaning and scope of the struggle for autonomy." *Latin American Perspectives*, 28 (2), 120–48.

Esteva, G. (2007) "Oaxaca: The path of radical democracy." *Socialism and Democracy*, 21 (2), 74–96.

Esteva, G. (2010) "Estado de cosas." *La Jornada*, May 5.

Ejército Zapatista de Liberación Nacional. (1994) "1st declaration of the Lacandon Jungle," in Subcomandante Insurgente Marcos, *Our word is our weapon*. London: Serpents Tail.

Ejército Zapatista de Liberación Nacional. (2012) "El EZLN anuncia sus pasos siguientes: Comunicado del 30 de diciembre del 2012." *Enlace Zapatista*, December 30, http:// enlacezapatista.ezln.org.mx/2012/12/30/el-ezln-anuncia-sus-pasos-siguientes -comunicado-del-30-de-diciembre-del-2012/ (accessed May 5, 2016).

Federici, S. (2004) *Caliban and the witch: Women, the body and primitive accumulation*. Brooklyn, N.Y.: Autonomedia.

Ferguson, N. (2004) *Empire: How Britain made the modern world*. London: Penguin.

Ffrench-Davis, R. (1994) "The Latin American economies 1950–1990," in L. Bethall (ed.), *The Cambridge history of Latin America*. Vol. 6, pt. 1. Cambridge: Cambridge University Press.

Fitzgerald, E. V. K. (1978) "The state and capital accumulation in Mexico." *Journal of Latin American Studies*, 10 (2), 263–82.

Foucault, M. (1979) *Discipline and punish: The birth of the prison*. Harmondsworth: Penguin.

Foucault, M. (1989) *The birth of the clinic: An archaeology of medical perception*. Translated by A. M. Sheridan. London: Routledge.

Frank, A. G. (1978) *Dependent accumulation and underdevelopment*. London: Macmillan.

Frye, D. (1994) "Speaking of the ejido: The modes of discourse about the Salinas Reforms." *Urban Anthropology*, 23 (2–3), 307–30.

Fukuyama, F. (1992) *The end of history and the last man*. London: Penguin.

Furtado, C. (1970) *Economic development of Latin America: From colonial times to the Cuban Revolution*. Translated by S. Macedo. Cambridge: Cambridge University Press.

Galeano, E. (2008) *Open veins of Latin America: Five centuries of the pillage of a continent*. New Delhi: Three Essays Collective.

García de León, A. (1994/2003) "Prólogo," in Ejército Zapatista de Liberación Nacional, *Documentos y comunicados*, 5 vols. Mexico City: Ediciones Era.

Gereffi, G. (1995) "Global production systems and Third World development," in B. Stallings (ed.), *Global change, regional response: The new international context of development*. Cambridge: Cambridge University Press.

Gereffi, G., and Evans, P. (1981) "Transnational corporations, dependent development, and state policy in the semiperiphery: A comparison of Brazil and Mexico." *Latin American Research Review*, 16 (3), 31–64.

Ghani, A. (1993) "Space as an arena of represented practices: An interlocutor's response to David Harvey's 'From space to place and back again,'" in J. Bird, B. Curtis, T. Putnam, G. Robertson, and L. Tickner (eds.), *Mapping the futures: Local cultures, global change*. London: Routledge.

Gibler, J. (2009) *Mexico unconquered: Chronicles of power and revolt*. San Francisco: City Lights.

Gibson, E. (2005) "Boundary control: Subnational authoritarianism in democratic countries." *World Politics*, 58 (1), 101–32.

Gibson-Graham, J. K. (2006a) *The end of capitalism (as we knew it): A feminist critique of political economy*. Minneapolis: University of Minnesota Press.

Gibson-Graham, J. K. (2006b) *A post-capitalist politics*. Minneapolis: University of Minnesota Press.

Gilbert, A., and Ward, P. (1984) "Community action by the urban poor: Democratic involvement, community self-help or a means of social control." *World Development*, 12 (8), 769–82.

Gilbert, A., and Ward, P. (1985) *Housing, the state and the poor: Policy and practice in three Latin American cities*. Cambridge: Cambridge University Press.

Gilbreth, C., and Otero, G. (2001) "Democratization in Mexico: The Zapatista uprising and civil society." *Latin American Perspectives*, 28 (4), 7–29.

Gill, S. (2008) *Power and resistance in the new world order*. 2nd ed. Basingstoke: Palgrave.

Gilly, A. (1983) *The Mexican Revolution*. Translated by P. Camiller. London: New Left Books.

Glade, W. (1963) "Revolution and economic development: A Mexican reprise," in W. Glade and C. W. Anderson (eds.), *The political economy of Mexico*. Madison: University of Wisconsin Press.

Glade, W. (1986) "Latin America and the international economy, 1870–1914," in L. Bethell (ed.), *Cambridge History of Latin America*, vol. 4. Cambridge: Cambridge University Press.

Glassman, J. (2006) "Primitive accumulation, accumulation by dispossession, accumulation by 'extra-economic' means." *Progress in Human Geography*, 30 (5), 608–25.

Gonzalez-Cassanova, P. (2005) "The Zapatista 'caracoles': Networks of resistance and autonomy." *Socialism and Democracy*, 19 (3), 79–92.

Goodale, M., and Postero, N. (2013) *Neoliberalism interrupted: Social change and contested governance in contemporary Latin America*. Stanford, Calif.: Stanford University Press.

Gramsci, A. (1971) *Selections from the prison notebooks*. Edited and translated by Q. Hoare and G. Nowell-Smith. New York: International Publishers.

Gramsci, A. (2011a) *Prison notebooks*. Vol. 1. Edited by J. Buttigieg. New York: Columbia University Press.

Gramsci, A. (2011b) *Prison notebooks*. Vol. 2. Edited by J. Buttigieg. New York: Columbia University Press.

Grandin, G. (2007) *Empire's workshop: Latin America, the United States and the rise of the new imperialism*. New York: Metropolitan Books / Henry Holt.

Green, D. (1995) *Silent revolution: The rise of market economics in Latin America*. London: Cassell.

Grindle, M. (1996) *Challenging the state: Crisis and innovation in Latin America and Africa*. Cambridge: Cambridge University Press.

Grugel, J. (1998) "State and business in neo-liberal democracies in Latin America." *Global Society*, 12 (2), 221–35.

Grugel, J. (2002) *Democratization: A critical introduction*. Basingstoke: Palgrave.

Gudynas, E. (2009) "Diez tesis urgentes sobre el nuevo extractivismo: Contextos y demandas bajo el progresismo sudamericano actual," in Centro Andino de Acción Popular and Centro Latino Americano de Ecología Social (eds.), *Extractivismo, política, y sociedad*. Quito: Centro Andino de Acción Popular y Centro Latino Americano de Ecología Social.

Gunder-Frank, A. (1966) "The development of underdevelopment." *Monthly Review* (September), 17–31.

Gutiérrez Aguilar, R. (2008) *Los ritmos del Pachakuti: Levantamiento y movilización en Bolivia (2000–2005).* Buenos Aires: Tinta Limón.

Hale, C. (2004) "Rethinking indigenous politics in the era of the 'Indio permitido.'" *NACLA Report on the Americas,* 38 (2), 16–21.

Hale, C. (2005) "Neoliberal multiculturalism: The remaking of cultural rights and racial dominance in Central America." *Political and Legal Anthropology Review,* 28 (1), 10–28.

Hall, G., and Humphrey, C. (2003) "Mexico: Southern States Development Strategy, volume 1: Synthesis report." World Bank, Documents and Reports, http://www-wds.worldbank.org/servlet/main?menuPK=64187510&pagePK=64193027&piPK=64187937&theSitePK=523679&entityID=000012009_20050105100328 (accessed September 14, 2009).

Hall, P., and Soskice, D. (2001) *Varieties of capitalism: The institutional foundations of comparative advantage.* Oxford: Oxford University Press.

Hamilton, N. (1982) *The limits of state autonomy: Post-revolutionary Mexico.* Princeton, N.J.: Princeton University Press.

Hamilton, N. (1986) "The limits of state autonomy," in N. Hamilton and T. Harding (eds.), *Modern Mexico: State, economy and social conflict.* London: Sage.

Hansen, R. (1971) *The politics of Mexican development.* Baltimore, Md.: Johns Hopkins University Press.

Hardt, M., and Negri, A. (2000) *Empire.* Cambridge, Mass.: Harvard University Press.

Hardt, M., and Negri, A. (2005) *Multitude: War and democracy in the age of empire.* London: Hamish Hamilton.

Hart, G. (2014) *Rethinking the South African crisis: Nationalism, populism, hegemony.* Athens: University of Georgia Press.

Hartley, L. P. (1953) *The go-between.* London: Penguin Classics.

Harvey, D. (1990) *The condition of postmodernity: An enquiry into the origins of social change.* Oxford: Blackwell.

Harvey, D. (1993) "From space to place and back again," in B. Bird, T. Curtis, G. Putnam, and L. Tickner (eds.), *Mapping the futures: Local cultures, global change.* London: Routledge.

Harvey, D. (1996) *Justice, nature and the geography of difference.* Oxford: Blackwell.

Harvey, D. (2000) *Spaces of hope.* Edinburgh: Edinburgh University Press.

Harvey, D. (2001) *Spaces of capital: Towards a critical geography.* Edinburgh: Edinburgh University Press.

Harvey, D. (2003) *The new imperialism.* Oxford: Oxford University Press.

Harvey, D. (2005) *A brief history of neoliberalism.* Oxford: Oxford University Press.

Harvey, D. (2006a) *The limits to capital.* Revised and fully updated. London: Verso.

Harvey, D. (2006b) *Spaces of global capitalism: Towards a theory of uneven geographical development.* London: Verso.

Harvey, D. (2010) *The enigma of capital.* London: Profile Books.

Harvey, N. (1998) *The Chiapas rebellion: The struggle for land and democracy.* Durham, N.C.: Duke University Press.

Harvey, N. (1999) "Resisting neoliberalism, constructing citizenship: Indigenous movements in Chiapas," in W. Cornelius, T. Eisenstadt, and J. Hindley (eds.),

Subnational politics and democratization in Mexico. San Diego: Centre for U.S.-Mexican Studies.

Harvey, N. (2005) "Who needs Zapatismo? State interventions and local responses in Marqués de Comillas, Chiapas." *Journal of Peasant Studies*, 32 (3–4), 629–50.

Harvey, N. (2006) "La disputa por los recursos naturales en el área del Plan Puebla-Panamá," in D. V. Solís and X. Leyva-Solano (eds.), *Geoeconómica y geopolítica en el área del Plan Puebla-Panamá.* Mexico City: CIESAS.

Held, D. (1993) "Democracy—from city-states to a cosmopolitan order?," in D. Held (ed.), *Prospects for democracy.* Cambridge: Polity.

Held, D. (2004) *Global covenant: The social democratic alternative to the Washington consensus.* Cambridge: Polity.

Held, D., and McGrew, A. (2002) *Globalization/anti-globalization.* Cambridge: Polity.

Heredia, B. (1996) "State-business relations in contemporary Mexico," in V. Bulmer-Thomas and M. Serrano (eds.), *Rebuilding the state: Mexico after Salinas.* London: Institute of Latin American Studies, University of London.

Hernández Castillo, R. A. (2001) *Histories and stories from Chiapas: Border identities in southern Mexico.* Austin: University of Texas Press.

Hernández Castillo, R. A. (2002) "Zapatismo and the emergence of indigenous feminism." *NACLA*, 35 (6), 39–43.

Hernández Castillo, R. A. (2003) "Between civil disobedience and silent rejection: Differing responses by Mam peasants to the Zapatista rebellion," in J. Rus, R. A. Hernández Castillo, and S. L. Mattiace (eds.), *Mayan lives, Mayan utopias: The indigenous peoples of Chiapas and the Zapatista rebellion.* Lanham, Md.: Rowman and Littlefield.

Hernández Navarro, L. (1999) "Reaffirming ethnic identity and reconstituting politics in Oaxaca," in W. Cornelius, T. Eisenstadt, and J. Hindley (eds.), *Subnational politics and democratization in Mexico.* San Diego: Centre for U.S.-Mexican Studies.

Hernández Navarro, L. (2012) "Zapatistas can still change the rules of Mexico's politics." *Guardian*, December 31, http://www.theguardian.com/commentisfree /2012/dec/31/zapatistas-mexico-politics-protest (accessed May 5, 2016).

Hernández Navarro, L. (2016) "Educación: El arte de la simulación." *La Jornada*, February 2, http://www.jornada.unam.mx/2016/02/02/opinion/014a2pol (accessed May 3, 2016).

Hesketh, C. (2016) "The survival of non-capitalism." *Environment and Planning D: Society and Space*, 34 (5), 877–94.

Hesketh, C., and Morton, A. D. (2014) "Spaces of uneven development and class struggle in Bolivia: Transformation or trasformismo?" *Antipode*, 46 (1), 149–69.

Higgins, N. P. (2004) *Understanding the Chiapas rebellion: Modernist visions and the invisible Indian.* Austin: University of Texas Press.

Hines, C. (2000) *Localization: A global manifesto.* London: Earthscan.

Hirsch, J. (1978) "The state apparatus and social reproduction: Elements of a theory of the bourgeois state," in J. Holloway and S. Picciotto (eds.), *State and capital: A Marxist debate.* London: Edward Arnold.

Hirst, P., and Thompson, G. (1999) *Globalization in question: The international economy and the possibilities of governance.* 2nd ed. Cambridge: Polity Press.

Hobbes, T. (1985) *Leviathan*. Edited and introduced by C. B. Macpherson. Harmondsworth: Penguin.

Hobsbawm, E., and Ranger, T. (1992) *The invention of tradition*. Cambridge: Cambridge University Press.

Holloway, J. (1998) "Dignity's revolt," in J. Holloway and E. Peláez (eds.), *Zapatista! Reinventing revolution in Mexico*. London: Pluto Press.

Holloway, J. (2002a) *Change the world without taking power: The meaning of revolution today*. London: Pluto Press.

Holloway, J. (2002b) "Zapatismo and the social sciences." *Capital and Class*, 26 (3), 153–60.

Holloway, J. (2005) "No." *Historical Materialism*, 13 (4), 265–85.

Holloway, J. (2010) *Crack capitalism*. London: Pluto.

Holloway, J., and Peláez, E. (eds.) (1998) *Zapatista! Reinventing revolution in Mexico*. London: Pluto Press.

Holloway, J., and Picciotto, S. (1977) "Capital, crisis and the state." *Capital and Class*, 2, 76–101.

Holloway, J., and Picciotto, S. (eds.) (1978) *State and capital: A Marxist debate*. London: Edward Arnold.

Howard, P. N., and Homer-Dixon, P. T. (1996) "Environmental scarcity and violent conflict: The case of Chiapas' project on environment, population and security, University of Toronto." http://faculty.washington.edu/pnhoward/publishing /articles/mexico.pdf (accessed February 14, 2010).

Huerta, M. (1999) "An interview with Subcomandante Insurgente Marcos, spokesperson and military commander of the Zapatista National Liberation Army (EZLN)." Translated by N. Higgins. *International Affairs*, 75 (2), 269–79.

Huntington, S. (1993) "The clash of civilizations?" *Foreign Affairs*, 72 (3), 22–50.

Instituto Nacional de Estadística y Geografía. (1994) *Estadísticas históricas de México*. Vol. 1. Aguascalientes: Instituto Nacional de Estadística y Geografía.

Instituto Nacional de Estadística y Geografía. (2014) *Anuario estadístico y geográfico de Oaxaca 2014*. Aguascalientes: Instituto Nacional de Estadística y Geografía.

Inter-American Development Bank. (2007) *Economic and social progress report*. New York: Inter-American Development Bank.

Ita, A. (2006) "Land concentration in Mexico after PROCEDE," in P. Rosset, R. Patel, and M. Corville (eds.), *Promised land: Competing visions of agrarian reform*. Oakland, Calif.: Food First Books.

Jameson, F. (1991) *Postmodernism, or, the cultural logic of late capitalism*. Durham, N.C.: Duke University Press.

Jenkins, R. (1979) "The export performance of multinational companies in Mexican industry." *Journal of Development Studies*, 15 (3), 89–107.

Jessop, B. (1990) *State theory: Putting capitalist states in their place*. Cambridge: Polity Press.

Jessop, B. (2005) "Gramsci as spatial theorist." *Critical Review of International Social and Political Philosophy*, 8 (4), 421–37.

Jones, G. A. (2000) "Between a rock and a hard place: Institutional reform and the performance of land privatization in peri-urban Mexico," in A. Zoomers and

G. Van der Haar (eds.), *Current land policy in Latin America: Regulating land tenure under neoliberalism*. Amsterdam: Royal Tropical Institute.

Joseph, G., and Nugent, D. (1994) "Popular culture and state formation in revolutionary Mexico," in G. Joseph and D. Nugent (eds.), *Everyday forms of state formation: Revolution and the negotiation of rule in modern Mexico*. Durham, N.C.: Duke University Press.

Kanoussi, D., and Mena, J. (1985) *La revolución pasiva: Una lectura del los cuadernos del caracel*. Puebla: Universidad Autónoma de Puebla.

Katz, F. (1986) "Mexico: Restored republic and Porfiriato, 1867–1910," in L. Bethell (ed.), *The Cambridge History of Latin America*, vol. 5. Cambridge: Cambridge University Press.

Katzenberger, E. (ed.) (1995) *First World, ha ha ha! The Zapatista challenge*. San Francisco: City Lights.

Kaufman, R. (1990) "How societies change developmental models or keep them: Reflections on the Latin American experience in the 1930s and the postwar world," in G. Gereffi and D. Wyman (eds.), *Manufacturing miracles: Paths of industrialization in Latin America and East Asia*. Princeton, N.J.: Princeton University Press.

Kautsky, K. (1914/1970) "Ultra-imperialism." *New Left Review*, 1 (59), 39–40.

Kemper, R. V., and Royce, A. P. (1979) "Mexican urbanisation since 1821: A macro-historical approach." *Urban Anthropology*, 8 (3–4), 267–89.

Kiely, R. (2007) *The new political economy of development: Globalization, imperialism, hegemony*. Basingstoke: Palgrave Macmillan.

King, T. (1970) *Mexico: Industrialization and trade policies since 1940*. Oxford: Oxford University Press.

Kipfer, S. (2002) "Urbanization, everyday life and the survival of capitalism: Lefebvre, Gramsci and the problematic of hegemony." *Capitalism Nature Socialism*, 13 (2), 117–49.

Kipfer, S. (2013) "City, country, hegemony: Antonio Gramsci's spatial historicism," in M. Ekers, S. Stipfer, and A. Loftus (eds.), *Gramsci: Space, nature, politics*. Oxford: Wiley Blackwell.

Klein, N. (2002) *Fences and windows: Dispatches from the front lines of the globalization debate*. London: Flamingo.

Knight, A. (1985) "The Mexican Revolution: Bourgeois? Nationalist? Or just a 'Great Rebellion'?" *Bulletin of Latin America Research*, 4 (2), 1–37.

Knight, A. (1986) "Mexican peonage: What was it and why was it?" *Journal of Latin American Studies*, 18 (1), 41–74.

Knight, A. (2002a) *Mexico: From the beginning to the Spanish conquest*. Cambridge: Cambridge University Press.

Knight, A. (2002b) *Mexico: The colonial era*. Cambridge: Cambridge University Press.

La Botz, D. (2015) "Oaxaca braces for conflict." *NACLA*, August 20, https://nacla.org/news/2015/08/20/oaxaca-braces-conflict (accessed May 3, 2016).

Lacher, H. (2006) *Beyond globalization: Capitalism, territoriality and the international relations of modernity*. London: Routledge.

Laclau, E. (1977) *Politics and ideology in Marxist theory: Capitalism, fascism, populism.* Norfolk: New Left Books.

Lander, E. (2000) *La colonialidad del saber: Eurocentrismo y ciencias sociales.* Buenos Aires: CLACSO.

Lander, E. (2006) "Marxismo, eurocentrismo y colonialismo," in A. Borón, J. Amadeo, and S. González (eds.), *Teoría Marxista hoy: Problemas y perspectivas.* Buenos Aires: CLACSO.

Larson, E. (2015) "In Oaxaca, teachers won't give up the fight." *NACLA*, https://nacla.org/news/2015/12/01/oaxaca-teachers-won't-give-fight (accessed April 20, 2016).

La Ventana, Investigación y Divulgación A.C., Tequio Jurídico A.C., and Servicios para una Educación Alternativa A.C. (2013) *Tierra y territorio: Una alternativa de vida.* http://tequiojuridico.org/tequiojuridico/2014/09/LIBRO-TIERRA-Y-TERRITORIO_small.pdf (accessed March 3, 2016).

Leal, J. F. (1986) "The Mexican state, 1915–1973: A historical interpretation," in N. Hamilton and T. Harding (eds.), *Modern Mexico: State, economy and social conflict.* London: Sage.

Lebowitz, M. (2003) *Beyond capital: Marx's political economy of the working class.* 2nd ed. Basingstoke: Palgrave Macmillan.

Lees, S. H. (1976) "Hydraulic development and political response on the valley of Oaxaca." *Anthropological Quarterly*, 49 (3), 197–210.

Lefebvre, H. (1947/2008) *The critique of everyday life.* Vol. 1. Translated by J. Moore. London: Verso.

Lefebvre, H. (1961/2008) *The critique of everyday life.* Vol. 2. Translated by J. Moore. London: Verso.

Lefebvre, H. (1964/2009) "The state and society," in N. Brenner and S. Elden (eds.), *State, space, world: Selected essays.* Minneapolis: University of Minnesota Press.

Lefebvre, H. (1966/2009) "Theoretical problems of autogestion," in N. Brenner and S. Elden (eds.), *State, space, world: Selected essays.* Minneapolis: University of Minnesota Press.

Lefebvre, H. (1970/2003) *The urban revolution.* Translated by R. Bononno. Minneapolis: University of Minnesota Press.

Lefebvre, H. (1975/2009) "The state in the modern world," in N. Brenner and S. Elden (eds.), *State, space, world: Selected essays.* Minneapolis: University of Minnesota Press.

Lefebvre, H. (1976) *The survival of capitalism: Reproduction of the relations of production.* Translated by F. Bryant. London: Allison and Busby.

Lefebvre, H. (1979/2009) "Comments on a new state form," in N. Brenner and S. Elden (eds.), *State, space, world: Selected essays.* Minneapolis: University of Minnesota Press.

Lefebvre, H. (1991) *The production of space.* Translated by D. Nicholson-Smith. Oxford: Blackwell Publishing.

Lefebvre, H. (1996) "The right to the city," in H. Lefebvre, *Writings on cities.* Translated and edited by E. Kofman and E. Lebas. Oxford: Blackwell.

Lefebvre, H. (2003) "Space and state," in N. Brenner, B. Jessop, M. Jones, and G. Macloed (eds.), *State/space: A reader.* Oxford: Blackwell.

Lenin, V. I. (1902/1987) "What is to be done," in H. M. Christman (ed.), *The essential works of Lenin*. New York: Dover Publications.

Lenin, V. I. (1917/1987a) "Imperialism the highest stage of capitalism," in H. M. Christman (ed.), *The essential works of Lenin*. New York: Dover Publications.

Lenin, V. I. (1917/1987b) "The state and revolution," in H. M. Christman (ed.), *The essential works of Lenin*. New York: Dover Publications.

Lewis, S. E. (2005a) *The ambivalent revolution: Forging state and nation in Chiapas, 1910–1945*. Albuquerque: University of New Mexico Press.

Lewis, S. E. (2005b) "Dead-end *caudillismo* and entrepreneurial *caciquismo* in Chiapas, 1910–1955," in A. Knight and W. Pansters (eds.), *Caciquismo in twentieth-century Mexico*. London: Institute for the Study of the Americas.

Leyva-Solano, X. (2001) "Communal and organizational transformations in Las Cañadas." *Latin American Perspectives*, 28 (2), 20–44.

Leyva-Solano, X., and Burguete, A. (2007) *La remunicipalización de Chiapas: Lo político y la política en tiempos de contrainsurgencia*. Mexico City: CIESAS.

Lipietz, A. (1984) "How monetarism has choked Third World industrialization." *New Left Review*, 1 (145), 71–87.

Lomnitz-Adler, C. (1992) *Exits from the labyrinth: Culture and ideology in Mexican national space*. Berkeley: University of California Press.

López Monjardin, A. (1993) "Juchitan: Histories of discord," in H. Campbell, L. Binford, M. Bartolomé, and A. Barabas (eds.), *Zapotec struggles: History, politics, and representations from Juchitán, Oaxaca*. Washington, D.C.: Smithsonian Institution Press.

Lorenzano, L. (1998) "Zapatismo: Recomposition of labour, radical democracy and revolutionary project," in J. Holloway and E. Peláez (eds.), *Zapatista! Reinventing revolution in Mexico*. London: Pluto Press.

Love, J. (1994) "Economic ideas and ideologies in Latin America since 1930," in L. Bethell (ed.), *Cambridge history of Latin America*, vol. 6, pt. 1. Cambridge: Cambridge University Press.

Luna, J. P., and Filgueira, F. (2009) "The left turns are multiple paradigmatic crises." *Third World Quarterly*, 30 (2), 371–95.

Luxemburg, R. (1913/2003) *The accumulation of capital*. London: Routledge.

Lyotard, J.-F. (1984) *The postmodern condition: A report on knowledge*. Manchester: Manchester University Press.

Mallon, F. (1995) *Peasant and nation: The making of postcolonial Mexico and Peru*. Berkeley: University of California Press.

Malloy, J. (1977) "Authoritarianism and corporatism in Latin America: The modal pattern," in J. Malloy (ed.), *Authoritarianism and corporatism in Latin America*. Pittsburgh: University of Pittsburgh Press.

Mandel, E. (1968) *Marxist economic theory*. Vol. 1. London: Merlin Press.

Marable, M. (2000) *How capitalism underdeveloped black America: Problems in race, political economy, and society*. Rev. ed. Cambridge, Mass.: South End Press.

Marcos, Subcomandante Insurgente. (2001) *Our word is our weapon*. London: Serpents Tail.

Marcos, Subcomandante Insurgente. (2003) "I shit on the revolutionary vanguards of

this planet." *Chiapas and the Zapatista Rebellion*, January 9–12, http://flag.blackened
.net/revolt/mexico/ezln/2003/marcos/etaJAN.html (accessed February 22, 2010).

Marcos, Subcomandante Insurgente. (2004) "Two flaws." *Chiapas and the Zapatista
Rebellion*, http://flag.blackened.net/revolt/mexico/ezln/2004/marcos/flawsAUG
.html (accessed February 2, 2010).

Marcos, Subcomandante. (2014) "Entre la luz y la sombra." *Enlace Zapatista*, May 25,
http://enlacezapatista.ezln.org.mx/2014/05/25/entre-la-luz-y-la-sombra/ (accessed
May 3, 2016).

Mariátegui, J. C. (1930/2011) "The new course of Mexican politics as seen from the
margins," in H. Vanden and M. Becker (eds.), *José Carlos Mariátegui: An anthology*.
New York: Monthly Review Press.

Mariátegui, J. C. (1984) *7 ensayos de interpretación de la realidad Peruana*. Lima:
Amuata.

Markman, S. D. (1984) *Architecture and urbanization in colonial Chiapas*. Philadelphia:
American Philosophical Society.

Martin, P. (2005) "Comparative topographies of neoliberalism in Mexico." *Environment
and Planning A*, 37 (2), 203–20.

Martin, P. (2006) "Mexico's neoliberal transition: Authoritarian shadows in an
era of neoliberalism," in H. Leitner, J. Peck, and E. Sheppard (eds.), *Contesting
neoliberalism: Urban frontiers*. New York: Guildford Publications.

Martínez, O. (1993) "Debt and foreign capital: The origin of the crisis." Translated by
L. Fierro. *Latin American Perspectives*, 20 (1), 64–82.

Martínez, V. L. J. (2013) "What we need are new customs: Multiculturality, autonomy,
and citizenship in Mexico and the lessons of Oaxaca," in T. Eisenstadt, M. S.
Danielson, M. J. B. Corres, and C. Sorroza Polo (eds.), *Latin America's multicultural
movements: The struggle between communitarianism, autonomy, and human rights*.
Oxford: Oxford University Press.

Martínez Vásquez, V. R. (1990) *Movimiento popular y política en Oaxaca 1968–1986*.
Mexico City: Consejo Nacional para la Cultura y las Artes.

Martínez Vásquez, V. R. (2007) *Autoritarismo, movimiento popular y crisis política:
Oaxaca 2006*. Oaxaca: Universidad Autónoma "Benito Juárez" de Oaxaca.

Marx, K. (1843/2000) "On the Jewish question," in D. McLellan (ed.), *Karl Marx:
Selected writings*. Oxford: Oxford University Press.

Marx, K. (1844/2007) *Economic and philosophical manuscripts of 1844*. New York:
Dover Publications.

Marx, K. (1845/1996) "Theses on Feuerbach," in D. McLellan (ed.), *Karl Marx, selected
writings*. Oxford: Oxford University Press.

Marx, K. (1847/1963) *The poverty of philosophy*. New York: International Publishers.

Marx, K. (1852/2000) "The eighteenth brumaire of Louis Bonaparte," in D. McLellan
(ed.), *Karl Marx, selected writings*. Oxford: Oxford University Press.

Marx, K. (1858/1973) *Grundrisse*. Harmondsworth: Penguin.

Marx, K. (1863/1972) *Theories of surplus value*. Pt. 3. Translated by J. Cohen. London:
Lawrence and Wishart.

Marx, K. (1867/1974) *Capital*. Vol. 1, *The process of production of capital*. London:
Lawrence and Wishart.

Marx, K. (1871/2000) "The civil war in France," in D. McLellan (ed.), *Karl Marx, selected writings*. Oxford: Oxford University Press.

Marx, K. (1875/1996) "Critique of the Gotha Program," in D. McLellan (ed.), *Karl Marx, selected writings*. Oxford: Oxford University Press.

Marx, K. (1894/1977) *Capital*. Vol. 3, *The process of capitalist production as a whole*. London: Lawrence and Wishart.

Marx, K., and Engels, F. (1845/2000) "The German ideology," in D. McLellan (ed.), *Karl Marx, selected writings*. Oxford: Oxford University Press.

Marx, K., and Engels, F. (1848/2000) *The communist manifesto*, in D. McLellan (ed.), *Karl Marx, selected writings*. Oxford: Oxford University Press.

Massey, D. (1993) "Power-geometry and progressive sense of place," in J. Bird, B. Curtis, T. Putnam, G. Robertson, and L. Tickner (eds.), *Mapping the futures: Local cultures, global change*. London: Routledge.

Massey, D. (1994) *Space, place and gender*. Cambridge: Polity Press.

Massey, D. (1995) *Spatial divisions of labour: Social structures and the geography of production*. 2nd ed. London: Macmillan.

Massey, D. (2005) *For space*. London: Sage.

McCaughan, E. (1993) "Mexico's long crisis: Towards new regimes of accumulation and domination." *Latin American Perspectives*, 20 (3), 6–31.

McMichael, P. (1990) "Incorporating comparison within a world-historical perspective: An alternative comparative method." *American Sociological Review*, 55 (3), 385–97.

McMicheal, P. (2000) "World-systems analysis, globalization and incorporated comparison." *Journal of World Systems Research*, 3, 68–99.

McNally, D. (2013) "The unity of the diverse: Working-class formations and popular uprisings from Cochabamba to Cairo," in C. Barker, L. Cox, J. Krinsky, and A. Nilsen (eds.), *Marxism and social movements*. Leiden: Brill.

Meadows, D. H., Meadows, D. L., Randers, J., and Behrens, W. W. (1972) *The limits to growth*. New York: Universe Books.

Merrifield, A. (2006) *Henri Lefebvre: A critical introduction*. London: Routledge.

Merrifield, A. (2012) *The politics of the encounter: Urban theory and protest under planetary urbanization*. Athens: University of Georgia Press.

Meyer, J. (1986) "Mexico: Revolution and reconstruction in the 1920s," in L. Bethell (ed.), *The Cambridge History of Latin America*, vol. 5. Cambridge: Cambridge University Press.

Millán, M. (1998) "Zapatista indigenous women," in J. Holloway and E. Peláez, (eds.), *Zapatista! Reinventing revolution in Mexico*. London: Pluto Press.

Modonesi, M. (2010) *Subalternidad, antagonismo, autonomía: Marxismos y subjetivación política*. Buenos Aires: CLACSO.

Modonesi, M. (2013) "Revoluciones pasivas en América Latina: Una aproximación gramsciana a la caracterización de los gobiernos progresistas de inicio de siglo," in M. Modonesi (ed.), *Horizontes gramscianos: Estudios en torno al pensamiento de Antonio Gramsci*. Mexico City: Universidad Nacional Autónoma de México.

Modonesi, M. (2015) "Fin de la hegemonía progresista y giro regresivo en América Latina: Una contribución gramsciana al debate sobre el fin del ciclo." *Memoria*, http://revistamemoria.mx/?p=658 (accessed April 10, 2016).

Mora, M. (2007) "The Zapatista anticapitalist politics and the 'other campaign':
    Learning from the struggle for indigenous rights and autonomy." *Latin American
    Perspectives*, 34 (2), 64–77.
More, T. (1997) *Utopia*. New York: Dover Publications.
Morton, A. D. (2002) "La ressurrección del maíz: Globalization, resistance and the
    Zapatistas." *Millennium: Journal of International Studies*, 31 (1), 27–54.
Morton, A. D. (2003) "Structural change and neoliberalism in Mexico: 'Passive
    revolution' in the global political economy." *Third World Quarterly*, 24 (4), 631–53.
Morton, A. D. (2005) "Change within continuity: The political economy of democratic
    transition in Mexico." *New Political Economy*, 10 (2), 181–202.
Morton, A. D. (2007a) "Global capital and the peasantry in Mexico: The recomposition
    of class struggle." *Journal of Peasant Studies*, 32 (3–4), 441–73.
Morton, A. D. (2007b) *Unravelling Gramsci: Hegemony and passive revolution in the
    global political economy*. London: Pluto Press.
Morton, A. D. (2007c) "Waiting for Gramsci: State formation, passive revolution and
    the international." *Millennium: Journal of International Studies*, 35 (3), 597–621.
Morton, A. D. (2010) "Reflections on uneven development: Mexican revolution,
    primitive accumulation, passive revolution." *Latin American Perspectives*, 37
    (1), 7–34.
Morton, A. D. (2013) *Revolution and the state in modern Mexico: The political economy
    of uneven development*. 2nd ed. Lanham, Md.: Rowman and Littlefield.
Motta, S. (2006) "Utopias re-imagined: A reply to Panizza." *Political Studies*, 54 (4),
    898–905.
Munck, R. (2013) *Rethinking Latin America: Development, hegemony, and social
    transformation*. New York: Palgrave Macmillan.
Muñoz, A. A. (2005) "The emergence and development of the politics of recognition of
    cultural diversity and indigenous peoples' rights in Mexico: Chiapas and Oaxaca in
    comparative perspective." *Journal of Latin American Studies*, 37 (3), 585–610.
Murphy, A., and Stepick, A. (1991) *Social inequality in Oaxaca: A history of resistance
    and change*. Philadelphia: Temple University Press.
Mutersbaugh, T. (2002) "Migration, common property, and communal labor: Cultural
    politics and agency in a Mexican village." *Political Geography*, 21 (4), 473–94.
Nacional Financiera. (1977) *Statistics on the Mexican economy*. Mexico City: Nacional
    Financiera.
Nash, J. (1994) "Global integration and subsistence insecurity." *American
    Anthropologist*, 96 (1), 7–30.
Nash, J. (2003) *Mayan visions: The quest for autonomy in an age of globalization*.
    London: Routledge.
Nitzan, J. and Bichler, S. (2009) *Capital as power: A study of order and creorder*.
    London: Routledge.
Norget, K. (2005) "Caught in the crossfire: Militarization, paramilitarization, and state
    violence in Oaxaca, Mexico," in C. Menijavar and N. Rodriguez (eds.), *When states
    kill: Latin America, the U.S. and technologies of terror*. Austin: University of Texas
    Press.

Norget, K. (2008) "Convergences and complicities: Local-national interactions in the 2006 Movement of the APPO." http://americas.irc-online.org/am/5366.

Norget, K. (2010) "A cacophony of autochthony: Representing indigeneity in Oaxacan popular mobilization." *Journal of Latin American and Caribbean Anthropology*, 15 (1), 116–43.

Noticias. (2009) "Paran en Zaachila el trazo del presunto 'Libramiento Sur.'" April 2, 2009.

Noticias. (2010a) "¿Libramiento Sur en villa de Zaachila?" January 24, 2010.

Noticias. (2010b) "Rechazan al Libramiento Sur." January 24, 2010.

O'Connor, J. (1998) *Natural causes: Essays in ecological Marxism*. New York: Guilford Press.

O'Donnell, G. (1977) "Corporatism and the question of the state," in J. Malloy (ed.), *Authoritarianism and corporatism in Latin America*. Pittsburgh: University of Pittsburgh Press.

Ohmae, K. (1999) *The borderless world: Power and strategy in the interlined economy*. Rev. ed. New York: Harper Business.

Olesen, T. (2004) "Globalising the Zapatistas: From Third World solidarity to global solidarity?" *Third World Quarterly*, 25 (1), 225–67.

Olivera, M. (2005) "Subordination and rebellion: Indigenous peasant women in Chiapas ten years after the Zapatista uprising." *Journal of Peasant Studies*, 32 (3–4), 608–28.

Ollman, B. (2003) *Dance of dialectic: Steps in Marx's method*. Urbana: University of Illinois Press.

Otero, G. (1999) *Farewell to the peasantry? Political class formation in rural Mexico*. Boulder, Colo.: Westview Press.

Otero, G. (2004) "Global economy, local politics: Indigenous struggles, civil society and democracy." *Canadian Journal of Political Science*, 37 (2), 325–46.

Ó Tuathail, G. (1996) *Critical geopolitics: The politics of writing global space*. London: Routledge.

Oxhorn, P. (1995) "From controlled inclusion to coerced marginalization," in J. Hall (ed.), *Civil society: Theory, history, comparison*. Cambridge: Polity Press.

Overmyer-Valázquez, M. (2006) *Vision of the Emerald City: Modernity, tradition and the formation of Porfirian Oaxaca, Mexico*. Durham, N.C.: Duke University Press.

Pansters, W. G. (2012) *Violence, coercion and state-making in twentieth-century Mexico: The other half of the centaur*. Stanford, Calif.: Stanford University Press.

Paulson, J. (2000) "Fake greenery: The Mexican government uses 'environmentalism' to repress the Zapatistas." *NACLA Report on the Americas*, 34 (1), 1.

Pearce, J. (2004) "Collective action or public participation? Complementary or contradictory democratisation strategies in Latin America." *Bulletin of Latin America Research*, 23 (4), 483–504

Peck, J., and Tickell, A. (2002) "Neoliberalizing space." *Antipode*, 34 (3), 380–403.

People's Global Action. (2007) "The history and importance of the San Andrés Accords." *Global Exchange*, http://www.globalexchange.org/countries/americas/mexico/SanAndres.html (accessed February 14, 2010).

Peterson, S. V. (2005) "How (the meaning of) gender matters in political economy." *New Political Economy*, 10 (4), 499–521.

Phillips, N. (1999) "Global and regional linkages," in N. Phillips and J. Buxton (eds.), *Developments in Latin American political economy: States, markets and actors*. Manchester: Manchester University Press.

Pickerill, J., and Chatterton, P. (2006) "Notes towards autonomous geographies: Creation, resistance and self-management as survival tactics." *Progress in Human Geography*, 30 (6), 730–46.

Piketty, T. (2014) *Capital in the twenty-first century*. Cambridge, Mass.: Harvard University Press.

Pisa, R. A. (1994) "Popular responses to the reform of article 27: State intervention and community resistance in Oaxaca." *Urban Anthropology*, 23 (2–3), 267–306.

Poole, D. (2007a) "Political autonomy and cultural diversity in the Oaxaca rebellion." *Anthropology News*, 48 (3), 10–11.

Poole, D. (2007b) "The right to be heard." *Socialism and Democracy*, 21 (2), 113–16.

Poole, D. (2009) "Affective distinctions: Race and place in Oaxaca," in D. Walkowitz and L. M. Knauer (eds.), *Contested histories in public space: Memory, race, and nation*. Durham, N.C.: Duke University Press.

Portes, A. (1985) "Latin American class structures: Their composition and change during the last decades." *Latin American Research Review*, 20 (3), 7–39.

Portes, A., and Hoffman, K. (2003) "Latin American class structures: Their composition and change during the neoliberal era." *Latin American Research Review*, 38 (1), 41–82.

Postero, N. G. (2004) *The struggle for indigenous rights in Latin America*. Eastbourne: Sussex Academic Press.

Poulantzas, N. (1978) *State, power, socialism*. London: New Left Books.

Proceso. (2013) "El 27% de mujeres indígenas esterilizadas sin su consentimiento: Conavim." *Proceso*, February 14, http://www.proceso.com.mx/333622 (accessed May 6, 2016).

Programa de las Naciones Unidad para el Desarrollo. (2009) *Indicadores de desarrollo humano y género en México 2005–2009*. Mexico City: Programa de las Naciones Unidad para el Desarrollo.

Rajchenberg, E., and Héau-Lambert, C. (1998) "History and symbolism in the Zapatista movement," in J. Holloway and E. Peláez (eds.), *Zapatista! Reinventing revolution in Mexico*. London: Pluto Press.

Renique, G. (2007) "Subaltern political formation and the struggle for autonomy in Oaxaca." *Socialism and Democracy*, 21 (2), 62–73.

Reyes Ramos, M. E. (1992) *El reparto de tierras y la política agraria en Chiapas, 1914–1988*. Mexico City: Universidad Nacional Autónoma de México.

Reynolds, C. (1978) "Why Mexico's 'stabilizing development' was actually destabilizing (with some implications for the future)." *World Development*, 6 (7), 1005–18.

Richard, A. (2008) "Withered Milpas: Governmental disaster and the Mexican countryside." *Journal of Latin American and Caribbean Anthropology*, 13 (2), 387–413.

Rios, P. M. (2009) "Unos 600 campesinos denuncian despojo para beneficiar a mineras de Canadá." *La Jornada*, April 6, 2009.

Rioux, S. (2013) "The fiction of economic coercion: Political Marxism and the separation of theory and history." *Historical Materialism*, 21 (4), 92–128.

Rioux, S. (2015) "Mind the (theoretical) gap: On the poverty of international relations theorising of uneven and combined development." *Global Society*, 29 (4), 481–509.

Roberts, P. (2015) "Passive revolution in Brazil: Struggles over hegemony, religion and development 1964–2007." *Third World Quarterly*, 36 (9), 1663–81.

Robinson, W. I. (1996) *Promoting polyarchy: Globalization, U.S. intervention, and hegemony*. Cambridge: Cambridge University Press.

Robinson, W. I. (2003) *Transnational conflicts: Central America, social change and globalization*. London: Verso.

Robinson, W. I. (2004a) "Global crisis and Latin America." *Bulletin of Latin American Research*, 23 (2), 135–53.

Robinson, W. I. (2004b) *A theory of global capitalism: Production, class, and state in a transnational world*. Baltimore, Md.: Johns Hopkins University Press.

Robinson, W. I. (2007) "Beyond the theory of imperialism: Global capitalism and the transnational state." *Societies without Borders*, 2 (1), 5–26.

Robinson, W. I. (2008) *Latin American and global capitalism: A critical globalization perspective*. Baltimore, Md.: Johns Hopkins University Press.

Robinson, W. I. (2013) "Global capitalism and its anti-human face: Organic intellectuals and interpretations of the crisis." *Globalizations*, 10 (5), 659–71.

Rocheleau, D. E. (2015) "Networked, rooted and territorial: Green grabbing and resistance in Chiapas." *Journal of Peasant Studies*, 42 (3–4), 695–723.

Rojas, R. (2005) "Penetran trasnacionales el corridor eólico con apoyo de prestanombres." *La Jornada*, October 3, 2010.

Rokkan, S. (1970) *Citizens, elections, parties: Approaches to the comparative study of the processes of development*. New York: David McKay Company.

Rosario Green, M. (1981) "Mexico's economic dependence." *Proceedings of the academy of political science*, 34 (1), 104–14.

Roseberry, W. (1994) "Hegemony and the language of contention," in G. Joseph and D. Nugent (eds.), *Everyday forms of state formation: Revolution and the negotiation of rule in modern Mexico*. Durham, N.C.: Duke University Press.

Rosenberg, J. (2006) "Why is there no international historical sociology?" *European Journal of International Relations*, 12 (3), 307–40.

Rosenberg, J. (2010) "Basic problems in the theory of uneven and combined development: Part II unevenness and political multiplicity." *Cambridge Review of International Affairs*, 23 (1), 165–89.

Rosenberg, J. (2013) "Kenneth Waltz and Leon Trotsky: Anarchy in the mirror of uneven and combined development." *International Politics*, 50 (2), 183–230.

Rubin, J. (1993) "COCEI against the state: A political history of Juchitán," in H. Campbell, L. Binford, M. Bartolomé, and A. Barabas (eds.), *Zapotec struggles: History, politics, and representations from Juchitán, Oaxaca*. Washington, D.C.: Smithsonian Institution Press.

Rubin, J. (1997) *Decentering the regime: Ethnicity, radicalism, and democracy in Juchitán, Mexico*. Durham, N.C.: Duke University Press.

Rubin, J. (1999) "Zapotec and Mexican: Ethnicity, militancy, and democratization in Juchitán, Oaxaca," in W. Cornelius, T. Eisenstadt, and J. Hindley (eds.), *Subnational politics and democratization in Mexico*. San Diego: Centre for U.S.-Mexican Studies.

Ruccio, D. (1991) "When failure becomes success: Class and the debate over stabilization and adjustment." *World Development*, 19 (10), 1315–34.

Ruccio, D. (2010) "Fordism on a world scale: International dimensions of regulation," in D. Ruccio, *Globalization and development: A Marxian class analysis*. London: Routledge.

Ruccio, D., and Gibson-Graham, J. K. (2010) "After development: Reimagining economy and class," in D. Ruccio, *Globalization and development: A Marxian class analysis*. London: Routledge.

Rus, J. (1994) "The comunidad revolucionaria institucional: The subversion of native government in highland Chiapas, 1936–1968," in G. Joseph and D. Nugent (eds.), *Everyday forms of state formation: Revolution and the negotiation of rule in modern Mexico*. Durham, N.C.: Duke University Press.

Rus, J. (1995) "Local adaption to global change: The reordering of Native society in highland Chiapas, Mexico." *European Review of Latin American and Caribbean Studies*, 58 (June), 71–89.

Rus, J. (2003) "Coffee and the recolonization of highland Chiapas, Mexico: Indian communities and plantation labour, 1892–1912," in W. G. Clarence-Smith and S. Topik (eds.), *The global coffee economy in Africa, Asia, and Latin America, 1500–1989*. Cambridge: Cambridge University Press.

Rus, J. (2004) "Rereading Tzotzil ethnography," in J. M. Watababe and E. F. Fischer (eds.), *Pluralizing ethnography: Comparison and representation in Maya cultures, histories and identities*. Santa Fe, N.M.: School of American Research Press.

Rus, J. (2005) "The struggle against indigenous caciques in highland Chiapas: Dissent, religion and exile in Chamula, 1965–1977," in A. Knight and W. Pansters (eds.), *Caciquismo in twentieth-century Mexico*. London: Institute for the Study of the Americas.

Rus, J., and Collier, G. A. (2003) "A generation of crisis in the central highlands of Chiapas: The cases of Chamula and Zinicantán 1974–2000," in J. Rus, R. A. Hernández Castillo, S. L. Mattiace (eds.), *Mayan lives, Mayan utopias: The indigenous peoples of Chiapas and the Zapatista rebellion*. Lanham, Md.: Rowman and Littlefield.

Sassen, S. (2006) *Territory, authority, rights: From medieval to global assemblages*. Oxford: Oxford University Press.

Sassen, S. (2007) "Introduction: Deciphering the global," in S. Sassen (ed.), *Deciphering the global: Its spaces, scales and subjects*. Abingdon: Routledge.

Sassoon, A. S. (1980) *Gramsci's politics*. London: Croom Helm.

Sassoon, A. S. (2001) "Globalisation, hegemony and passive revolution." *New Political Economy*, 6 (1), 5–17.

Scott, J. (1985) *Weapons of the weak: Everyday forms of peasant resistance*. New Haven, Conn.: Yale University Press.

Scott, J. (1998) *Seeing like a state: How certain schemes to improve the human condition have failed*. New Haven, Conn.: Yale University Press.

Semo, E. (2012) *México: Del antiguo régimen a la modernidad—reforma y revolución*. Ciudad Juárez: Universidad Autónoma de Ciudad Juárez.

Serrano, M. (1996) "The legacy of gradual change: Rules and institutions under Salinas," in V. Bulmer-Thomas and M. Serrano (eds.), *Rebuilding the state: Mexico after Salinas*. London: Institute of Latin American Studies, University of London.

Shanin, T. (1984) *Late Marx and the Russian road: Marx and the peripheries of capitalism*. London: Routledge and Kegan Paul.

Silver, B. J. (2003) *Forces of labour: Workers' movements and globalisation since 1870*. Cambridge: Cambridge University Press.

Skidmore, T., and Smith, P. (1992) *Modern Latin America*. 3rd ed. Oxford: Oxford University Press.

Smith, N. (1993) "Homeless/global: Scaling places," in J. Bird, B. Curtis, T. Putnam, G. Robertson, and L. Tickner (eds.), *Mapping the futures: Local cultures, global change*. London: Routledge.

Smith, N. (2000) "What happened to class?" *Environment and Planning A*, 32, 1011–32.

Smith, N. (2006) "The geography of uneven development," in B. Dunn and H. Radice (eds.), *100 years of permanent revolution*. London: Pluto Press.

Smith, N. (2008) *Uneven development: Nature, capital and the production of space*. 3rd ed. Athens: University of Georgia Press.

Snyder, R. (1999) "After the state withdraws: Neoliberalism and subnational authoritarian regimes in Mexico," in W. Cornelius, T. Eisenstadt, and J. Hindley (eds.), *Subnational politics and democratization in Mexico*. San Diego: Centre for U.S.-Mexican Studies.

Snyder, R. (2001) "Scaling down: The subnational comparative method." *Studies in Comparative International Development*, 36 (1), 93–110.

Sorroza Polo, C., and Danielson, M. S. (2013) "Political subsystems in Oaxaca's usos y costumbres municipalities: A typology based on the civil-religious service background of mayors," in T. Eisenstadt, M. S. Danielson, M. J. B. Corres, and C. Sorroza Polo (eds.), *Latin America's multicultural movements: The struggle between communitarianism, autonomy, and human rights*. Oxford: Oxford University Press.

Soto, V., and Banister, J. M. (2016) "Building cities, constructing citizens: Sustainable rural cities in Chiapas, Mexico." *Journal of Latin American Geography*, 15 (1), 111–31.

Sousa Santos, B. de (ed.) (2006) *Democratising democracy: Beyond the liberal democratic canon*. London: Verso.

Stahler-Sholk, R. (2007) "Resisting neo-liberal homogenization: The Zapatista autonomy movement." *Latin American Perspectives*, 34 (2), 48–63.

Stahler-Sholk, R. (2014) "Autonomy, collective identity, and the Zapatista social movement," in R. Stahler-Sholk, H. E. Vanden, and M. Becker (eds.), *Rethinking Latin American social movements: Radical action from below*. Lanham, Md.: Rowman and Littlefield.

Stahler-Sholk, R., Vanden, H., and Kuecker, G. (2007) "Globalizing resistance: The new politics of social movements in Latin America." *Latin American Perspectives*, 34 (2), 5–14.

Stallings, B. (2005) *Finance for development: Latin America's banks and capital markets after liberalization*. Washington, D.C.: Brookings Institution Press.

Stanford, L. (1994) "The privatization of Mexico's ejidal sector: Examining local impact, strategies, and ideologies." *Urban Anthropology*, 23 (2–3), 97–119.

Stephen, L. (1997) "Redefined nationalism in building a movement for indigenous autonomy in southern Mexico." *Journal of Latin American Anthropology*, 3 (1), 72–101.

Stephen, L. (1998) "The cultural and political dynamics of agrarian reform in Oaxaca and Chiapas," in R. Snyder and G. Torres (eds.), *The future role of the ejido in rural Mexico*. San Diego: Center for U.S.-Mexican Studies.

Stephen, L. (2013) *We are the face of Oaxaca: Testimony and social movements*. Durham, N.C.: Duke University Press.

Stout, R. J. (2010) "Awakening in Oaxaca: Stirrings of the people's giant." *Monthly Review*, 62 (2), 29–39.

Strange, S. (1996) *The retreat of the state: The diffusion of power in the world economy*. Cambridge: Cambridge University Press.

Tansel, C. B. (2015) "Deafening silence? Marxism, international historical sociology and the spectre of Eurocentrism." *European Journal of International Relations*, 21 (1), 76–100.

Tapia, L. (2011) *El estado de derecho como tiranía*. La Paz: CIDES/UMSA.

Taylor, W. B. (1972) *Landlord and peasant in colonial Oaxaca*. Stanford, Calif.: Stanford University.

Teschke, B. (2002) "Theorizing the Westphalian system of states: International relations from absolutism to capitalism." *European Journal of International Relations*, 8 (1), 5–48.

Teschke, B. (2003) *The myth of 1648: Geopolitics, and the making of modern international relations*. London: Verso.

Teschke, B. (2005) "Bourgeois revolution, state formation and the absence of the international." *Historical Materialism*, 13 (2), 3–26.

Thomas, P. (2013) "Hegemony, passive revolution and the modern prince." *Thesis 11*, 17 (1), 20–39.

Thorp, R. (1986) "Latin America and the international economy from the First World War to the world depression," in L. Bethell (ed.), *Cambridge history of Latin America*, vol. 4. Cambridge: Cambridge University Press.

Tilly, C. (1984) *Big structures, large processes, huge comparisons*. New York: Russell Sage Foundations.

Tormey, S. (2004) *Anti-capitalism: A beginners guide*. Oxford: Oneworld.

Trotsky, L. (1919/1962) "Results and prospects," in L. Trotsky, *The permanent revolution and results and prospects*. London: New Park.

Trotsky, L. (1930/1962) "The permanent revolution," in L. Trotsky, *The permanent revolution and results and prospects*. London: New Park.

Tutino, J. (1986) *From insurrection to revolution in Mexico: Social bases of agrarian violence 1750–1940*. Princeton, N.J.: Princeton University Press.

Tutino, J. (1993) "Ethnic resistance: Juchitán in Mexican history," in H. Campbell, L. Binford, M. Bartolomé, and A. Barabas (eds.), *Zapotec struggles: History, politics, and representations from Juchitán, Oaxaca.* Washington, D.C.: Smithsonian Institution Press.

Twomey, M. (1998) "Patterns of foreign investment in Latin America in the twentieth century," in J. Coatsworth and A. M. Taylor (eds.), *Latin America and the world economy since 1800.* Cambridge, Mass.: Harvard University, David Rockefeller Center for Latin American Studies.

United Nations. (1949) *Economic survey of Latin America.* London: United Nations.

United Nations. (1957) *Economic survey of Latin America.* London: United Nations.

United Nations Conference on Trade and Development. (2000) *World investment report.* New Delhi: Academic Foundations.

United Nations Conference on Trade and Development. (2003) *Trade and development report.* New York: United Nations Publications.

United Nations Conference on Trade and Development. (2004) *World investment directory.* Vol. 9, *Latin America and the Caribbean.* Pts. 1 and 2. New York: United Nations.

United Nations Conference on Trade and Development. (2005) *World investment report.* New Delhi: Academic Foundations.

United Nations Conference on Trade and Development. (2006) *Trade and development report.* New York: United Nations Publications.

United Nations Conference on Trade and Development. (2007) *World investment report.* New Delhi: Academic Foundations.

Van der Haar, G. (2005) "Land reform, the state, and the Zapatista uprising in Chiapas." *Journal of Peasant Studies,* 32 (3–4), 484–507.

Van der Pijl, K. (2007) *Nomads, empire, states: Modes of foreign relations and international political economy.* Vol. 1. London: Pluto.

Varas, A. (1995) "Latin America: Towards a new reliance on the market," in B. Stallings (ed.), *Global change, regional response: The new international context of development.* Cambridge: Cambridge University Press.

Veltmeyer, H. (1997) "Latin America in the new world order." *Canadian Journal of Sociology,* 22 (2), 207–42.

Veltmeyer, H. (2012) "The political economy of natural resource extraction: A new model or extractive imperialism?" *Canadian Journal of Development Studies / Revue canadienne d'études du développement,* 34 (1), 79–95.

Vilar, P. (1971) "The age of Don Quixote." *New Left Review,* 68, 59–71.

Villafuerte Solís, D. (2005) "Rural Chiapas ten years after the armed uprising of 1994: An economic overview." *Journal of Peasant Studies,* 32 (3–4), 461–83.

Viqueria, J. P. (1994) "Tributo y sociedad en Chiapas, 1680–1712." *Historia Mexicana,* 44 (2), 237–67.

Wainwright, J. (2008) *Decolonizing development: Colonial power and the Maya.* Oxford: Blackwell Publishing.

Wallerstein, I. (1974) *The modern world system.* Vol. 1, *Capitalist agriculture and the origins of the European world-economy in the sixteenth century.* London: Academic Press.

Wallerstein, I. (1984) *The politics of the world-economy: The states, the movements and the civilizations*. Cambridge: Cambridge University Press.

Walton, J., and Shefner, J. (1994) "Latin America: Popular protest and the state," in J. Walton and D. Seddon (eds.), *Free markets and food riots: The politics of global adjustment*. Oxford: Blackwell.

Washbrook, S. (2005) "The Chiapas uprising of 1994: Historical antecedents and political consequences." *Journal of Peasant Studies*, 32 (3–4), 417–49.

Wasserstrom, R. (1983) *Class and society in central Chiapas*. Berkeley: University of California Press.

Waterbury, R. (1975) "Non-revolutionary peasants: Oaxaca compared to Morelos in the Mexican revolution." *Comparative Studies in Society and History*, 17 (4), 410–42.

Waterbury, R. (2007) "The rise and fracture of the Popular Assembly of the Peoples of Oaxaca." *Anthropology News*, 48 (3), 8–10.

Webber, J. (2011) *From rebellion to reform in Bolivia: Class struggle, indigenous liberation, and the politics of Evo Morales*. Chicago: Haymarket Books.

Weinert, R. (1981) "Foreign capital in Mexico." *Proceedings of the Academy of Political Science*, 34 (1), 115–24.

Weiss, L. (1998) *The myth of the powerless state: Governing the economy in a global age*. Cambridge: Polity Press.

Whitecotton, J. (1977) *The Zapotecs: Princes, priests and peasants*. Norman: University of Oklahoma Press.

Wilde, O. (1891/2009) *The soul of man under socialism*. Auckland, New Zealand: Floating Press.

Williamson, J. (1990) *Latin American adjustment: How much has happened?* Washington, D.C.: Institute for International Economics.

Wilpert, G. (2006) *Changing Venezuela by taking power: The history and policies of the Chávez government*. London: Verso.

Wilson, J. (2011) "Notes on a rural city: Henri Lefebvre and the transformation of everyday life in Chiapas, Mexico." *Environment and Planning D: Society and Space*, 29 (6), 993–1009.

Winant, H. (1994) *Racial conditions: Politics, theory, comparisons*. Minneapolis: University of Minnesota Press.

Wolf, E. (1955) "Types of Latin American peasantry: A preliminary discussion." *American Anthropologist*, 57 (3), 452–71.

Wolf, E. (1959) *Sons of the shaking earth*. Chicago: University of Chicago Press.

Wolf, E. (1997) *Europe and the people without history*. Berkeley: University of California Press.

Womack, J., Jr. (1978) "The Mexican economy during the revolution, 1910–1920: Historiography & analysis." *Marxist Perspectives*, 1 (4), 80–123.

Wood, E. M. (1995) *Democracy against capitalism: Renewing historical materialism*. New Delhi: Aakar Books.

Wood, E. M. (2002) *The origins of capitalism: A longer view*. London: Verso.

Wood, E. M. (2005) *The empire of capital*. New ed. London: Verso Books.

Wright, M. W. (2006) *Disposable women and other myths of global capitalism*. London: Routledge.

Yashar, D. J. (1999) "Democracy, indigenous movements, and the postliberal challenge in Latin America." *World Politics*, 52 (1), 76–104.

Yashar, D. J. (2005) *Contesting citizenship in Latin America: The rise of indigenous movements and the postliberal challenge.* Cambridge: Cambridge University Press.

Zepeda, E. (1995) "It comes from afar," in E. Katzenberger (ed.), *First World, ha ha ha! The Zapatista challenge.* San Francisco: City Lights.

Zibechi, R. (2004) "The impact of Zapatismo in Latin America." *Antipode*, 36 (3), 392–99.

Zibechi, R. (2010) *Dispersing power: Social movements as anti-state forces.* Oakland, Calif.: AK Press.

Zibechi, R. (2012) *Territories in resistance: A cartography of Latin American social movements.* Oakland, Calif.: AK Press.

Zibechi, R. (2015) "Las tormentas que vienen." *La Jornada*, November 27, http://www .jornada.unam.mx/2015/11/27/opinion/024a2pol (accessed November 30, 2015).

Žižek, S. (1997) "Multiculturalism, or the cultural logic of multinational capitalism." *New Left Review*, 225, 28–51.

INDEX

Radio Universidad, 129
Recession, 49, 60, 61
Redistribution: land, 68, 86, 113, 114, 123,
    146–47, 149, 167; wealth, 58
Repartimiento, 108, 144
Representations of space, 24, 25, 106
Repression, 92, 116, 122, 127, 130–31, 150; of
    teacher's union in Oaxaca, 101, 128
Revolution. *See* Mexican Revolution; Passive
    revolution
Rural cities, 168

Salinas de Gortari, Carlos, 6, 97, 117, 123, 156,
    167
San Andrés Accords, 171–72, 180
San Jose del Progreso, 131
Section 22, 101, 129, 131, 178
Selva Lacandona, 140, 143, 153, 168, 190n24
Silva-Herzog, Jesús, 95
Sindicato Nacional de Trabajadores de la
    Educación (SNTE, National Union of
    Education Workers), 129
"Sixth Declaration of the Lacandon Jungle,"
    161, 179, 190n19
Slums, 14, 100
Social contract, 123
Socialism, 10, 48
Social property relations, 9, 27–28, 33
Social relations of production, 11, 13, 22,
    25–27, 78
Southern Cone countries, 54
Soviet Union, 15, 19
Spatial practices, 24, 45, 48, 53, 70, 106–7, 140,
    144
States system, 9, 27–28
Surplus value, absolute and/or relative, 38

Tariff barriers, 51, 55, 97
Tehuantepec, Isthmus of, 114, 125
Tequios, 121, 188n7
Territorialization, 68
Territory, 116, 127, 132–133, 138, 151–53, 169
Tierras communales, 106
Tlatelolco Plaza, 92, 156
Trade union, 53, 102, 128; social movement
    unionism, 178

Transnationalism: capitalist class and,
    90; solidarity and, 166; transnational
    corporations (TNCS), 8, 66, 89–90, 92, 94,
    125, 132, 133
Tribute, 26, 36, 106, 107–8, 138–40, 142
Trotsky, Leon, 9, 79, 116

Unemployment, 57, 65, 100
Uneven and combined development, 3–5, 8–9,
    36–37, 144, 175–76; Latin American state
    formation and, 50, 58, 60; Mexican state
    formation and, 77, 97–98
Uneven and combined hegemony, 5, 104, 112,
    117, 120, 137, 175. *See also* Gramsci, Antonio;
    Hegemony
United States of America (USA), 36, 46, 48, 49,
    60, 89, 98, 100, 169
Urbanization, 47, 114, 115, 169
Urbina, Erasto, 152
Usos y costumbres, 105, 122, 125, 188n3
Utopian space, 180–84

Vanguardism, 103, 166, 179
Venezuela, 10, 58, 64, 65, 67, 69, 182
Violence, 27, 35, 84, 86, 150, 172, 179; domestic,
    160
Volcker, Paul, 60

Wage labor, 39, 76, 79, 85, 111, 112, 131, 149, 152,
    155
War on drugs, 178
War on terror, 173
Wind farms, 117–18
Working class, 6, 31, 47, 49, 51, 56, 57, 67, 83,
    103, 178
World Bank, 60–61, 119, 124
World Social Forum (WSF), 10
World War I, 47
World War II, 48–49, 57, 86, 89, 90, 154

Zaachila, 125–27
Zapata, Emiliano, 78, 161
Zapatismo, 159–61, 162–63, 167, 169, 170, 179–80
Zapatistas. *See* Ejército Zapatista de Liberación
    Nacional
Zapotec, 117

GEOGRAPHIES OF JUSTICE AND SOCIAL TRANSFORMATION

CPSIA information can be obtained
at www.ICGtesting.com
Printed in the USA
LVOW07s2043301117
558173LV00002B/187/P